EAST SUS

1837.

LIST

OF THE

REGISTERED ELECTORS,

WITH THE

VOTES OF SUCH AS ACTUALLY POLLED

AT THE

ELECTION

FOR

KNIGHTS OF THE SHIRE,

TO REPRESENT THE

EASTERN DIVISION

OF THE

COUNTY OF SUSSEX

IN THE FIRST PARLIAMENT

OF

HER MAJESTY, QUEEN VICTORIA THE FIRST,

Summoned to be holden at Westminster,

On the Eleventh day of September, 1837, (being the Third Parliament
under the Reform Act, passed the Seventh of June, 1832.)

WITH A MAP OF THE POLLING PLACES OF EAST SUSSEX.

Sussex Press:
BAXTER AND SON, LEWES.

1837.

NOTES.

The Names of the Electors are correctly copied from the Register of 1836, arranged alphabetically in parishes, with the places in which the Electors reside.

The Voters marked thus * polled on the second day.

The Names of those who did not poll are printed in italics; these include many persons who are dead, as well as those who have lost their qualification by a change of residence, and various other causes.

It will no doubt appear that some of the Names are spelt incorrectly, which is attributable in most instances to the Lists sent in by the Overseers, and the unavoidable differences made in copying, over which the Editor could not exercise any control.

The Nomination took place at Lewes, on TUESDAY, the first day of August, 1837,

GEORGE PALMER, Esq.,

High Sheriff of the County, presided; when

THE HON. CHARLES COMPTON CAVENDISH,

(Of Latimers, Buckinghamshire),

Was nominated by Mr. Serjeant D'OYLY, of Rottingdean, and seconded by Sir CHARLES RICHARD BLUNT, Bart., M.P., of Heathfield Park.

HERBERT BARRETT CURTEIS, Esq.,

(Of Peasmarsh),

Was nominated by Sir CHARLES FOSTER GORING, Bart., of Highden, and seconded by HENRY SHIRLEY, Esq., of Pippingford.

GEORGE DARBY, Esq.,

(Of Markly),

Was nominated by WILLIAM COURTHOPE MABBOTT, Esq., of Uckfield, and seconded by JAMES INGRAM, Esq., of Rottingdean.

AUGUSTUS ELIOTT FULLER, Esq.,

(Of Rose Hill),

Was nominated by Sir CHARLES MONTILIEU LAMB, Bart, of Beauport, and seconded by GEORGE COURTHOPE, Esq., of Lewes.

The shew of hands being in favour of George Darby, Esq., and Augustus Eliott Fuller, Esq., a Poll was then demanded on behalf of the Hon. Charles Compton Cavendish, and Herbert Barrett Curteis, Esq., and was taken at Lewes, Brighton, Cuckfield, East Grinstead, Mayfield, Battle, Hastings, and Rye, on Friday and Saturday, the 4th and 5th days of the same month.

The Poll was kept open until four o'clock in the afternoon of Saturday; and on Monday, the 7th, on casting up the Poll, the numbers were declared to be, for—

George Darby, Esq. 2256
Augustus Eliott Fuller, Esq. 1749
The Hon. Charles Compton Cavendish.........1793
Herbert Barrett Curteis, Esq. 1619

The Sheriff then declared that George Darby, Esq., and the Hon. Charles Compton Cavendish were duly elected.

EAST SUSSEX POLLING DISTRICTS,

With the number of Registered Electors in each Parish.

The Poll at Lewes was taken in *three* Booths, at Cuckfield in *one*, at Brighton in *two*, at East Grinstead in *two*, at Mayfield in *two*, at Battle in *two*, at Hastings in *one*, and at Rye in *one*. The several Parishes were allotted to the respective Booths, as under, every Voter being required to poll in the Polling Booth to which the Parish wherein he was registered was allotted.

LEWES POLLING DISTRICT.

BOOTH A.		BOOTH B.	BOOTH C.	
Alciston	5	Falmer	11	Laughton	18	Seaford Town and Port	29

BOOTH A.

Alciston	5	Falmer	11
Alfriston	16	Folkington	4
Arlington	23	Framfield	50
Barcombe	21	Friston	2
Beddingham	3	Glynde	8
Berwick	8		
Bishopstone	3		
Blatchington, East	3		
Chailey	36		
Chalvington	9		
Chiddingly	36		
Chiltington	10		
Denton	3		
Ditchling	37		
Eastbourne	81		
Eastdean	5		
Easthoathly	18		

BOOTH B.

Hailsham	80
Hamsey	18
Heighton	2
Hellingly	45
Iford	4
Isfield	10
Jevington	9
Kingston	3
All Saints	63
Lewes { St. John	67
St. Michael	36
St. Peter & St. Mary Westout	18

BOOTH C.

Laughton	18	Seaford Town and Port	29
Littlington	3	Selmeston	5
Little Horsted	8	Southease	5
Lullington	1	Southmalling	18
Newhaven	15	Southover	33
Newick	26	Stanmer	1
Piddinghoe	3	Street	5
Plumpton	8	Tarring Neville	3
Ringmer	45	Telscomb	4
Ripe	14	Uckfield	40
Rodmell	5	Westdean	6
Rottingdean	22	Westfirle	9
St. Thomas-a-Becket in the Cliffe	49	Westmeston	8
		Willingdon	25
		Wilmington	10

CUCKFIELD POLLING DISTRICT.

Ardingly	9	Cuckfield	69	*Slaugham, that part which lieth in the Eastern Division of the County	18	Twineham	11
Balcombe	15	Hurstperpoint	38			Wivelsfield	19
Bolney	19	Keymer	24				
Clayton	17	Lindfield	42				
Crawley	17						

* That part of the Parish which is in the Western Division of the County, is in the Horsham Polling District·

BRIGHTON POLLING DISTRICT.

BOOTH A.

Aldrington, East 0
Blatchington, West 3
Brighthelmstone, *all the voters in the parish whose Surnames begin with A, B, C, D, E, F, G, H, I, J, K, L, M.* 451

BOOTH B.

Brighthelmstone, *all the voters in the parish whose Surnames begin with N, O, P, Q, R, S, T, V, U, W, X, Y, Z,* 298

Fulking	6	Patcham	11
Hangleton	0	Piecomb	6
Hove	36	Portslade	19
Newtimber	3	Poynings	6
Ovingdean	2	Preston	7

EASTGRINSTEAD POLLING DISTRICT.

BOOTH A.

Eastgrinstead 180
Fletching 57

BOOTH B.

Horstedkeynes 24

Hartfield	55	Maresfield	35	Withyham	39
Westhoathly	29	Worth	93

MAYFIELD POLLING DISTRICT.

BOOTH A.

Burwash 71
Buxted 52

Frant	50	Mayfield	117
Heathfield	71	**BOOTH B.**	
Lamberhurst	26	Rotherfield	104

Ticehurst	76
Wadhurst	78
Waldron	47
Warbleton	61

BATTLE POLLING DISTRICT.

BOOTH A.

Ashburnham	15
Battle	87
Bodiam	10
Brightling	18
Catsfield	17

		BOOTH B.	
Crowhurst	10		
Dallington	17	Mountfield	12
Etchingham	20	Ninfield	26
Ewhurst	28	Penhurst	2
Herstmonceux	49	Pevensey	19
Hooe	20	Salehurst	69

Sedlescomb	17
Wartling	34
Westfield	30
Westham	27
Whatlington	13

HASTINGS POLLING DISTRICT.

All Saints	57	Saint Leonard	6	Saint Michael	0	Hollington	7
Holy Trinity	5	Saint Mary in the Castle	65	Bexhill	81	Ore	19
Saint Andrew	0	Saint Mary Bulverhithe	0	Fairlight	13	Pett	10
Saint Clement	60	Saint Mary Magdalen	19	Guestling	18	

RYE POLLING DISTRICT.

Beckley	39	East Guildeford	8	Peasmarsh	29	Saint Leonard and Saint Thomas the Apostle	0
Brede	34	Icklesham	16	Playden	19	Udimore	13
Broomhill, that part which lies in Sussex	4	Iden	24	Rye	130	
		Northiam	65	Winchelsea	31	

On the First of July, previous to the Dissolution of Parliament, HERBERT BARRETT CURTEIS, Esq., the late Member, declared his intention, by public Advertisement, of not again offering himself as a Candidate for the representation of the Eastern Division of Sussex, when GEORGE DARBY, Esq., of Markly, published the following Address :—

TO THE ELECTORS OF THE EASTERN DIVISION OF THE
COUNTY OF SUSSEX.

GENTLEMEN,—Having been called upon to offer myself as a Candidate for the representation of East Sussex at the ensuing Election, in a manner which precludes my declining that honor, I now take the opportunity of declaring the principles on which I solicit your suffrages.

I believe it to be the sacred duty of every man to use his utmost energies to defend the Protestant Constitution against the attacks of those Roman Catholic Agitators who obtained power under the promise of peace, even if those attacks be sanctioned by the Government of a Protestant State.

Should I have the honor to become one of your REPRESENTATIVES, I shall consider myself called upon to attend with diligence to the varied interests of the country at large, and of every class of Society; but feel it a peculiar duty and sincere pleasure, to make the welfare of this County the first and constant object of my solicitude, and shall lose no opportunity of promoting to the best of my ability, the prosperity of the Agriculturists, of which the Trade will, I am convinced, especially in this County, feel the beneficial effect.

I am persuaded of the NECESSITY of adequate protection to British capital and labour, whether employed in Agriculture or Manufactures, and am most decidedly opposed to free trade in either the one or the other.

I shall direct my utmost efforts to maintain, unimpaired, the CONSTITUTION OF THE KINGDOM—the stability of the PROTESTANT CHURCH—and the honor and independence of the CROWN.

I have the honor to remain,

Your obliged and faithful servant,

GEORGE DARBY.

Lewes, 8th July, 1837.

Although Mr. CURTEIS had declined offering himself as a Candidate for East Sussex, yet on the 18th of July, to the surprise of all parties, he announced his intention of contesting this Division of the County, and his partizans and friends commenced an active canvass, and every preparation was made for the approaching contest :—upon this a requisition on the part of the Conservatives, was, immediately forwarded to AUGUSTUS ELIOTT FULLER, Esq., of Rose-Hill, who waving all personal considerations, accepted the invitation of the requisitionists, and addressed the Electors as follows :—

TO THE INDEPENDENT ELECTORS OF EAST SUSSEX.

GENTLEMEN,—From the peculiar situation in which East Sussex is placed at the present moment, I am induced to wave all personal considerations, and at once to comply with the numerous and respectable Requisitions I have received, to offer myself as a Candidate for your Suffrages, at the approaching Election.

An anxious desire to support the Constitution and Protestant Religion against the attacks of their foes, open and covert; and to maintain the Agricultural and Commercial Interests of the Country, alone actuate me in taking this step.

Should I become one of your Representatives, my votes on all occasions will be given conscientiously and independently; and I shall exert myself, to the utmost of my power, to promote the welfare and prosperity of the Eastern Division of the County of Sussex, with which my own interests are completely identified.

The sudden and alarming illness of a member of my family prevents my immediately returning to Rose-Hill and paying my respects to you personally; I trust that I shall be able to do so in a few days, and in the mean time I entreat my friends to strain every nerve in promoting our common cause.

I have the honor to be,

Gentlemen, your faithful servant,

AUGUSTUS ELIOTT FULLER

Clifford Street, 20th July, 1837.

At the conclusion of the Poll the following Addresses were issued by Mr. DARBY and Mr. FULLER :—

TO THE ELECTORS OF EAST SUSSEX.

GENTLEMEN,—Your great exertions to secure my return demand my warmest gratitude. For them, and for your personal kindness towards myself, I return you my heartfelt thanks, and humbly trust that my conduct, as your Representative, will never cause one of my supporters to regret that he assisted to place me at the head of the poll.

I remain, Gentlemen,

Your sincere and obliged faithful servant,

GEORGE DARBY.

Baker-street, Portman-square, August 9th, 1837.

INDEPENDENT ELECTORS OF EAST SUSSEX.

GENTLEMEN,—You have nobly supported me in the late contest, and I thank you most sincerely

Although we are beaten by a small majority, the independence of my native county will be secure for a future Election.

I beg to offer my sincere thanks to the Gentlemen of the different Committees, for their strenuous exertions in my favor.

I am, Gentlemen,

Your obliged and faithful humble servant,

AUGUSTUS ELIOTT FULLER.

INDEX TO PARISHES.

ANALYSIS OF THE POLL.

	Darby.	Fuller.	Cavsh.	Curteis	Total.
Plumpers for - - - - - - -	118	16	106	83	323
Divided votes for Darby and Fuller - -	1675	1675	—	—	1675
,, ,, Darby and Cavendish	299	—	299	—	299
,, ,, Darby and Curteis -	164	—	—	164	164
,, ,, Fuller and Cavendish	—	37	37	—	37
,, ,, Fuller and Curteis - -	—	21	—	21	21
,, ,, Cavendish and Curteis	—	—	1350	1350	1350
Total - -	2256	1749	1792	1618	3869

REGISTERED VOTES IN 1836.		Unpolled	Polled
Lewes District - - - - - - - - - -	1135	194	941
Cuckfield - - - - - - - - -	298	71	227
Brighton - - - - - - - - - -	848	249	599
East Grinstead - - - - - - - - - -	482	76	406
Mayfield - - - - - - - - - - -	753	115	638
Battle - - - - - - - - - - -	540	105	435
Hastings - - - - - - - - - -	361	58	303
Rye - - - - - - - - - - - -	404	84	320
Total - - -	4821	952	3869

NOTE.—There is included in the Register upwards of 100 duplicate names, as well as those who tendered their votes, the latter are inserted in the different Parishes in which their supposed qualification is specified.

THE POLL

FOR

KNIGHTS OF THE SHIRE,

FOR THE

EASTERN DIVISION

OF

THE COUNTY OF SUSSEX, 1837.

LEWES POLLING DISTRICT.

NAMES.	D.	F.	Ch	Cs.	QUALIFICATION AND WHERE SITUATE.
ALCISTON.					
Farhill, George, Esq., Chichester ..					Leasehold great tithes of Alciston.
Fears, Thomas					Copyhold house and land.
Mockett, George					Copyhold houses and land.
Ridge, Henry					Land as occupier, Court Farm.
Stephens, William					Copyhold houses and land.
ALFRISTON.					
Brooker, Charles					Freehold land and copyhold houses, E. and W. side, High-street.
Brooker, Chas. Springate, Litlington					Copyhold houses, E. & W. side High-st.
Cooley, Joseph					Copyhold ho., bg. & gdn., north end.
Hilton, Richard					Copyhold houses, west side.
Haryott, Richard					Copyhold house, east side.
Kidd, William					Cp. house & land, N. end & W. side.
*Lidbetter, Thomas					Land as ocp, Burnt-house Farm & Little Sutton, Seaford.
Marchant, William					Copyhold house, west side.
Pagden, Henry					Ld. as ocp., south end, Frog-firle Farm
Reeds, William					House & ld. as ocp. W. side & N. end.
Woodhams, William					Freehold house and land, east side.
Woodhams, John					H., bgs., & land, as ocp., E. & N. side.
Woodhams, George					Copyhold house, east side.
Wilson, John, East Blatchington ..					Fr. house & gn., Winton-st. N. end.
Winch, Ralph					Copyhold, east side.
Woodhams, Walter, Lullington Court-house					Land as ocp. Lullington Court

B

NAMES.	D.	F.	Ch	Cs	QUALIFICATION AND WHERE SITUATE.

LEWES—ALL SAINTS.

NAMES.	D.	F.	Ch	Cs	QUALIFICATION AND WHERE SITUATE.
Acland, P. P. F. P., Bart., Fairfield, near Bridgewater, Somerset					Freehold house.
Adams, George, East-street				—	Fr. shop & warehouse, Market-street.
Adams, John, High-street				—	Freehold land, Church-street.
Ade, John, Preston-street, Brighton..					Freehold house, High-street.
Attwood, William, High-street				—	Freehold land, Eastgate-lane.
Bates, John, North-street, St. John..				—	Freehold house, Friars'-walk.
Berry, James, South Malling				—	Freehold house, Albion-street.
Berry, Henry, High-street			—		Freehold house, High-street.
Bridger, Wm, St. Mary's-lane, St. John's				—	Freehold house, St. Mary's-lane.
Browne, Henry, High-street				—	Freehold house, 214, High-street.
Carter, Wm., South-parade, Lewes ..					Two freehold houses, Walwer's-lane.
Comber, Benj., High-st., St. Ann's ..					Freehold house, Little East-street.
Corner, Wm., West-street, St. John's				—	Freehold house, West-street.
Dadswell, Robert, York-street ..				—	Freehold house, York-street.
Duplock, Stephen, Fisher-street				—	Freehold house, Lansdown-place.
Fairhall, Joseph, St. Nicholas-lane ..				—	Freehold shop, St. Nicholas-lane.
Fuller, William, St. Nicholas-lane ..				—	Freehold house, Wellington-street.
Godlee, Burwood, Cliffe, Lewes ..				—	House and land, Friars'-walk.
Gest, Richard, Cliffe, Lewes				—	Freehold warehouse, Eastgate-street.
Gooding, Lewis, St. John's-street ..		—			Freehold house, Dolphin-lane.
Gosling, Jesse, Church-street					Freehold house, Church-street.
Gwynne, George, esq., Marlborough-place, Brighton					Freehold house, High-street
Hammond, Nathan, High-street ..				—	Fr. sta. & coach-h., St.Nicholas-lane.
Harman, George, North-street					Freehold house, North-street.
Harvey, John, Cliffe, Lewes					Freehold house, East-street.
Hicks, Thomas, Eastgate-street ..					Freehold house, Eastgate-street.
Hobden, John, Keere-st., St. Michael's	—				Freehold house, Waterloo-place.
Hoper, George, Esq., High-street ..	—				Freehold house, Eastgate-street.
Hother, Charles, New-street	—				Freehold house, New-street.
Hother, Geo., High-st., St. Michael's	—				Freehold land, Church-street.
Hother, John, High-street	—				Freehold garden, Eastgate-lane
Huggett, Thomas, High-street ..	—				Freehold house, Friars'-walk.
Isted, Edmund, Southover	—				Freehold houses, St. Nicholas-lane.
Inskip, J. S., High-street, St. John's	—				Two fourth parts of a fr., h., Ch.-st.
Johnston, Thomas, St. Michael's ..					Freehold house, High-street.
King, Thomas, St. Michael's					Freehold house, Dolphin-lane.
*Lowdell, Stephen, High-street	—				Freehold house, North-street.
Madgwick, John Chatfield, High-st.	—				Freehold house, High-street.
Marten, Fred., Burlington-st, Brighton					Fr. hs. Green-wall, York-st. & West-st.
Martin, Thomas, Friars'-walk				—	Freehold house, Friars'-walk.
Moon, Rt., 34, Preston-st., Brighton				—	Freehold house, 40, High-street.
Paine, James, Eastgate-st., Lewes..	—				Freehold house, Albion-street.
Parker, William, St. Michael's	—				Freehold house, Wellington-street.
Parsons, Latter, Eastgate-street ..				—	Freehold house, Albion-street.
Penford, James, Market-street				—	Freehold house & gn., St.Nicholas-lane
Slight, Julian, Portsmouth, Hants ..				—	Freehold house, East-street.
Smart, George, Herstmonceux					Freehold house, New-street.
Smart, Richard, Bath-st., St. Luke's, Middlesex					Annuity arising out of a freehold house, Church-street.
Smart, William, Market-street ..				—	Freehold workshop, New-street.
Soule, Israel May, North-street ..				—	Fr. Chapel, as Minister, Eastgate-st.
Stedman, James, Friars'-walk				—	Freehold house & garden, Norfolk-st.
Steere, James, East-street				—	Freehold house, West-street.
———, William, East-street				—	Freehold house, West-street

NAMES.	D.	F.	Ch	Co	QUALIFICATION AND WHERE SITUATE.
Taylor, William, Clapham, Surrey ..					Freehold house, Little East-street.
Traft, Edward, North-street, Cliffe..					Freehold house, Friars'-walk,
Verrall, Plumer, High-street				—	Freehold house, Friars'-walk.
Watts, George, Little East-street ..				—	Freehold house, Norfolk-street
Weston, Edward, East-street					Freehold house, High-street.
Wheeler, Robert, Aylesbury, Bucks..					Two fourth parts of a fr. h. High-st.
Whiteman, Thos., High-st., St. Mich.		—			Freehold house, High-street.
Whitfeld, Thomas, High-street ..		—			Freehold house, Market-lane.
Wille, Charles, sen., North-street ..				—	Freehold house, North-street.
Wimble, Nehemiah, High-street ..				—	Freehold houses, Eastgate-street.

ARLINGTON.

Ade, Charles, Milton-house				—	Copyhold land, near Milton-street.
Barber, John, Wilbees Farm-house..				—	Ld. as ocp., Wilbees farm, near the Ch.
Barber, William, Wilbees Farm-house				—	Ld. as ocp., Wilbees farm, near the Ch.
Bodle, Charles, Milton-street				—	Copyhold house and land, Milton-st.
Body, James, Upper Dicker				—	Copyhold house and land and carpenter's shop, Upper Dicker.
Child, Thomas, Michelham Priory ..				—	Cp. ld., Goodberries, nr. the Up. Dicker
Cruttenden, William, New Claberham				—	Land as ocp., New Claberham farm.
Cruttenden, Leonard				—	Land as ocp., New Claberham farm.
Fox, John, Cane-heath				—	Copyhold house and land, Caneheath.
Fears, George, Arlington-street ..				—	Fr. & cp. h. & ld., near Arlington-st.
Fox, Arthur, Upper Dicker				—	Land as occupier, High Barn farm, near the Upper Dicker.
Gosden, John, Arlington-street ..				—	Cp. h. & ld. Arlington-st. near the Ch.
Gutsell, William, Upper Dicker ..				—	Land as occupier, the Plough Inn, and houses and land, Upper Dicker.
Gosden, Thomas, Arlington-street ..				—	Freehold and copyhold house & land, Arlington-street, near the Church.
Gosden, Thomas, Caneheath				—	Copyhold houses and land, Caneheath.
Goldfinch, Harry, Esq., 11, Up. Wimpole-street, Marylebone, London ..				—	Freehold house & land, Milton-street and Hempstead farms.
Hide, William, sen., Millton-street ..				—	Freehold woodland & copyhold house & land, Hailsham-lane, & nr. the Ch.
Pagden, Thomas, Chilver-bridge ..				—	Land as occupier, Chilver Bridge farm
Scutt, Thomas White, Esq., Glynde, near Lewes				—	Copyhold house and land, Milton-st.
Store, Thomas, Heathfield				—	Fr. and cp. house & land, Up. Dicker
*Willard, Leonard Kilham, Esq. 46, Ship-street, Brighton				—	Freehold houses & land, Milton-street and Hempstead farms
*Shoosmith, Thomas, Old Claberham				—	Land as ocp., Old Claberham farm.
*Shoosmith, Walter, Wick-st. House				—	Land as occupier, Wick-street and Sessingham farms.

BARCOMBE.

Allen, (Rev.) Robert Rectory ..		—			Rectorial Tithes of Barcombe.
Barnes, Thomas		—			Land as occupier, Spithurst.
Constable, John		—			Copyhold land, Carpenters.
Coppard, James		—			Land as ocp. Longford and Old Park.
Cox, Thomas				—	Copyhold house, Cooksbridge.
Fuller, James		—			Land as ocp. Scuffings & Covels farm.
Funnell, James		—			House and land as occupier, Anchor Inn, and St. Helena.
Gray Russell, Esq., ...		—			Mills as occupier, Barcombe Mills.
Goring, Ch., Foster, Bart., Highdean				—	Freehold farm, Balneath.

NAMES.	D.	F	Ch	Cs.	QUALIFICATION AND WHERE SITUATE.
Harmer, John, Newick					Freehold land.
Holroyd, John Borrett					Land as ocp., Barcombe Place farm.
Jenner, Richard, sen.					Land as ocp., Banks and Peakins farm.
Knight, Richard, jun.					Land as occupier, Church farm.
Morris, Philip, Newick					Freehold land.
Reed, William					Land as ocp., Haysland near the Mill.
Richardson, Thos. Esq., Lewes					Fr., land, Vuggels and Bradneys farm.
Rogers, Henry, Kingston					Land as ocp. Groveland & Stepneys.
Skinner, Barnard					Freehold house, Barcombe-street.
Westgate, William					Copyhold land, Firzely farm.
*Wigney, George, Esq.,					Freehold land, Beaches farm.
*Wood, Jn., Martin, All Saints, Lewes					Copyhold land, Bunces farm.

BEDDINGHAM.

Body, George					Land as ocp. Itford & Asheam farms.
Hoper, John, Esq., Lewes					Freehold lands.
Jenner, John					Land as ocp. Little Preston farm.

BERWICK.

Duly, Henry					Copyhold house and land.
Jenner, William					Land as occupier, near the Church.
King, John					Land as occupier, Court farm.
Stace, William					Land as occupier, near the Church.
Stace, George					Land as occupier, near the Church.
West, Harvey, Rev., Southover					Freehold land.
Westgate, William					Freehold land and house.
White, Henry					Freehold house and land.

BISHOPSTONE.

Catt, William					Freehold Mill, Tide Mill.
Cooper, Thomas, Norton					Land as occupier, Norton farm.
Farncombe, George					Ld., as ocp. Bishopstone Manor farm.

BLATCHINGTON, EAST.

King, John					Freehold land, Blatchington farm.
Lewis, John, Rev.					Rectorial Tythes of Blatchington.
Sampson, William King					Land as occupier, Blatchington farm

CHAILEY.

Alcorn, John, Hornslodge					Copyhold house and land.
Anscomb, Allen, Plumbtree House.					Copyhold house and land.
Avery, John					Land as occupier, Bowers farm.
Avery, Charles					Cp., house and lds., Long Ridge farm.
Beard, George, Mill House					Copyhold Mill and land.
Beard, Thomas Rootes					Freehold house, Jervis's.
Beard, John, Cinder Farm					Land as occupier, Cinder farm.
*Best, Gabriel					Land as ocp., part of Ade's farm.
Brook, Henry					Land as ocp. Laylands and Osborns.
Brown, Stephen					Land as occupier, Bush and Riddens farms part in Lindfield.
*Champnes, Thomas Edward					Land as occupier, Allington-house.
Dudeney, Edward					Land as occupier, Waningore farm.
Feist, James					Land as occupier, Warrs farm.
Gell, Francis Harding, Esq., Lewes.					Freehold house and land.
Hamshar, Harry, Chailey-green					Copyhold Mill, South Common Mill.

NAMES.	D.	F.	Ch.	Cs.	QUALIFICATION AND WHERE SITUATE.
Hindley, Samuel, Charity S. Com.,					Cp., house and land, South Common.
Hobden, William					Land as occupier, Great Lodge farm.
Jones, David					Copyhold house and lands, Wildfields.
Knight, Edward					Land as occupier, Townings farm.
Knight, Thomas					Ld., as ocp. Breens's & the Hole farm.
Markham, John, Esq.,Fladong's Hotel, Oxford-street, London					Freehold lands.
Marshall, Thomas, Chailey N. Common					Copyhold premises.
Millyard, John, Chailey N. Common					Freehold house and land.
Morley, James					Land as occupier, Waspbourn farm.
Pannett, Thomas, South Common ..					Copyhold land.
Pannett, William, Southease ..					Cp., house and ld., the Hundred Acres.
Perry, Chas., Castle-terrace, Hastings					Two copyhold houses and land.
*Saint John, Frederic, Hon., Roe Heath Cottage ..					Freehold house and land.
Searlet, Robert Campbell, Esq., 1, Park-street, Westminster ..					Copyhold land, Pouch lands.
*Shelley, John Castle-banks, Lewes					Copyhold farm, Tomkins and Markstakes farm.
Thomson, Wm., School-hill, Lewes					Ld., as ocp., Shoulders & Fridges farms
Trebeck, Thomas, Rev., the Parsonage					Rectorial Tithes of Chailey.
*Valentine, Charles Porteus, Rev.					Land as occupier, Woodsbrook farm.
Walls, Joseph					Freehold house and land, Snatts farm.
Waterman, Edward					Copyhold house and land, Snells farm.
Weston, Henry					House and land as occupier, Swan Inn.

CHALVINGTON.

NAMES.	D.	F.	Ch.	Cs.	QUALIFICATION AND WHERE SITUATE.
Carpenter, James					Land as occupier, near the Church.
Carpenter, Thomas					Cp., house and land, near the green.
Fuller, Rev. Rt. Eitzherbert, East Grinstead					Rectorial Tithes of Chalvington.
Guy, Thomas					Freehold land, N. and E. Hurst farm.
Marten, Michael					Fr., house and land, near the green.
Medhurst, Michael					Fr., house and land, below the Church.
Picknall, Robert					Cp., house and land, near the green.
Vine, John					Fr., house and land, New-house farm.
Woollgar, John Webb, East-st. Lewes					Fr., ld., Lovers farm & North Binns.

CHIDDINGLY.

NAMES.	D.	F.	Ch.	Cs.	QUALIFICATION AND WHERE SITUATE.
Baxhill, John, the Dicker ..					Freehold h., and land on the Dicker.
Christmas, James, the Friths Farm					House and ld., as occupier, the friths.
Day, Thomas, Esq., Burghill ..					Freehold houses and land, Burghill.
Davies, Thomas, Kingston nr. Lewes					Freehold land, Willetts farm.
Dray, Edward, Muddles Green ..					Land as occupier, Farleighs farm.
Frost, John, the Dicker					Fr., and cp. h. & ld. on the Dicker.
Funnell, Samuel, Chiddingly Park					Copyhold house and land, Hale.
Gwynne, George, Esq., 7, Marlbro' place, Brighton					Copyhold h. and ld., Millhouse farm.
Guy, Thomas, Chiddingly-place					Land as ocp., Parsonage and Pickhill.
Guy, George, Chiddingly-street ..					Freehold h., and land, the Place farm.
					Freehold and copyhold houses and land, Nash-street, and Chiddingly-street.
Guy, William, Highlands Farm ..					Land as occupier, Highlands farm.
Guy, Robert, Nash-street ..					House and land as ocp., on the Dicker.
Hicks, Richard, Hilder's Farm ..					Freehold house and land, Hilders farm
Hide, Richard, the Dicker ..					Mill h. and ld. as ocp., on the Dicker
Holman, John, the Dicker ..					Copyhold h., and land, on the Dicker

NAMES.	D.	F.	Ch	Cs	QUALIFICATION AND WHERE SITUATE.
Holman, William, Gatehouse Farm	—				House & ld., as ocp.; Gatehouse farm
Holman, Samuel, Pickhill		—			Copyhold house and land, Pickhill
Knight, John, Peaks Farm			—		House and land as ocp., Peaks farm.
Knight, Peter, the Dicker			—		Copyhold house and ld., on the Dicker
*Lower, Richard Muddles Green			—	—	Fr. and cop. houses, Middles green.
Moon, William, Bat and Ball Inn	—				House and land as ocp., on the Dicker
Morris, Joseph, Beeding Court Farm	—				Fr. house and land, on the Dicker.
Noakes, George, Holms Hill			—		Freehold house, Holmshill.
Page, Peter, Holms Hill			—		Copyhold house, Holmshill.
Pelling, Richard, the Strood Farm	—				Freehold house and land, Strood farm
Price, Jerh., Hadlow Down, Mayfield	—				Fr., h. & ld., Higlers-den, near West-st
Reeves, Robert, the Stream Farm	—				Fr. h. and ld., the Stream and Hale.
Russell, Whitworth, the Rev., Millbank, Westminster					Vicarage of Chiddingly.
Russell, John Clifford, Chiddingly-st.			—		Freehold house, Chiddingly-street.
Smith, Stephen, Park River		—			Copyhold house and land, Beard's.
Thorpe, William, on the Dicker		—			House and land as ocp., on the Dicker
Verral, Edward, Esq., Lewes					Freehold house and land, Whitesmith.
Weston, John, on the Dicker			—		Fr., house and land, on the Dicker.
White, James, Muddles Green		—			Freehold house, Middles green.
Woodward, John, Esq., Uckfield		—			Freehold house and land, Peaks.

CHILTINGTON.

NAMES.	D.	F.	Ch	Cs	QUALIFICATION AND WHERE SITUATE.
*Avery, Thomas, Yokehurst			—		Land as occupier, Homewood farm.
Egles, Edward, Cleveland			—		Freehold ld., Cleveland & Chapel farm
Elphick, Samuel, Whitehouse			—		Land as occupier. White-house farm.
Hoadley, William			—		Freehold house and ld., late Hoadleys
Martin, John, Stantons			—		Land as occupier, Stanton's farm.
*Mighell, Joseph Hurstbarns			—		Land as occupier, Hurstbarns farm.
Uridge, Henry, Brookhouse			—		Land as occupier, Brookhouse farm.
Walder, James, Northbarns			—		Land as occupier, Northbarns farm.
Welfare, Thomas, Hartsland					House and land as ocp., Hartsland farm
Wood, Richard, Hattons Green			—		Fr., house and garden, Triangle land.

DENTON.

NAMES.	D.	F.	Ch	Cs	QUALIFICATION AND WHERE SITUATE.
Bates, William Henry, Clarence-place, Brighton					Freehold land and buildings.
*Doughty, Henry Hepworth Newhaven	—			—	Land as occupier, Courthouse farm.
*Putland, William Denton.	—			—	Copyhold house and shop, Denton-st.

DITCHELLING.

NAMES.	D.	F.	Ch	Cs	QUALIFICATION AND WHERE SITUATE.
Attree, John, Ringmer			—		Fr., Tythes of Park and Court farms.
Attree, Wm., Wakeford, Ship-street, Brighton			—		Copyhold land.
Burtenshaw, Thomas			—		Land as occupier, Freeborough.
Browne, John, Horsham			—		Copyhold land, Norman's.
Burtenshaw, Henry, 31, Leicester-square, London			—		Freehold house and land, Folders.
*Boddington, Robert			—		Copyhold house.
Crosskey, William, Lewes			—		Freehold land, Popes farm.
Comber, Thomas			—		Freehold land, Honeys-wood.
Cripps, Rush Marten, Novington, Westmeston			—		Freehold land, Beards fields.
Dean, John			—		Land as ocp., Old Yard and Breaches.
Elliott, William			—		Copyhold house, Normans.
Ellis, Frederick Charles, 56, East-street, Brighton	—		—		Freehold house, East-field house.

NAMES.	D.	F.	Ch	Ca.	QUALIFICATION AND WHERE SITUATE.
*Gravett, William				—	Land as occupier, Shortfrith.
Grinyer, Thomas				—	Freehold house in Cox's meadow.
Hunt, James				—	Freehold land, Court gardens.
Hebbern, William			—		Copyhold land.
Hebbern, Henry			—		Copyhold land.
Hubbard, William				—	Copyhold house, Bull Inn.
Illman, Thomas				—	House and land as ocp., the Rookery.
Jenner, William				—	Copyhold house and land.
Kensett, Jesse				—	Copyhold house and buildings.
Lindfield, George, Horsham				—	Copyhold land, Sawyers farm.
Muddle, Thomas				—	Copyhold house, East-end lane.
Mancer, Francis, 17, Crescent-street, Brighton				—	Freehold land, the Fleet's and part of Pope's farm.
Mercer, Richard				—	Ld. as ocp., Shortfrith & Jointer fms.
*Michell, John			—		Copyhold house and shop.
Parsons, Daniel				—	Freehold house.
*Randalls, George St. Pancras, near Chichester				—	Copyhold land.
Randalls, John, St. Pancras, near Chichester				—	Copyhold land.
Rowland, Peter				—	Copyhold house and Malt-house.
Scrace, John		—			Land as ocp., Court and Park farms.
Scrace Francis				—	Land as ocp., Court and Park farms.
Turner, James				—	Land as occupier, North-end.
Tester, Thomas				—	Copyhold house and land, in the Town
Vallance, Henry, Chippenham, Wilts				—	Cp., house and land, Royal Oak Inn.
Wood, John				—	Land as occupier, East-end land.
Wood, John, 3, Nelson-place, Brixton Hill, Surrey				—	Fr. & cop. h. & ld., East-end farm.

EASTBOURNE.

NAMES.	D.	F.	Ch	Ca.	QUALIFICATION AND WHERE SITUATE.
Butcher, John, Eastbourne Town				—	Copyhold houses.
Baker, Thomas, Eastbourne Town				—	Copyhold houses, Lamb Inn.
Beck, Henry, Russell-street, Hastings				—	Freehold land, South-street.
Bently, Henry, Eastbourne Town				—	Freehold house, the Town.
Baker, William, Eastbourne Town				—	Copyhold house, Town.
Brodie, Alfred, Sea-side				—	Leaseholdhouses and land, Sea-side.
Brown, Joseph, Sea-side, Eastbourne				—	Copyhold houses, Sea-side.
Ceaplin, Henry, Eastbourne Town		—			Copyhold houses, the Town.
Cavendish, Richard, Hon., Belgrave-square, London				—	Freehold land, Meads.
*Cavendish, Charles Compton, Hon., Burlington-house, London				—	Freehold land.
Cavendish, George Henry, Hon., Belgrave-square, London				—	Freehold land, Meads.
Coppard, Thos., All Saints, Hastings				—	Part freehold house and garden, Meads
Coppard, Dennis, Meads				—	Freehold house and garden, Meads.
Coppard, Richard, jun., Meads				—	Freehold house, Meads.
Caldecott, Rt. Marriott, Esq., Meads		—			Copyhold house, Meads.
Colman, John, South-street				—	Freehold land, Cow Brook land.
*Drury, George Vandeputt, Esq., 5, Terrace, South-street					House as occupier, South-street.
Dumbrill, John Neville, South-street				—	Freehold house and cottages the Wish
Dumbrill, Edward, South-street				—	Copyhold house, South-street.
*Dumbrill, William South-street				—	Freehold cottages & gardens, Sea-side
Dobree, Saml., Esq., South-field Lodge		—			Freehold house & land, Prentice-street
Frederick, Thomas, Esq., the Greys				—	House as occupier, the Town.
Ford, Henry, Sea-side			—		Copyhold house, Sea-side.

NAMES.	D.	F.	Ch.	Cs.	QUALIFICATION AND WHERE SITUATE.
Gilbert, Davies, Esq., Eastbourne town					Fr. lands, the Town and Southbourne.
Gilbert, John Davies, Esq., Ditto					One third part of fr. h., the Poor h.
Graham, John, Esq., Rose Cottage					Freehold lands, in the Marsh.
Gell, F.Harding, Esq., High-st. Lewes					Copyhold house, South-street.
*Gorringe, John 2, St. George's-place, Brighton					Copyhold house, South-street.
Gorringe, Jn. Pennington, Farm House					Land as occupier, South-street.
Hoad, Charles, Sea-side					Fr. h. & land, Highwormy, Sea-side.
Handley, Jos, Burlington-h., London					Freehold house and garden, the Town
*Head, John, South-street ..					Freehold house, South-street.
Hart, George, Eastbourne Town ..					Copyhold house, Holywell, Meads,
Hart, Richard, Eastbourne Town ..					Freehold house, the Town.
Hurst, Thomas, Radmell Farm					Land as occupier, Radmell farm.
Hurst, George, Eastbourne Town ..					Freehold house, Star Inn and garden
Hurst, Harry, Windmill, Eastbourne					Freehold house and garden, the Town
Hurst, Robert, Eastbourne Town ..					Freehold house and garden, the Town
Heathfield, William, Sea-side ..					Freehold Chapel, South-street.
Heatherly, John,* Eastbourne Town					Freehold house, the Town.
Hyland, William, Eastbourne Town					Freehold house, the Town.
Hussell, John, Sea-side					Fr. cottages and ld., Sea-side, Hides.
Jones, William, Eastbourne Town					Freehold house and land, the Town.
Luck, Thomas, Meads					Freehold house, Meads.
Manger, John, Sea-side					House as occupier, Sea-side.
Mann, John, Sea-side					Freehold house and land, Sea-side, Goose Marsh, & inner Chaw-brook.
Maynard, George, Eastbourne Town					Freehold house and garden, the Town
Maynard, Edward, South-street ..					Copyhold tenements Holywell, Meads.
Morris, William, South-street ..					Freehold houses, Meads.
Mockett, Richard, South-street ..					Freehold land, Sea-side.
Mockett, Henry, Sea-side ..					Houses and land as occupier, Sea-side
Newman, John, Eastbourne Town					Copyhold house and land, Upwick.
Newman, William, Eastbourne Town					Copyhold house and land, the Town.
Newman, James, Eastbourne Town					Freehold land, Sparrows-lane.
Prodger, William, sen., South-street					Freehold shop, South-street.
Prodger, William, jun., South-street					Freehold house, South-street.
Pitman, Rev. Thos., Eastbourne town					Vicarage of Eastbourne.
Pagden, James, Meads ..					Ld. as ocp., Meads & Prentice-street.
Reed, John, Eastbourne Town					Copyhold houses, the Town.
Rawdon, Chs. Wyndham, Esq. the Wish					Land as occupier, the Wish.
Richardson, John, Eastbourne Town.					Freehold houses, the Town.
Reed, Richard, Sea-side					Freehold land, Marsh.
Row, John, Sea-side					Houses as occupier, Sea-side.
Rason, William, Sprays Farm ..					House and land as occupier, Meads.
Swann, James, South-street					Fr. h. & School-room, South-street.
Stevens, Thomas, Goffs					Copyhold houses, Meads.
Stone, Richard Buckley, South-street					Copyhold house, South-street.
Stretton, John, Eastbourne Town					Freehold house, the Town.
Smith, Jeremiah, Cadborough, nr. Rye					Freehold land, Meads.
Turner, Joseph, South-street ..					Fr. house and garden, South Bowen.
Thorncroft, James, Goffs					Leasehold property, Sea-side.
Towner, James, Eastbourne Town					Copyhold houses, the Town.
Vine, Thomas, Sea-side					Fr. h. & gn., Reed Cottage, Sea-side
White, Thomas, Yalding, Kent ..					Copyhold houses and land, South-st.
Webster, John Charles. Compton-pl.					Freehold land.
Willard, Jno. Hy. Esq., Eastbourn town					Freehold house and land, the Town.
Willard, Chas., Esq., Sevenoaks, Kent					Freehold house and garden.
Waters, Benjamin, Eastbourne Town					H. and ld. as ocp., Motcombe house.
Wilkins, Joseph, Eastbourne Town					Copyhold house, the Crown Inn.
*Whiteman, George, South-street ..					H. and gn. as ocp., South-street.
John, South-street ..					Copyhold house, South-street.

NAMES.	D.	F.	CR	Cs.	QUALIFICATION AND WHERE SITUATE.

EASTDEAN.

Gärdner, Rev., Christopher   .. — Vicarage house, Eastdean.

Hills, John William   .. — Freehold house, and Blacksmiths shop, Eastdean-street.

Hodson, James   .. — House and land as ocp., Birling farm

Scrase, Richard, Gore farm. — Land as occupier, Gore farm.

Willard, Charles, No. 8, Marine-place, Brighton   ..   . — Freehold land and house, Eastdean-st.

EASTHOATHLY.

*Brown, Richard, Amberstone farm, Hailsham .   ..   .. — Cp., h., and ld., Hawkhurst Common.

Colgate, Robert ..   .   .. — Freehold house and land, Sellens.

Holman, Henry .   ..   .. — Copyhold house, Easthoathly-street.

King, John, Southover, Lewes   .. — Freehold house and land, Nursery.

Langdale, Rev. Edward ..   .. — Rectory of Easthoathly.

Martin, Joseph ..   .   . — House and Mill as ocp., Easthoathly-st

Martin, Matthew   ..   .. — Fr., & cp., lds., Penfold & Hesmead fm.

Moon, Néri   ..   .. — Land as ocp., Easthoathly & Waldron

Paine, David, King's Head Inn   .. — Land as occupier, near the Church.

Parr, Wm., Throgmorton-st., London — Copyhold house.

Raynes, Edward, Rev.   ..   .. — Freehold house and land, Belmont.

Raikes, Henry   ..   .. — House and land as occupier, Gatehouse

Rich, Henry .   ..   .. — Two cp., h , and ld., near the Church.

Smith, John Curtis   ..   .. — Copyhold house and land, Park-gate.

Tester, Edward ..   ..   .. — Land as occupier, Scallowbridge farm.

Turner, Hy. Martin, Doddington, Kent — Copyhold house, Easthoathly-street.

Wickerson, John   ..   .. — Two copyhold houses.

Weller, Alexander .   .. — Land as ocp., Easthoathly & Waldron.

FALMER.

Carter, William   ..   . — Copyhold house, East-street.

Dale, Edward   ..   ..   .. — Copyhold house, Middle-street.

Filder, George   ..   ..   .. — Land as occupier, Hodshrove farm.

Goodday, John William, Rev.,   . — Vicarial Tithes of Falmer cum Stanmer

Hodson, James   ..   .. — Land as occupier, Falmer Court farm.

Madgwick, William   ..   .. — Land as occupier, Balmer farm.

*Moon, William   ..   .. — Land as occupier, Mary farm.

Mott, George   ..   ..   . — Freehold h., and land, near the Mill.

Pite, James, ... — House and land as occupier, Swan Inn

Whitfeld, James   .. — Land as occupier, Housdean farm

*Willard, William Rogers   .. — Land as occupier, Bevendean farm

FOLKINGTON.

Dennes, Henry   ..   .. — Copyhold house and land, Dennes.

Harison, Wm., Esq., Folkington St. — Freehold lands, Folkington-place and Wootton farms.

Kelson, Henry, Rev., Folkington St. — Rectory of Folkington.

Pagden, John, Folkington-place   .. — Land as ocp., Folkington-place farm.

FRAMFIELD.

*Adams, John Honeys Green   .. — Copyhold h., and land, Honeys green.

Banks, Joseph, Framfield Street   .. — Copyhold house, Framfield-street.

Barton, William, Stile Reed   .. — Cp., house and land, Teelings Common

Boorman, Copping, Vine Farm   .. — 100 acres of land as ocp., Vine

NAMES.	D.	F.	Ch	Cs.	QUALIFICATION AND WHERE SITUATE.
Berwick, Edward, Barnet Wood ..	—				Copyhold land, Barnet Wood.
Bonney, George, Hammonds Green	—				139 acres of ld., as ocp., Highlands fm.
Bradford, John, Blackboys Common			—		House and land, as occupier, Blackboys Common.
Brooke, Daniel Thompson, High-street Croydon					Fr., house and land, Framfield-street.
Browne, Henry, Barnet Wood ..					Copyhold house & land, Barnet Wood.
Burton, Benjamin, Hundred House					100 acres of land, as occupier, Hundred House and Cyder House.
*Burton, Wm., jun., Mount Ephraim	—			—	Cp., house and land, Mount Ephraim.
Collins, John, Eastons Green ..			—		Freehold house and ld., Easton's green.
Cornwell, Stephen, Waldron Down					Copyhold house and land, Vine farm.
Dapp, Isaac, Pounsley ..	—				Land as occupier, Pounsley.
Donovan, Alex., Esq., Framfield Park					Fr. house and land, Framfield-park.
Farrant, Abraham, Eastons Green					Copyhold h. and ld., Easton's green.
Foster, J. H., Ridgwood Hill, Uckfield		—			Land as occupier, Tarbledown farm.
*Galloway, John, High-st., Croydon					
Guy, Samuel, Arches				—	260 acres of ld. as ocp., Arches farm.
Hemsley, Samuel, Barnett Wood ..	—				Copyhold house and land, Barnett Wood and Easton green.
Hoare, Henry, Rev., Vicarage House	—		—		Vicarial Tithes of Framfield.
Hughes, Wm., Esq., Brownings Grove					Fr. & cp. h. & ld., Brownings grove.
Kenward, William, Little Streele					Cp. house and land, Little Streele.
Leadner, Wm. Driver, Easton's Green					Copyhold house and ld., Easton's green
Lingwood, Robert, Esq., Highlands					Highlands house on lease, Highlands.
Martin, William, Gate House ..			—		160 acres of land, as occupier, Gatehouse farm.
Marchant, Charles, Birdnye .					60 acres of land as occupier, Birdnye.
*Maitland, John, Esq., Bridge street Westminster					Freehold house and land, Tarble Down
Jenner, Thomas, Bentley					300 acres of ld., as ocp., Bentley farm.
Newnham, Robert, Framfield Street			—		2 cp. hs. and gns., Framfield-street.
*Newnham, Henry Upton's Mill ..					Copyhold h. and land, Upton's Mill.
Normaman, Thomas, Pounsley ..					Mill, h. and ld. as ocp., Pounsley.
Packham, Thomas, Tickeridge Mill					H., Mill & ld., as ocp., Tickeridge Mill
Page, John, Church Stile ..					85 acres of ld., as ocp., Church-stile.
Peters, James, Framfield Street ..					Copyhold house and land, Spriggs.
Reed, George, Foxhunt, Waldron ..					Copyhold h. and ld., Easton's green.
Relf, William, Blackboys Common					Cp. h. and land, Blackboy's Common
*Salter, Joseph, Mount Ephraim, Tonbridge Wells					Cp. h., and ld., Blackboy's Common.
Smith, John, Sharelands					Copyhold house and land, Sharelands.
Stapley, Henry, Framfield Street ..			—		H., and land as ocp., Framfield-street.
Stapley, Robert, Honey's Green ..					Cp. house and land, Bridge lands.
*Stephens, John, Mount Ephraim ..				—	Cp. house and land, Mount Ephraim.
Stevenson, Richard, Pale House ..					Farm and glebe land, Pale house.
Stone, Wm. Thos., Esq., Stone Bridge	—				Freehold houses, and lands, Stonebridge and Newplace.
Tapp, Thomas, Barnett Wood ..	—				Cp. house and land, Barnett Wood.
Thompson, Philip, Barnett Wood ..	—				Cp. house and land, Barnett Wood.
Thompson, Stephen, Cliffe, Lewes	—				Cp., houses and land, Barnett Wood.
Wallis, Thomas, Framfield Street					Cp. house and land, Framfield-street.
Waller, John, Mount Ephraim ..				—	88 acres of ld. as ocp., Mount Ephraim
Woodward, William Packham, Rev., Rectory House, West Grinstead ..	—				Freehold farm, Arches farm.

FRISTON.

Ashby, George, Eastdean ..	—			—	Freehold land.
William . ..	—			—	Land as occupier, Friston farm

NAMES.	D.	F.	Ch	Cs.	QUALIFICATION AND WHERE SITUATE
GLYNDE.					
*Ellman, John, Esq.					Land as occupier, Glynde farm.
Ellman, Thomas, South Malling					Freehold house.
*Ellman Frederick, Battle					Freehold land.
Ellman, George, Watlington					Freehold house.
Rose, William, Rev.					Vicarial Tythes and Glebe of Glynde.
Trevor, Henry Otway, Hon.					Freehold estate, Glynde-place.
Tugwell, Richard, Lewes					Freehold house.
Wisdom, Thomas					Freehold house.
HAILSHAM.					
Baker, Walter					Freehold house and land, Town.
Burfield, Thomas					Freehold house and garden, Town.
Baker, James Bray					House as occupier, Town.
Barnett, John					Land as occupier, Harebeating.
*Barton, Harry, Goudhurst, Kent					Freehold marsh land, Newbridge.
Breads, George					H. yard & ld. as ocp. near the Ch.,
Bovis, Joseph					Land as ocp., near the Salt Marsh.
Constable, Rev. Richard, Cowfold					Vicarial Tithes of Hailsham.
Clare, John Gibson					Freehold house and garden, Town.
Carey, John-Nicholas					Fr. house and land, near Sayerland.
Cunningham, James Mackey					Freehold house, Town.
*Davies, William					Trustees of a fr. chapel, Baptist chapel
Elmes, Edwin, Seaford					One fr. and five cp. houses, Town.
Field, James, Kennington, Surrey					Freehold land and buildings.
Gurnett, Caleb, Cuckfield					Cp. house and garden, Harebeating.
Godden, Edward, Seaford					Freehold farm and house, Hawks.
Goldsmith, William					Freehold house and shop, Town.
Geering, Thomas					Leasehold house and shop, Town.
Hoad, James					One fr. and one copyhold house, Town
Hollebone, Charles, West Firle					Freehold house, Town.
James, Samuel					Freehold house, Town.
Kenward, Robert					House and land as ocp., near the Marsh
Kenward, John					Land as occupier, Harebeating.
Lade, Luke					Land as occupier, Town.
Lively, Joseph					House as occupier, the Crown Inn.
Longley, Jeremiah					Freehold house and farm, Harebeating
Mynn, John, Esq.					Fr. house and land, Otham Quarter.
Osborne, Bartholomew					Fr. house and land, Otham Quarter.
Pagden, Peter					Brewhouse as occupier, Harebeating.
Pitcher, John, Westham					Freehold marsh land, in the Marsh.
Perigoe, Samuel, Uckfield					Freehold land.
*Pierce, Thomas					House and ld. as ocp., Magham Down
Rhoods, Henry Crowhurst, Petworth					Fifth share of freehold marsh land, Loose marshes.
Rickman, Edwin					House and land as ocp., Amberstone
Sampson, Richard King, Esq.					Fr. house and land, near the Common.
*Slye, Matthias, Westham					Freehold marsh land, Marsh.
Sinnock, Samuel, Hailsham					Freehold house and garden, Town.
Stafford, William Whitmore					Freehold house, Town.
Slye, William					Freehold house and land, Town.
Stredwick, Thomas					Copyhold house, Cacklebury.
Shoosmith, John					House and land as occupier, Downash
Terry, Samuel					Freehold cottages, Cacklebury.
Tanner, William					Freehold house, Town.
Verrall, William					House and land as ocp., Harebeating.

NAMES.	D.	F.	Ch	Cs	QUALIFICATION AND WHERE SITUATE.
Weller, George		—			Freehold house and land, Harebeating
Weller, John		—			Freehold house and land, Cold Thorn.
Welch, Rev. Thomas Robinson		—			Freehold house and garden, Town.
*Wratten, David, Herstmonceux				—	Copyhold house, Summerheath.
White, Thomas		—			Freehold house and warehouses, Town
Willard, Thomas Rogers		—			Freehold house and land, Town.

HAMSEY.

NAMES.	D.	F.	Ch	Cs	QUALIFICATION AND WHERE SITUATE.
Aylwin, James				—	Land as occupier, Offham farm.
*Cheesman, John		—			Fr. h. and Brewhouse, Cooksbridge.
Guy, Henry		—			Land as occupier, Hamsey-place farm.
Guy, Nathaniel		—			Land as occupier, Cowlease farm.
Holmden, Thomas		—			Land as occupier, Hewen-street farm.
Harmer, George		—			Land as occupier, Offham lane.
Kell, Thomas Smith		—			Land as occupier, Cooksbridge farm.
Lambe, William		—			Land as occupier, Tulleys Wells farm.
Lashmar, James				—	Land as ocp., Great Hewen-street farm
Merricks, George				—	Freehold house, Friendly Hall.
Partington, Thomas, Esq.				—	Freehold house and land, Offham.
Shiffner, Sir George, bart.		—			House and land, Combe-place.
Shiffner, George, Rev., the Rectory		—			Rectorial Tithes of Hamsey.
Shiffner, Henry, Esq., Brighton		—			Rent charge out of Hewen-street farm
Shiffner, Thomas, Esq., Windsor Castle		—			Rent charge out of Hewen-street farm
*Steere, John, jun. West-street, Lewes	—				Mill and premises as ocp., Race-hill.
Uridge, Henry, Lewes				—	Freehold h., and land, Funnell's land.
Verrall, Henry				—	Copyhold h., and ld., Boundary Hall.

HEIGHTON.

NAMES.	D.	F.	Ch	Cs	QUALIFICATION AND WHERE SITUATE.
Geere, William					Fr. land, Geere's farm, Heighton.
Woolgar, George		—			Freehold h. and shop, Heighton-street

HELLINGLY.

NAMES.	D.	F.	Ch	Cs	QUALIFICATION AND WHERE SITUATE.
Arkcoll, William, South Malling				—	Freehold land and house, Horsebridge
Ashdown, Daniel				—	Copyhold houses, near Cockslow.
Bishop, James				—	Freehold house, Dicker.
Beeny, William				—	H., Mill and ld., as ocp., Horsebridge
*Blunden, John	—				Freehold house, Vicarage-street.
Bishop, James, Esq., Westburton				—	Freehold land, Shawpits.
Bennett, John, Esq.				—	Freehold house and land, Horsebridge
*Cumberbatch, Abraham Parry, Esq.				—	House as ocp., near the Church-yard.
Calverley, Thomas, Esq., Ewell Castle, Surrey				—	Freehold hou c and land, the Broad.
Clapson, John				—	Freehold land, Lyeshurst farm.
Clapson, George				—	Cp. house, mill and land, North-street
Comber, Joseph				—	Freehold houses, near the Church-yard
*Dunk, Thomas				—	Freehold house and land, Homestall.
*Dunk, James				—	Fr. house and land, School-house.
Douch, Samuel				—	Freehold house and land, Lee Bridge.
Ellis, Henry				—	Copyhold house and land, West-street
Goodwin, Thomas				—	House as occupier, White Hart Inn
Gosden, John				—	H. & ld. as ocp., Winkinghurst farm.
*Gilbert Benjamin Woodyer				—	Freehold house and land, Vicarage st.
Hart George Edward, West-st., Lewes				—	Freehold land, Grovebridge farm.
Hall, Thomas Colbran				—	House and land as ocp., Grovehill fm.
Humphrey, David				—	Cp. hs. and land, Dicker Brickyard.
Humphrey, William				—	Copyhold house, Horsebridge.
Huggett, William				—	House and land as ocp., Horsebridge.

NAMES.	D.	F.	Ch	Co	QUALIFICATION and WHERE SITUATE.
Huggett, William					Copyhold house and land, Dicker
Kennard, Stephen					Fr. house, land and mill, Church-mill.
Knight, Reuben					Freehold house and land, Dicker.
Martin, Thomas					Freehold house and land, Vicarage-st.
Martin, Thomas, jun.,					H. and land as ocp., West-st., farm.
Miller, William					Cp. houses and ld., Boreship Pottery
Mitchell, John					Cp. house and land Dicker Pottery.
Noakes, Robert					House and land as ocp., Cockslow fm.
Norman, Wm., 104, All Saints-street, Hastings					Freehold land, Back-lane.
*Olive, John, Rev.					Vicarage of Hellingly.
Page, Richard					House and land as occupier, Dicker.
Pattenden, John					H. and ld. as ocp., Knightsbridge fm.
Pitcher, Robert					Copyhold house and lds., Horsebridge
Russell, William					House and land as ocp., Hackhurst fm
Ripley, Mark					Copyhold house and land, Amberstone
Stapley, John					House and ld. as ocp., Horselunges fm
Todd, T.Esq.,Twickenham Pk., Midsx.					Freehold land, Horselunges.
Thorpe, William					Freehold and cp., land, Horsebridge.
*Thatcher, Thomas					House and land as ocp., Starnash fm.
Wheeler, F. James					H. and land as ocp., Boreship-house.
Watkins, Charles, Esq.					Freehold house and land, Lee Lands.

IFORD.

Donald, (The Rev.) Mathewman Hodgson					Vicarial Tythes of Iford.
Hurly, Henry					Freehold land.
Ridge, Henry, Alciston					Copyhold land.
Verrall, Richard					Land as occupier, Swanborough.

ISFIELD.

Attree, Richard					Freehold lands, Boathouse farm.
Gaunt, Charles, Rev.					Rectorial Tithes of Isfield.
Heaver, Benjamin					Land and mill as occupier, Isfield.
Hallett, James					Land as ocp., Batchelor's Hall farm.
*Heaver, Edward					Land as ocp., Buckham Hill farm.
*Hemsley, Abraham					Copyhold land.
Huntley, George					Land as occupier, New house farm.
King, John, Esq., Loxwood, Wisboro' Green					Freehold land, Isfield-place, Buckhorn, old mill and Pridie's farms.
Mannington, Peter, Isfield-place					Land as occupier, Isfield-place, Buckhorn, old mill and Pridie's farms.
Markwick, Ebenezer					Freehold land, late Diplocks.

JEVINGTON.

Ade, Henry, Willingdon					Fr. h. & ld., & ld. as ocp., Jevington-st
Filder, John Turner					Land as ocp., Jevington-place farm.
Grace, Thomas Henry, Rev., Westham					Rectorial Tithes of Jevington.
Mockett, Richard, Eastbourne					Freehold house, Jevington-street.
Noakes, Thomas					Land as occupier, Wannock farm.
Peerless, James					Copyhold house & Blacksmith's shop, Jevington-street.
Plasted, Henry, Haydon-st., London					Freehold house and ld., Jevington-st.
Reed, John					Land as ocp., Jevington-street farm.
Reed, Samuel					Freehold house, Jevington-street.

NAMES.	D.	F.	Ch	Cs.	QUALIFICATION and WHERE SITUATE.

KINGSTON.

Knight, Ewd., Godmersham Pk., Kent					Freehold Tythe.
Rogers, Henry					Land as occupier, Kingston farm.
Wise, Thomas					Copyhold house and land.

LAUGHTON.

Alcorn, George					Copyhold house and ld., Little Com.
Barrow, Joseph, Brickhouse					Copyhold land, Brickhouse.
Bishop, Thomas, Whitesmith					Copyhold house and land, Whitesmith
Downman, Sir Thomas, K.C.B., Dublin, Ireland					Cp. house and land, Laughton lodge.
Hide, William, Stonecross					Land as occupier, Stone Cross.
Hoad, Henry, Broomham					Copyhold house & fr. land Broomham
Johnston, Thomas, Lewes					Cp. house and land, Laughton-pound.
Kingman, James, Whitesmith					Cp. and fr. h. and land, Whitesmith.
Marchant, Richard					Land as occupier, Edinborough.
Randall, William, Whitesmith					Copyhold houses, Whitesmith.
Susans, John, Lewes					Freehold land, Laughton-pound
Starnes, Thomas					Freehold land.
*Starnes, Stephen					Freehold land.
Shoosmith, John					Land as occupier, Chambers-court.
Scrace, Edward					Land as occupier, Colbrans.
Wood, Rowland					Land as occupier, Laughton-place.
*Winton, William					Land as occupier, Halland.
Waters, Obadiah					Land as occupier, Millwards.

LITLINGTON.

Parris, Alfred, High-street					Parish Clerk of Litlington.
Robinson, William Beauclerk, Rev., Jevington					Rectorial Tithes of Litlington.
Scutt, Thomas, Rev., Clapham House					Freehold land, Clapham house.

LITTLE HORSTED.

Allchin, Thomas					Land as occupier, Horsted-pond farm.
Barry, Chas. Upham, Benit-pl., Cambridge					Fr. land, Hunington and Bradford fms.
Catt, Henry					Land as occupier, Owlsbery farm.
Homewood, John					Land as occupier, Wicklands farm.
Moon, Humphrey					Land as occupier, Worth farm.
Martin, John					Land as ocp., Plasket-park farm.
*Simpson, Rev. Joseph					Freehold house and land, Parsonage.
Skinner, James					Land as occupier, Hunington and Bradford farm.

LULLINGTON.

Woodhams, Walter					Land as ocp., Lullington Court farm.

NEWHAVEN.

Bond, Richard Massy					Freehold land, near the the Glebe land
Brooker, Richard					Copyhold house, High-street.
Cole, William					Ls. warehouse, Bonding warehouse.
*Eagles, Thomas Hadlow					Copyhold house, High-street.
Elphick, William, Steyning					Copyhold house.
Elphick, William, Esq.					Copyhold house and land, Newhaven.

NAMES.	D.	F.	Ch	Cs.	QUALIFICATION AND WHERE SITUATE.
Knight, Broho, 17, High-st., Lewes					Copyhold houses.
Knight, William					Copyhold house.
Smith, John, Rev.					Rectorial Tithes of Newhaven.
Stevens, William					Copyhold house.
Stone, William.. ..					Copyhold house, High-street.
Towner, Charles William					Copyhold house, High-street.
Vinall, Edward					Copyhold house, High-street..
Willard, Nicholas					Land as occupier, Court-house farm.
Woolgar, Richard					House and land as occupier, Glebe.

NEWICK.

NAMES.	D.	F.	Ch	Cs.	QUALIFICATION AND WHERE SITUATE.
*Attree, Thomas					Copyhold house and shop.
Blaauw, William Henry, Esq. ..					Freehold land, Beechlands.
Brook, James, sen., Barcombe ..					Copyhold land.
Best, William, Chailey ..					Dissenting Chapel, Newick Common
*Brooks, John					Copyhold house and garden.
Bish, William, sen., ...					Copyhold house and garden.
Collings, Thomas					Copyhold land, Painters farm.
Dudeney, Philip					Land as occupier, Lane-end farm.
Deane, James, Esq., Tunbridge Wells					Fr. and cp. lds., Snells & Ketches fms
Ellis, John .. .					Land as occupier, Church farm.
Hamshar, Edward					Land as occupier, Broomly farm.
Harmer, John					Copyhold land.
Hall, John					Copyhold land.
Hall, Henry, jun.					Freehold land, Goldbridge farm.
Hart, Edward					Freehold and copyhold land.
Impey, Elijah Barwell, Esq., Clapham Common					Copyhold house and land.
Isard, William, ...					Copyhold house and land
Morris Philip,					Land as occupier, Brit's farm
Powell (Rev.), Thomas Baden ..					Freehold glebe, Rectory
Slater, James Henry, Esq. ..					Freehold land, Newick Park
Sturt, John, ...					Freehold house, Colonel's-bank
Springett, Stephen					Land as occupier, School-house farm
Siffleet, Stephen					Freehold land
Siffleet, Michael					Copyhold house and land
Weston, Thomas					Copyhold house and land
Wheeler, Edward					Copyhold house and land

PIDDINGHOE.

NAMES.	D.	F.	Ch	Cs.	QUALIFICATION AND WHERE SITUATE.
Croft, Hugh					Land as occupier, Lodge farm
Tompsett, Joseph					Land as occupier, Dean's farm
Waterman, Edward					Copyhold land

PLUMPTON.

NAMES.	D.	F.	Ch	Cs.	QUALIFICATION AND WHERE SITUATE.
Avery, William					Inholmes farm, Plumpton Green
Bates, Edward					Oc. of ld. at a rental of £50 per ann., Plumpton Crossways
Baxter, John					Freehold house & lds, Plumpton Cross
Burtenshaw, John Martin ..					Land as occupier, Ashurst farm
Jenner, John					Copyhold house & lds, Plumpton-green
Martin, James ..					Land as occupier, Ridden's farm
Woodward, Rev. William ..					Freehold land, above 40s. per annum
Woolgar, Philip					Freehold house & ld., Plumpton-lane

NAMES.	D.	F.	Ch.	Ct.	QUALIFICATION AND WHERE SITUATE.
RINGMER.					
Baber, J., Esq., S. Bourne, Eastbourne					Freehold house & land, Middle-broyle
Bannister, John					Freehold house & land, Wellingham
Bannister, Thomas					Copyhold, Wellingham and Clayhill
*Berry, Ebenezer Henry					Freehold land, Ringmer-green
Berry, J., sen., Southmalling, Lewes,					Copyhold land, Winter's land
Berry, William					Two copyhold houses, Ringmer-green and back green
Blunt, Sir Chas. R. Bart., Heathfield,					Freehold house & ld., Ringmer-green
Brand, Henry B. W., Glynde-place,					Copyhold land, Mount farm
Brand, Thomas C. W., Glynde-place,					Copyhold land, Mount farm
Constable, Rev. John					Freehold house and land, Middleham
Cooke, John					Land as occupier, Plashet Park farm
*Cooper, Thos, St. Michael's, Lewes					Fr., lsd., & cp. house & ld, Moor-lane
Cosham, William					Freehold house & gar. Ringmer-green
Davies, James, Cliffe, Lewes					Freehold house & land, Ringmer-green
Fuller, Joseph					Land as occupier, Wellingham
Greenfield, William					Three copyhold houses, Ringmer-green
Green, Araunah, St. Michael's, Lewes,					Freehold houses & land, Broyle-lane, and near Dog-kennel & Park-gut
Hassell, John					Freehold house and land, Broyle-lane
Hillman, T. North-st, Cliffe, Lewes,					Land as ocp. Goat & Old-house farms
Hillman, John, Jun.					Land as ocp. Goat & Old-house farms
Holman, George					Land as ocp., Broyle, & ld., by Plashet
Howell, Robert					Freehold house and land, Norlington
Inskip, George					Freehold house and land, Moor-lane
King, Thomas, Cliffe, Lewes					Freehold house and land, Swingate
Lupton, John, Rev.					Fr. & cp. ld., Ashton and Broyle-lane
*Lewis, Charles Goring, Esq.					
Maitland, Robert, Esq., Middle Temple, London					Freehold and copyhold land, Bottenscrook, and near Green Man Inn
Martin, William, Jun.					Leasehold houses & ld. Ringmer-green
Martin, William,					Freehold land, near Chamberlaynes
Martin, David					Cp. houses, Ashton & near the church
Martin, Henry					Land as ocp., Upper-broyle Lodge farm
Merricks, James					Three cp. tnts. and ld. Ringmer-green
Morris, Benjamin, All Saint's, Lewes,					Freehold land, Norlington-field
Packett, John, Sen.					Fr. house & gn. & cp. ld., Clay-hill
Paine, Henry					Land as occupier, Broyle-place farm
Pelham, William					Two fr. houses & 1 gn., Broyle-side
Randalls, Joseph					Freehold house and land, Moor-lane
Rickman, John					Freehold house and land, Wellingham
*Rogers, Thomas, Southover					Land as occupier, Broyle-side
Saxby, Charles					Land as occupier, Middle Broyle, and Lower Lodge farms
Stevens, Richard					House and land as occupier, with Lee's land in Isfield, Old Ship Inn
Stevens, Walter					Seven fr. houses, Ringmer-green
Tasker, William					Two freehold houses, Broyle-lane
Verrall, George Henry					Land as occupier, Norlington farm
Weller, Henry					Two copyhold houses, Ringmer-green
* Withers, William					Land as oc., Withgate Moor-lane
RIPE.					
Bolton, Gillmore William, Esq., 25, Austin Friars', London					Freehold house and land
*, Edward					Land as occupier, Ripe

NAMES.	D.	F.	Ch	Cx	QUALIFICATION AND WHERE SITUATE.
Cane, William					Freehold land, Ripe-street
Feist, William					Freehold house and land, Ripe-street
Fuller, Joseph Paine, Laughton					Land as occupier, Lullhams
* Geall, John					Freehold house and land, Ripe-street
Mannington, Matthew					Land as occupier, Ripe
* Mannington, William, Lansdowne-place, Lewes					Freehold house and land, Darp
Martin William					Land as occupier. Ripe-street
Raynes, Rev. W., Rectory-house					Rectorial Tythes of Ripe
* Tourle, James, Sheer, Surrey					Freehold house, Ripe-street
Weeden, T., Bloomsbury-pl.,Brighton					Freehold land, Lullhams
Weller, James					Mill as occupier, Ripe
Westgate, Samuel					Two freehold houses

RODMELL.

NAMES.	D.	F.	Ch	Cx	QUALIFICATION AND WHERE SITUATE.
Fears, William					Copyhold house & gn., Rodmell street
Glazebrook, William					Copyhold house & gn., Rodmell-street
Marten, John					Freehold land, Rodmell-brooks
Saxby, Charles					Freehold house & land, Rodmell-street
Saxby, John, Northease					Leasehold land, Northease

ROTTINGDEAN.

NAMES.	D.	F.	Ch	Cx	QUALIFICATION AND WHERE SITUATE.
Beard, Thomas, Esq.					Copyhold land, West-side-land
Beard, Charles					Copyhold land, East-side-land
Beard, Stenning					Copyhold land
Belton, Joseph					Copyhold houses
Cracknell, William, Esq.					Copyhold houses
Coppard, Thomas					Freehold house
Cowley, Charles					Copyhold houses
D'Oyly, Thomas, Esq.					Copyhold houses
*Dedman, William, Shoreham					Freehold land, Norton farm
Dumbrell, William					Land as occupier, Manor farm
Finch, J., 33, Dean-st., Soho, London					Vicarial Tythes of Rottingdean
Farnecomb, John					Freehold land
Hooker, Rev. Thos., Redmond, D.D.					Copyhold houses
Ingram, James, Esq.					Copyhold houses
*Knight, Henry, Esq.					Copyhold houses
Lennard, Thomas, Esq.					House as occupier, in the street
Martin, Stephen					Copyhold house
Piper, Samuel					Copyhold houses
Richardson, Thomas					Copyhold houses
Rusbridge, Henry, West-st., Brighton					House as occupier
Smith, Gavin, Rottingdean-house					Copyhold houses, in the street
Stevens, John					Copyhold house

SAINT ANN, LEWES.

NAMES.	D.	F.	Ch	Cx	QUALIFICATION AND WHERE SITUATE.
Barchard, Francis, Esq., Ashcombe					House and ld. as ocp., Ashcombe h.
Boxall, John, High-street					Freehold house.
Davey, Edw., Black Lion-st., Brighton					Freehold land adjoining Church-yard.
Dicker, Thomas, High-street					Freehold land, West Laine.
Fold, John, sen., High-street					Freehold house.
Gear, Robert, (Esq.), High-street					Freehold house.
Gillham, James, 10, Nelson-street, Greenwich					4 Freehold houses.
Langridge, William, High-street					Freehold house, High-street.
Langridge, Wm. B., Esq., High-street					Freehold stable.

NAMES.	D.	F.	Ch.	Cs.	QUALIFICATION AND WHERE SITUATE.
Leney, Isaac, Cliffe					Land as occupier, Spital farm.
Lintott, James, High-street					Freehold houses, High-street.
Maxfield, Joseph, High-street					Freehold houses.
Medhurst, Samuel, High-street					Freehold house.
*Molineux, George, Esq., High-st.					Freehold house.
Scobell, John, Rev., St. Ann					Freehold land, Winterbourne lane.
Sickelmore, John, High-street					Mill as Lessee and occupier, Southern-street, Ann's mill.
Sturt, William, Chailey					Freehold house.
Winter John, High-street					Freehold houses.

ST. MICHAEL, LEWES.

NAMES.	D.	F.	Ch.	Cs.	QUALIFICATION AND WHERE SITUATE.
Alderton, Richard, Keere-street					Freehold house, High-street.
Avenall, Abhm., Church-st., Croydon					Freehold house, 71, High-street
Bailey, George, sen., High-street					Freehold house, High-street.
Blaker, John, Castle-place					Freehold house, 65, High-street.
*Brown, Richard, St. Ann					Freehold house.
*Carey, John, North-st., All Saints					
Carter, William, South-parade					2 copyhold houses, South-parade.
Cooper, Thomas, High-street					Freehold houses.
*Davey, William, 162, High-street					Freehold house.
Duplock, Thomas, High-street					Freehold house.
Goldsmith, Edward, 99, High-street					Freehold house.
Hammond, James, High-street					Freehold house, High-street.
Harvey, Daniel Whittle, Esq., Great George-street, Westminster					Freehold house, High-street.
Hobden, Charles, Keere-street					Freehold house.
*Holmden, George, Westerham, Kent					Freehold house, High-street.
Lee, Fred. Wm., Friars Wk., All Saints					Freehold house, 64, High-street.
Lee, Stewart Warren, High-street					Freehold house, 64, High-street.
*Lowdell, Stephen, High-street					Freehold house.
Mantell, Gideon, Old-steyne, Brighton					Freehold house, High-street.
*Mercer, William, Saint Michael,					Freehold house, High-street.
*Moon, Robert, Brighton					Freehold house, Saint Michaels.
Neal, Robert, High-street					Freehold house, 70, High-street.
Patchin, Thomas, Saint Ann					Freehold house, 87, High-street.
Pelham, John Cresset, Esq., Warren's Hotel, London					Freehold houses, High-street.
Porter, John, East-street					Freehold houses, Westgate-lane.
Proctor, G. Rev.D.D., Brighthelmston					Rectory of Saint Michael.
Robinson, William, South-parade					Freehold house.
Shelly, John, Precinct of the Castle					Copyhold house, Castle Banks.
Smart, William, High-street					Freehold house, High-street.
Smart, Samuel Hide, High-street					Freehold house, Saint Martins-lane.
*Waters, John High-st., St. Michael					Freehold stable, Bull-lane.
Willard, Richard, High-street					Freehold house.
*Williams, Chas. Kevern, Rev., High-street, St. Ann					Rent charge on a house, High-street.
Wood, John, High-street, Cliffe					Freehold house.
Wood, T. Daynes, Pentonville, London					Freehold house.
Wood, William, Bristol					Freehold house.

ST. JOHN UNDER THE CASTLE, LEWES.

NAMES.	D.	F.	Ch.	Cs.	QUALIFICATION AND WHERE SITUATE.
Adams, John, High-Street, All Saints.					Freehold house, St. John-street
Ancell, Thomas, North-street					Freehold house, Lancaster-street.
Baker, Robert Whiteman, North-st.					Freehold house, North-street.

LEWES POLLING DISTRICT.

19

NAMES.	D.	F.	Ch	Ca	QUALIFICATION AND WHERE SITUATE.
Barber, Edward, St. Nicholas-lane, All Saints					Freehold house, North-street.
Beard, Edward, High-st., St. Michael					Freehold stable and yard, Fisher-street
Bein, John, East-street, All Saints					Freehold house, Wellington-street.
Blackman, Henry, Esq., High-street, All Saints					Freehold house, High-street.
Blaker, Edgar, High-street, All Saints					Part of fr. coach house, West-street.
Blaker, John, jun., High-st., All Saints					Part of fr. coach house, West-street.
Boore, Chas., High-street, All Saints					Freehold house, North-street.
Boore, Edward, West-street					Freehold house, West-street.
Boore, Frederick, Sun-street					Freehold house, Sun-street.
Bristow, John, Wellington-street					Freehold house, Wellington-street.
Bull, Peter, High-street, St. Michael					Freehold houses, North-street.
•Butland, James, Lancaster-street					Freehold house, Lancaster-street.
*Card, Henry, North-street, All Saints					Freehold house, Lancaster-street.
Chatfield, Thomas, High-st., All Saints					Freehold houses, Brook-street.
Cooke, William, North-street					Copyhold houses, Mount Pleasant.
Corner, Richard, Cliffe, Lewes					Freehold houses, Brook-street.
Cowper, John, High-street					Freehold houses, Church-street.
Cox, William, High-street, St. Michael					Copyhold houses, New-road.
Crofts, Peter Guerin, Rev., Malling-hs.					Rectory of St. John under the Castle.
Dudeney, John, St John-street					Freehold house, St. John-street.
Ellis, Thomas, Court-house					Land as occupier, Court-house farm.
Every, John, North-street.					Freehold houses, North-street.
*Evershed, Thomas, Cliffe, Lewes					Part of fr. hs., St. John-st. and Sun-st.
Fennell, James, Lancaster-street					Freehold house, Brook-street.
Fowle, William, Cliffe, Lewes					Freehold house, St. John-street.
Francis, Philip, St. John-street					Freehold houses, Spring gardens.
Fuller, John, Barcombe					
Gell, Francis Harding, Esq., High-street, All Saints					Freehold house, Sun-street.
Gibbs, James, Sun-street					Pt. of fr. hs. St. John-st. and Sun-st.
Hackman, George, Allington					Land as occupier, Allington farm.
*Harman, Sargent, Fisher-street					Freehold house, Fisher-street.
*Hillman, Samuel, South-malling					Freehold house, Church-street.
Hilton, John, All Saints, Lewes					Cp. yard and gn., with a cp. h. and ld. in Horsted Keynes, St. John.
*Howell, Richard, Alciston					Freehold house, North-street.
Hollands, John, All Saints, Lewes					Freehold house, North-street.
Holmes, William Esq., Brookfield, in the parish of Leominster, Sussex					Five freehold cottages, North-street.
Huggett, William, Lancaster-street.					Freehold house, Lancaster-street.
Inskip, John, Eastgate-st., All Saints					Freehold house, St. John-street.
Knight, Richard, St. John-street					Freehold house, St. John-street.
Langford, John, Precinct of the Castle					Freehold house, North-street.
Levett, George, Southover					Freehold house, St. John-street.
Lower, Reuben Wm., Lansdown-place, All Saints					Freehold house, Church-street.
Marsh, Thomas, Poor-hs., All Saints					Freehold house, Lancaster-street.
Martin, Fred., Burlington-st., Brighton					Fr. Slaughter-house, St. John-street.
Martin, Selven, Fisher-street					Freehold house, Fisher-street.
Merricks, George, Hamsey					Freehold houses, North-street.
Neal, Edwin, High-street, St. Michael					Freehold house, Lancaster-street.
Porter, Henry, Cliffe, Lewes					Freehold house, Spring-gardens.
Porter, Richard, Cliffe, Lewes					Freehold Chapel St. John-street.
Potter, Isaac, Green-wall					Freehold house, Spring-gardens.
Potter, Peter, Green-wall					Freehold house, Spring-gardens.
Robinson, George, Mount Pleasant					Freehold house, West-street.

NAMES.	D.	F.	Ch.	Cs.	QUALIFICATION AND WHERE SITUATE.
Rogers, William, North-street, Westminster		—			Freehold house, Sun-street.
Rooke, John, Sun-street ..		—			Freehold house, Sun-street.
Rusbridge, Stephen, North-street ..		—			Freehold house, North-street.
Short, Henry, North-street ..		—			Freehold houses, Brook-street.
Smith, Wm., Market-st., All Saints..		—			Fr. hs., North-street, Green Wall.
Smith, William, Cuckfield & Brighton					Freehold houses, Sun-street.
Stephens, Charles, West-street ..		—			Freehold houses, West-street.
*Tourle, Thomas, Esq., Landport ..		—			Freehold land, Beechwood farm.
*Waller, James, Sun-street		—			Freehold house, Sun-street.
Willis, John, Essex-street, Strand, Westminster					Freehold land, Mountfield.
Winch, John, North-street ..		—			Freehold houses, North-street.
Wright, William, North-street ..		—			Freehold house, Brook-street.

SAINT THOMAS-A-BECKET IN THE CLIFFE, LEWES.

NAMES.	D.	F.	Ch.	Cs.	QUALIFICATION AND WHERE SITUATE.
Ade, Durrant, East-street, Lewes ..		—			Freehold house, High-street.
Berry, Thomas, Malling-st, Lewes ..		—			Freehold house, High-street.
Brown, Nicholas, Chepstow, Monmouthshire					Freehold house, Foundry road.
Bunting, Charles Kennard..		—			Rent charge freehold houses.
Farnes, John		—			Freehold house, North-street.
Farnes, John, jun.		—			Freehold Wharf, Foundry road.
Flint, Samuel, High-street, Lewes ..					Moiety of freehold house, High-street.
Frankland, Samuel, High-st., Lewes		—			Fr. building or chapel, Chapel-hill.
Freeman, John					Freehold house.
Garnham, Barnard		—			Freehold houses.
Gaston, William.. . ..		—			Freehold house, North-street.
Geering, John		—			Freehold cottages.
Godlee, Burwood .. .					Freehold house, High-street.
Goodyer, Richard ..		—			Annuity charged on fr. hs. High-street
Green, Henry		—			Freehold house.
Grover, John			—		Freehold cottage.
Grover, Simon			—		Freehold house.
Gurnett, John, Hailsham			—		Freehold house.
*Harvey, Daniel.. ..		—			Freehold house, High-street.
*Hicks, George		—			Freehold house, North-street.
Hillman, Henry		—			Freehold house.
Hillman, James, Great St. Andrews, Cambridge		—			Two freehold houses.
Hillman, John		—			Freehold house.
Hillman, Thomas Reeves, Trinity College, Cambridge, & Cliffe, Lewes		—			Freehold house and shop, High-street.
Hother, Charles, New-street ..					Freehold house, North-street.
Johnston, Thomas, jun. ..		—			Freehold factory.
Lambe, Richard, High-street ..		—	—		Share of freehold factory.
Lambe, William, High-street ..		—	—		Share of freehold factory.
Leney, Samuel		—			Freehold houses.
Madgwick, Thomas, High-street ..		—			Freehold warehouse.
Martin, Richard		—			Freehold house.
Mitchell, John, Hurstperpoint		—			Freehold house, Chapel-hill.
Morris, Ebenezer		—			Freehold house.
Nutley, Edward, Southover ..		—			Freehold house.
*Peckham, Edwin		—			Freehold houses
Povey, William, St. Martin's-lane ..		—			Two freehold houses.
Rusbridge, Charles . ..		—			Freehold houses.
Rusbridge, William ! ..			—		Freehold house, South-street

NAMES.	D.	F.	Ch.	Cs.	QUALIFICATION AND WHERE SITUATE.
Rusbridge, Benjamin					Freehold houses
Simmonds, William					Freehold house.
Smart, Thomas, Horsham			—		Freehold house, North-street.
*Spencer, Chris., 40, Ship-st., Brighton					Freehold house.
Venus, John					Freehold houses.
Verrall, George Henry, Ringmer					Freehold house.
Verrall, Alexander					Freehold house.
Whatley, Richard, North-street					Two freehold houses, North-street.
Wille, George					Six freehold houses, Soap factory-lane.
Wood, Thomas, High-street					Freehold inn, High-street.
Woollgar, John Webb, East-street					Freehold house, High-street.

SEAFORD TOWN, AND PORT.

NAMES.	D.	F.	Ch.	Cs.	QUALIFICATION AND WHERE SITUATE.
Allwork, Thomas, sen.					Freehold houses.
Allwork, Thomas, jun.					Freehold houses.
Atkinson, Jas. Simmons, 212, Regent-street, London					Freehold warehouse
Beal, Richard					Freehold house.
*Bingham, Rev. Rd., Gosport, Hants					Tithe and glebe.
Brooker, James, Esq.					Freehold house, near the Town-hall.
Buckwell, Henry, Sutton					Land as occupier, North Sutton farm.
Bull, Henry					Freehold house, late the Ship.
Bull, Thomas Henry, Newhaven					Freehold house, High-street.
*Carnegie, Rev. James					Tithe and glebe of Sutton cum Seaford.
Chambers, Thos. Wm., Esq., Chinting					Freehold house and land, Town farm.
Ceaplin, Charles					Freehold house.
Champion, William					Freehold house and land.
Colwell, James					Freehold house.
Ellis, Edward					Land as occupier, Lodge farm.
Fitz Gerald, John, Esq., Portland-pl., London					Freehold house and land, the Lodge.
Gorring, James					Freehold house.
Gorring, Thomas			—		Freehold houses.
Hubard, Joseph					Freehold house.
Haine, John					Freehold house.
Horn, Emanuel, Sutton					Land as occupier, South Sutton farm.
King, John, Berwick-court					Land as occupier, Chownes farm.
Redman, Richard					Freehold houses.
Roberts, Daniel					Freehold house, High-street.
Simmonds, James					Freehold house.
Stevens, Joseph					Freehold houses, High-street.
Stevens, George					Freehold houses, High-street.
Towner, William					Freehold houses, High-street.
Towner, W., jun.					Freehold houses.

SELMESTON.

NAMES.	D.	F.	Ch.	Cs.	QUALIFICATION AND WHERE SITUATE.
Gorringe, James, Tilton farm					Land as occupier, Tilton farm.
Hilder, Thomas, Mays farm					Land as occupier, Mays farm.
Hillman, Thomas, North-street, Cliffe					Land as occupier, Part of Goat farm.
Latham, Rev. Henry, the Vicarage					Vicarial Tythes of Selmeston.
Skinner, James, Sherrington					Land as occupier, Sherrington farm.

SOUTHEASE.

NAMES.	D.	F.	Ch.	Cs.	QUALIFICATION AND WHERE SITUATE.
Funnell, William Baker					Land as occupier, Southease.
Kent, John					Copyhold land.
Kent, James					Copyhold land.
Tourle, Knight William, Buxted					Rent charge, 60l. per ann., Southease.
Verrall, Miles, All Saints, Lewes					Land as occupier, Southease.

NAMES.	D.	F.	Ch	Cc.	QUALIFICATION and WHERE SITUATE.

SOUTHMALLING.

NAMES.	QUALIFICATION and WHERE SITUATE.
Berry, Henry Ebenezer	Freehold house & land.
*Burrell, C. M., Bt., KneppCas., Shipley	Freehold farm, Upper Stoneham.
Cruttenden, *William*, Peasmarsh	Freehold cottage, Malling-street.
Grantham, Stephen	Land as oc., Lower Stoneham farm
Hamlin. John, Spring-gardens. Lewes	Freehold house, mill, and land.
Hoey, Geo. Beard, Cliffe, Lewes	Freehold garden, pleasure garden.
Hoey, George, jun., Cliffe, Lewes	Freehold houses.
*Lewis, Charles Goring, Esq.	House and land as oc., Ryder's Well.
Madgwick, Wm., sen., All Saints, Lewes	Freehold land, Ryder's Well.
Pettet, Thomas, sen.	Freehold houses.
Philcox, Moses	One-fourth part of freehold houses.
Relf, Samuel, tendered for Darby and Fuller	
	Hs. & ld. as oc., Upper Stonham farm.
Ridge, William	Freehold house, South-street.
Robinson, Samuel	Freehold house and garden.
*Robinson, Thos., All Saints, Lewes	Freehold house.
Saunders, John,	Freehold house & land, Malling-house and Lower Stoneham.
Spence, Henry Hume, Esq., Earl's-terrace, Kensington	
Wille, Charles, jun., Cliffe, Lewes	Freehold house & land, Ryder's Well.

SAINT JOHN THE BAPTIST, SOUTHOVER.

NAMES.	QUALIFICATION and WHERE SITUATE.
Baker, James	Freehold cottage, Spring-gardens
Carter, John, Walwer's-lane, Lewes	Freehold house, Ham-lane.
Cheal, Alexander, Uckfield	Freehold houses, High-street.
*Cheal, Charles	Freehold warehouse, High-street.
Collins, James, Chiddingly	Freehold houses, Spring-gardens.
Cook, David, High-street, St. Anns	Land, as occupier, Quarry Brooks.
Cruttenden, Thomas	Freehold houses, Spring gardens.
Durrant, John Mercer Bosville, Portland Cottage, Hammersmith	Freehold farm.
Fairhall, John.	Fr. h. & gn., back of High-street.
Francis, T. Spring, West-st., St. John's	Freehold house, Eastport-lane.
Goldsmith, John.	Freehold-houses, High-street.
Goldsmith, Henry, Friar's-walk, Lewes	Freehold houses, Spring-gardens.
Grantham, George, High-street, Lewes	Freehold land, Quarry Brooks.
Heseltine, Wm., Turret-h., S. Lambeth	Freehold houses, High-street.
Huggett, John, High-street, Lewes	Freehold houses, Garden-street.
Ingram, Hugh, Steyning	Freehold house, High-street.
Leonard, Jas., Little East-st., Lewes	Freehold house, Ham lane.
Mercer, John	Freehold house, High-street.
Morris, James	Land as occupier, Priory farm.
Moreton, William	Freehold house, St. James's-street.
Penfold, William	Freehold houses, East-port lane.
Pollard, Jas., St. Nicholas-lane, Lewes	Freehold houses, Spring gardens.
Pumphrey, George	Freehold house, St. James's-Street.
*Reed, Thomas	Freehold house, Ham lane.
Robinson, Charles	Freehold Brewhouse, Spring gardens.
Shoesmith, John	Freehold stable, East-port lane.
Smith, William, High-street, Lewes	Freehold land, Quarry Brooks.
Swaysland, Thomas, sen.	Freehold shop, High-street.
Tillman, John	Freehold house, Ham-lane.
Verrall, William,	Freehold land.
Verrall, Wm., jun., Keere-st., Lewes	Freehold houses, High-street.
*Verrall, Harry	Freehold house, High-street.
'eller, Isaiah	Freehold house, High-street.

NAMES.	D.	F.	Ch.	Cs.	QUALIFICATION AND WHERE SITUATE.

STANMER.

NAMES.	D.	F.	Ch.	Cs.	QUALIFICATION AND WHERE SITUATE.
Woodman, Richard					Land as occupier, Park farm.

STREET.

NAMES.	D.	F.	Ch.	Cs.	QUALIFICATION AND WHERE SITUATE.
Fitzhugh, Wm. A., Rev., Parsonage					Rectorial Tithes of Street.
Ridge, Benjamin, St. Ann's, Lewes..					Copyhold land, Captains farm.
Knight, Thomas					Land as occupier, Combers farm.
Sturt, William					Freehold lands, Elm Grove farm.
Trower, John					Freehold land, Godman's farm.

TARRING-NEVILLE.

NAMES.	D.	F.	Ch.	Cs.	QUALIFICATION AND WHERE SITUATE.
Fuller, Robert					H. and ld. as ocp., Tarring Court farm
Ranger, George					Fr. house and garden in Tarring-street
Wynch, Hy., Belle Vue Hall, Brighton					The glebe and tithes of Tarring Neville

TELSCOMBE.

NAMES.	D.	F.	Ch.	Cs.	QUALIFICATION AND WHERE SITUATE.
Hutchins, Jas., the Rev., Rottingdean					Rectorial Tithes of Telscombe.
Kent, George					Land as occupier, Telscombe farm.
*Osborne, William . ..					House and land as ocp., Warren farm.
Tompsett, James, Piddinghoe ..					House and land as ocp., Pond farm.

UCKFIELD.

NAMES.	D.	F.	Ch.	Cs.	QUALIFICATION AND WHERE SITUATE.
Best, James, High-street ..					H. and ld. as ocp., Bell-Inn, High-st.
Cameron, James, Uckfield Nursery..					Fr. house & Nursery, North entrance
Cloake, Henry ,High-street ..					House as occupier, Maidenhead Inn.
Covey, William Henry, High-street..					House and land as ocp., High-street.
Eade, George, Church-street ..					Two copyhold hs., Ch-st. and Budlets.
Fenner, William, Ridgewood Hill ..					Two copyhold hs., at Ridgewood-hill.
Gosling, William, High-street ..					Freehold and Cp. houses, High-street.
Hart, Richard, Esq., Beddingham ..					Fr. and cp. land, Uckfield and Buxted.
Hurdis, George Clarke, Esq., High-st.,					Copyhold house, High-street.
How, William, High-street ..					Five fr. hs., High-street & Church-st.
Hastings, Thomas Martin, Church-st.,					Cp. house and garden, South entrance
Jenner, John, Fir Cottage.. ..					H. and ld. as occupier, Olive's farm.
*Jarratt, John, Ringles Cross ..					Cp. buildings and ld., at Ringles Cross.
Kenward, Edward, Church-street ..					Copyhold h. & Malthouse, Church-st.
Kenward, John, Ridgewood ..					Copyhold house and land, Ridgewood.
Kenward, William, Ridgeland farm..					Four cp. hs., at Ridgewood Common.
Lidbetter, George, Tunbridge Wells					Copyhold Warehouse, Hempsted lane.
Lidbetter, Samuel, High-street ..					Freehold houses, High-street.
Lidbetter, William Henry, High-street					Copyhold houses and ld., High-street.
Mabbott, W. Courthope, Esq., High-st.					Freehold house, High-street.
Mannington, John, High-street ..					Copyhold h. and shop, High-street.
Mannington, George, Uckfield Mill..					Fr. house & Mill near Uckfield bridge.
Markwick, John, High-street ..					Four copyhold houses, High-street.
Markwick, Rd., North-entrance ..					Copyhold house
Markwick, Stephen, Church-street ..					Fr. house, Copt-hall, North-entrance
Merricks, T. near Uckfield-bridge ..					Fr. house and shop, South-entrance
Newnham, John, Uckfield Brewery..					Fr. & cp.hs. King's Head & Bell Inns
Pentecost, Thomas, High-street ..					Copyhold houses, Church-street
Prince, Charles, High-street ..					Copyhold house, High-street
Streatfield, Rd. S., Esq., The Rocks					Fr. & cp. lands, Uckfield & Framfield
Smith, William, Esq., Hempsted ..					Fr. & cp. lands, Uckfield & Framfield
Shephard, Thomas, High-street ..					Copyhold house & garden, High-street

NAMES.	D.	F.	Ch	Cs.	QUALIFICATION AND WHERE SITUATE.
Simes, Edmund, Harland's farm					Land as occupier, Harland's farm
Simes, Henry, High-cross					Land as occupier, Harland's farm
Shipton, John, High-street					Freehold house, High-street
Turner, James, North-entrance					Copyhold h. & gn., North-entrance
Underwood, John, Rev., Church-st.					Two copyhold houses, Church-street
Woodward, John, Esq., High-street					House as occupier, High-street
Waterman, James, nr. Uckfield-bridge					Copyhold house, South-entrance
Whapham, John, High-street					Copyhold house and land, High-street

WESTDEAN.

NAMES.	D.	F.	Ch	Cs.	QUALIFICATION AND WHERE SITUATE.
*Ade, Charles, Charlston					Land as occupier, Charlston farm
Ellis, John, Exceat					Land as occupier, Exceat
Ellis, John Thomas, Jun., Exceat					Land as occupier, Exceat
Newman, William, Charlston					Land as occupier, Charlston
Saxby, Richard,					Land as occupier, Westdean
Wells, George, Rev., Wiston, Sussex					Prebend of Exceat & rent charge of £5

WESTFIRLE.

NAMES.	D.	F.	Ch	Cs.	QUALIFICATION AND WHERE SITUATE.
Berry, George					Land as occupier, Newhouse farm
Davy, William, Southover, Lewes					Freehold house and garden
Ellis, Charles Marchant					Land as occupier, Bushy-lodge farm
Hutchinson, Charles Edward Rev.					Vicarial Tithes of Westfirle
Langridge, John					Land as occupier, Charlston-farm
Langridge, Joseph, Union-st., Brighton					Copyhold land, Strong's-farm
Putland, John					Land as occupier, Place-farm
Stephens, John					Land as occupier, Preston-farm
*Saxby, William					Land as occupier, Church-farm

WESTMESTON.

NAMES.	D.	F.	Ch	Cs.	QUALIFICATION AND WHERE SITUATE.
Botting, William					Land as occupier, Blackbrook farm
Botting, William					Land as oc., Westmeston-place farm
Cripps, John Marten, Esq.					Freehold house & ld., Blackbrook farm
Courthope, Wm., Rev., the Parsonage					Rectorial Tithes of Westmeston
Faulkener, William					Land as occupier, Common-farm
Hunter, William					Fr. house & land, Wm. Carter, tenant
Springate, John					Land as occupier, Hayligh-farm
Tomlinson, Nicholas					House & land as oc., Middleton-place

WILLINGDON.

NAMES.	D.	F.	Ch	Cs.	QUALIFICATION AND WHERE SITUATE.
Ade, Charles					Land as occupier, Chalk-farm
Adams, William,					Freehold house & gn., Willingdon-st.
Adams, William, jun.					Houses & cottages as occupier, Willingdon-street
Bartholomew, William					Freehold house & gn. Willingdon-st.
Bates, John Ellison, Rev., Eardiston, near Worcester					Freehold & copyhold lands, Rapson's-farm
Denman, Arnold					Land as occupier, Park-farm
Elphick, Henry					Copyhold house and garden
Filder, Joseph, Eastbourne					Copyhold lands, Lotbridge-marsh
Moore, Henry, Rev.					Vicarage of Willingdon
*Newman, Robert, Brighton					Freehold house & lds, Willingdon-st.
Putland, John, Westfirle					Land as occupier, New-barn farm
Page, Richard					Freehold house, self occupier
Rason, William, Eastbourne					Copyhold lands
Rippington, Edward					Freehold house & lds., Willingdon-st.
Seymour, Joseph					Freehold and copyhold land

NAMES.	D.	F.	Ch	Cg.	QUALIFICATION AND WHERE SITUATE.
Symms, William, West Grinsted					Freehold house and garden
Shoosmith, Joseph, Willingdon					Land as occupier, Willingdon-street
Thomas, Inigo, Esq.					Freehold house and land, Ratton
Ticehurst, William					Copyhold house and garden
* Terry, Thomas					Freehold house and land
Vine, James					Copyhold house and garden
Verrall, Charles					Copyhold house & gn., Willingdon-st.
Verrall, Henry					Copyhold house and garden.
Willard, James Dippery					Freehold house and lands.
Webster, John Charles, Eastbourne					Copyhold house & lds., Willingdon-st.

WILMINGTON.

NAMES.	D.	F.	Ch	Cg.	QUALIFICATION AND WHERE SITUATE.
Alfrey, George, Esq., 34, Great St. Helen's, London					Freehold land, Copthall farm.
Ade, James					Land as occupier, Hayreed farm.
Cavendish, William George, the Hon., Burlington-house, London					Copyhold house
Cooper, George Miles, Rev., Vicarage					Vicarial Tithes of Wilmington.
Davis, William					Copyhold house & ld., Wilmington-st.
Lambe, William					Copyhold land, Sand-pit, land.
Lambe, John					Copyhold land, Newfield & other land.
Lambe, Richard					Land as oc., Chawhams & other land.
Peerless, William					Copyhold house, Wilmington-street
* Vine, William					Copyhold house & ld., Wilmington-st.

CUCKFIELD POLLING DISTRICT.

ARDINGLY.

NAMES.	D.	F.	Ch	Cg.	QUALIFICATION AND WHERE SITUATE.
Betchley, Richard					Ocp. of land, Stroodgates & Newhouse
Comber, Thomas					Occupier of land, Town-house.
*Comber, William					Fr. h. & land, part of Jenkins Croft.
Hamilton, Rev. James					Rectorial Tithes, &c., of Ardingly.
Leppard, John					Land, Avens farm.
Marchant, Henry					House & land, Hill-house farm.
Robinson, W. Sanders, Reigate, Surrey					Freehold messuage, &c., Town-house
Stanbridge, Thomas, West Hoathly					Leasehold house and shop, Hapstead Green.
Uwins, Richard, Lingfield					Fr. h. and ld., Hapstead green.

BALCOMBE.

NAMES.	D.	F.	Ch	Cg.	QUALIFICATION AND WHERE SITUATE.
Booker, John					Fr. h. & ld., in the parish of Balcombe.
Brown, Jos., jun.					Copyhold house and land in the Street.
Bones, William					Fr. house and garden, High-street.
*Coomber, Thomas					Copyhold house and land, Stone Hall, Newhouse, and others.
Coomber, John					Copyhold house and lands in the Street

E

NAMES.	D.	F.	Ch.	Cs.	QUALIFICATION AND WHERE SITUATE.
Gibb, Thomas					Copyhold houses in the Street.
Humphry, Michael					Cp. h. & lds., Little Cooper's Corner, in the parish of Balcombe.
Ireland, John					Fr. house & other property, North lane
Newham, William					Cp. farm and lands, yearly 10l. value, North lane.
Pennifold, John					Copyhold house and lands, Rocks lane
Sarel, Rev. Henry Rule					Rectorial tithes of Balcombe.
Strong, Rev. Clement					House and land, Balcombe house.
Tester, Charles,					House and land, Green Trees.
Unwins, William					House & land, Spices farm.
Webber, John					Copyhold house and shop in the Alley.

BOLNEY.

NAMES.	D.	F.	Ch.	Cs.	QUALIFICATION AND WHERE SITUATE.
Agate, Thomas, Bolney-street					Freehold lands, Gravelies farm.
Beeching, John					H. & ld. as occupier, Hulks land.
Baker, Jn., 19, Lavender-st., Brighton					Freehold cottage.
*Borrer, John Hamlin, Gloucester-place, Brighton					Freehold land.
Chittenden, Andrew, 13, Charles-street, Middlesex Hospital, London.					Fr. ld., Bolney farm or Hulks land.
Cragg, Richard					Land as occupier, Brooklands farm.
Geering, John, Twineham					Occupier of Marsh lands in Bolney.
Holroyd, John, sen., 23, Northumberland-street, Strand, London					Freehold house and shop.
Jeffery, Richard					Ld. as oc., Hill house, Gravelies and Jerimees farm.
Leppard, James					Land as occupier, Bolney place farm.
Marshall, Wm. Esq., Hurstperpoint.					Freehold land, Garsons farm.
Pierce, Stephen					Land as occupier, Brookers farm
Ryecroft, Sir Henry, Bart., Priory, Kew, Surrey					3 fr. cottages, Bolney-st. and Cm.
*Tredcroft, Henry Esq., Warnham Court, Warnham					Freehold house.
*Tribe, William, Worthing					Moiety of a freehold farm.
Tufnell, Rev. Jn. Chas., Hurstperpoint					Freehold land.
Vincent, Rev. Wm Saint Andrew					Glebe land and small tithe.
*Waller, James, Horsham					Fr. fms., Egglands & Cheetsgrove.
Winter, William					Land as ocp., Holmwood house farm.

CLAYTON.

NAMES.	D.	F.	Ch.	Cs.	QUALIFICATION AND WHERE SITUATE.
Avery, Thomas					Copyhold land, Fowls and Barbers.
Bayntain, Chas., North-st., Brighton					Freehold land.
Bayntain, Lawrence C. jun., I.U.S.C., London					Freehold house.
Brooker, Wm., St. John's Common					Copyhold house & land, late Daniels.
Burthenshaw, James					Land as occupier, Ham farm.
Dewey, Henry					Land as occupier, Clayton Wickham.
Ede, John, Clayton-street					Freehold building, Clayton windmill.
*Elwood, C., Lt.-Col., Priory, Clayton					Fr. h. and ld., Hammonds farm.
Ford, Thos. sen., St. John's Common					Fr. h. & gn., St. John's Common.
Gainsford John, Hammonds Mill					Fr. bg. and land, Hammonds Mill.
Jeffery, James, St. John's Common					Cp. h. and land, St. John's Common.
Kinchen, William					Copyhold house and land, Birds hole.
Ockenden, William, Coldharbour					Land as ocp., Cold Harbour farm.
Pronger, Edmond					Land as occupier, Bridge farm.
*Shuttelworth, George Esq., Poultry, London					Copyhold house and land.

NAMES.	D.	F.	Ch	Cs.	QUALIFICATION AND WHERE SITUATE.
Stubbs, Hasted, Mill lane		—			Land as occupier, Friars Oak farm.
Whiteman, Thos. Dominick, Spring Cottage			—		Fr. house and land, Spring cottage.

CRAWLEY.

NAMES.	D.	F.	Ch	Cs.	QUALIFICATION AND WHERE SITUATE.
Bisshopp, Robert		—			Freehold houses, Magazines.
*Biggs, Thomas, Reigate, Surrey ..			—		Freehold houses, Underhill & Weeks.
Broadwood, T. Esq., Holmbush, Sussex					Freehold farms, Buckenhill or Wynd farm and Shelley.
Buckle, Mathew, City of Bath ..					Jurdens farm.
Caffin, John, Ifield					Leashold stables.
Clitherow, Jas., Boston h., Brentford					Freehold lands Place farm.
Holder, James, Crawley		—			Freehold houses.
*Johnson, Joseph, Ifield		—			Freehold houses and land.
Lewin, Rev., Spencer James, Ifield ..					Rectorial tithes of Crawley.
*Midleton, Charles, Lowfield Heath			—		Fr. cottages, N. entrance of Crawley.
Mitchell, John, Crawley ..					H. & ld., 50l. a-yr., in Crawley & Worth
Newman, James		—			H. and ld. as occupier, the Sun Inn.
Robinson, John					Land as occupier, Crawley place.
*Smith, Thomas		—			Freehold land, Church Croft.
Snelling, James		—			2 freehold houses.
Swan, Edward, Dorking, Surrey ..					Freehold houses.
Tusler, James, Crawley ..		—			Freehold house, Crosskeys.

CUCKFIELD.

NAMES.	D.	F.	Ch	Cs.	QUALIFICATION AND WHERE SITUATE.
Agate, Thomas, Westup ..				—	Land as occupier.
Anscombe, Joseph				—	Copyhold house, Cuckfield town.
Bannister, John				—	House and land as occupier, Sparks, Courtlands, and Denmans farms.
Barber, Phillip, Mallions				—	Copyhold land, Langleys or Mallions.
Baynton, Samuel Adlam, U.S.C., London					Rent charge on ld., part in Cuckfield & in Balcomb, Worth and Keymer.
Bellamy, T. Jones, Esq., Willies, ..					Freehold h. and land, Clevars lane.
Best, Faulkner				—	Freehold house, Talbot Inn.
Bray, Henry, Bolney		—			Freehold house, Cuckfield Town.
Bray, Henry, jun.				—	Copyhold house, Church-street.
Brigden, Thomas.. ..				—	Fr. house and garden, Church-street.
Broad, William, Dorking, Surrey ..					Freehold messuages and gardens.
*Broomfield, Thomas, Cuckfield ..				—	H. & ld. as ocp., Great Hayward fm.
Botting, William, Moon Hill ..					Land as occupier, Moonhill farm.
Betchely, Edward ..				—	Copyhold farm, Westlands farm.
Caffyn, Jacob, Lucas farm ..				—	Freehold land near Haywards heath.
Cherry, John Peter, Esq., Pilsty ..			—		Copyhold land and tithes of Pilsties Lakes, Hopes and Rowhill.
Clutton, Wm., Hartswood, Buckland, Surrey					Copyhold fm. and corn tithes, Hallies and tithes of Lanes farm.
Cook, John English, Bolnors farm ..					Copyhold land, Staplefield Common.
Cooper, George, Nymans ..					Copyhold land, Nymans farm.
Croucher, Thomas, Balcombe, Sussex					Copyhold h. & ld., nr. Whitemans green
*Crunden, Henry, Reigate, Surrey ..				—	Freehold house, Cuckfield town.
*Chatfield, Robert, Stockwell, Surrey				—	Freehold land, Sidny farm.
Chart, Richard				—	Freehold house, Cuckfield town.
*Elliott, William..				—	Copyhold house, Cuckfield town.
Field, James, Bloxmead farm ..				—	Freehold land, Bloxmead farm.
Fieldwick, William, Slough farm ..				—	Land as occupier, Slough farm.
Ford, William, Vinals farm ..				—	Land as ocp., Vinals farm & Rowland, near Staplefield Common.

NAMES.	D.	F.	Ch.	Cs.	QUALIFAICATION AND WHERE SITUATE.
Greenfield, Edmund, Barnhall cottage					Freehold h. & ld., Staplefield green.
Hobden, James					Cp. h. and ld., Haseldean farm.
Holden, Stephen, North-street, Lewes					Freehold house, Cuckfield town.
Hoper, J. Jun., Esq., High-st. Lewes					Freehold house & land, Kenmead farm
Hearn, Rev. Robert, Broadfield, St.					Freehold and Cp. land, Heasewood,
George, Suffolk					Easeland, & Lower Moonhill farms
Jeffery, Joseph, Cuckfield..					House and land as occupier, Horse-gate and Old Park farms.
Jeffery, Joseph, Jun.					Fr. h. & ld., near Whitemans green.
Jenner, Charles					Copyhold house and garden, Broad-st.
Juniper, Charles, Rose and Crown ..					Freehold houses.
*Juniper, Charles, Jun. ..					Copyhold land near Slough green, and at Whitemans green.
Kennard, Richard, Hayward's-heath					Fr. house and garden, Lindfield lane.
Knight, Stephen, Whiteman's-green					Fr. house and land, Whitemans green.
Lency Isaac					Fr. h. & ld., N. end of Cuckfield town
Marchant, William, Moorfields ..					Land as occupier, Moorfields, Humphries and Fowlers.
Martin, Thomas, Hookhouse farm ..					2 copyhold farms and rectorial tithes, Hookhouse & Burnt house farms.
Marshall, Rev. J. Wm. H., Ovingdean					Cp. h. & ld., Little Horsemanhoads.
Norman, James O., Esq., Brookside, Cuckfield					Copyhold house and land, Brookside.
Norris, William, Broad-st., Cuckfield					Copyhold h. & fr. ld., Broad-street.
Noble, Richard, Harvest-hill ..					Copyhold farm, Harvest hill.
Packham, John					H. & ld. as ocp., Pains-place farm.
Packham, R., Hodshirf farm, Cuckfield					Freehold house, Broad-street.
Packham, William					House and land as occupier, Old Furnace and Southlands.
Penfold, Philip					House and land as occupier, Great and Little Bentley farms.
Pennifold, Michael ..					H. & ld. as ocp., Lyes & Upper Ridges and part of Little Ease farms.
Potter, Peter					Freehold house, Cuckfield town.
Parkhurst, Thomas, Cuckfield-town..					Copyhold house, Cuckfield town.
Picknell, James, ...					Freehold house, Cuckfield town.
Taylor, George					Land as ocp., Part of Bridge farm.
Taylor, William					House and land as occupier, Riddens, and part of Little Ease farms.
Turner, John					Fr. mill & land Hayward's heath.
Tulley, Charles, Staplefield-common					Land as occupier, Staplefield common
Upton, Stephen					House & land as ocp., part of up. and lr. little East farms.
Upton, William, Challoner farm ..					Copyhold house and land, Ansty.
Uwins, William, Cuckfield					
Waller, John Champion, 8, Grove-street, Camden town, Middlesex ..					Freehold land, Woodcrofts.
Waller, Samuel					Freehold house and land, Banks.
Waller, Thos. Geo., 48, Great Russell-street, Bloomsbury-square, London					Copyhold farm, Jarretts.
Wells, Sir John, K.C.B., Bolnore Hs.					Freehold house and land, Bolnore.
Wood, Stephen, Handley farm ..					Lands as occupier, Handly, Gravely, Sugswarths and Harlands.
*Wileman, John, Leonards farm ..					Cp. and fr. land., Brook-street.
Webber, George					Freehold land, Highlands farm.
*Wileman, Stephen Cuckfield ..					House as occupier, King's Head Inn

HURSTPERPOINT.

NAMES.	D.	F.	Ch.	Cs.	QUALIFAICATION AND WHERE SITUATE.
—·rer, Nathl., Esq., ...					Freehold land, Churchfield.
·er, Wm., Esq., Henfield ..					Fr. house and ld., Westown or Pacons.

NAMES.	D.	F.	Ch.	Cs.	QUALIFICATION AND WHERE SITUATE.
Brooke, Rev. Jno. Shaw, Eltham, Kent		—			Freehold tithe and land, Glebe house
Campion, William John, Esq. ..		—			Freehold land, Danny.
Chandler, William ..					Freehold land, Church lane.
Crosskey, Thomas Page ..					Freehold land, Church lane.
Dodson, Sir John, Doctors Commons, London					Freehold land, Hoads.
•Davies, Richard					Land as occupier, Randells.
Ede, Thomas, Shermanbury ..					
Ellis, William					Freehold house and land, Church field
Fabian, John		—			Freehold house and land in the street.
Goodman, Samuel					Leasehold land, Stroods farm.
Hider, Henry		—			Land as occupier, Eastfield and Pitts.
Holman, Henry					Freehold house and land.
Jenner, William		—			Land as occupier, Town lands.
Knight, Jesse		—			Copyhold house, in the street.
Lee, Thomas, Horsham					Fr. house & stables, Sayer's Common.
Lempriere, John Sturch ..					Leasehold h. and land, Royal Oak Inn.
Marchant, John		—			Freehold land, Little Park farm.
•Marshall, James					Cp. ld. & Malthouse, part of Russells.
Mitchell, John, Goose lease.		—			Freehold house, Gooselease.
•Mitchel!, James		—			Leasehold mill, Ruckford mill.
Mitten, William		—			Fr. house and land, Townfield cottage.
Nye, Richard					Land as occupier, Mill house.
Packham, Henry ..		—			Land as occupier, Washbrooks.
Pierce, John		—			Land as occupier, Hurst Wickham.
Roberts, Avery, Esq.					Freehold house, Brick house.
Randell, John		—			Freehold house, in the street.
Randell, William		—			Fr. house and gn., part of Little Park.
Spratly, John ..					Freehold house, in the street.
•Uwins, Thomas ..					Ld. as ocp., Cobbs mill and Black h.
Vallance, Edward					Freehold farm, Chates.
Webber, George		—			Land as occupier, Lock's farm.
Weekes, Hampton		—			Freehold house, Matts.
Weekes, Richard, jun.		—			Freehold house and land, Washbrook
Weekes, Richard, Esq.		—			Freehold house, Mansion house.
Wells, Peter		—			Freehold house, in the street.
Wickham, Thomas		—			Land as occupier, Wanbarrow.
KEYMER.					
Attree, William, Western-rd., Brighton					Freehold land, Saint John's Common.
Baynton, H., Bronfort, Devises, Wilts					Freehold house and land, Brooklands.
Bine, Stephen, Sadlescombe, Newtim.	—				Freehold land, Rookery farm.
Brent, John, Canterbury, Kent ..					Freehold land, Ashen ground.
Brooker, Wm. Keymer and Cuckfield.					
Ellman, Jno., Landport Cottage, Lewes	—				Fr. land, Warners, St. John's Com.
Ford, Thos. Welfare, Vails Bridge Mill					Cp. land and mill, Vails Bridge mill.
Garbett, Jas., Brazennose Col., Oxford	—				Rectory of Clayton cum Keymer.
Hammond, George, the Lodge ..					land as occupier, the lodge farm.
Jenner, Philip, New Close ..					land as occupier, New close farm.
Jeffry, Thos., St. John's Common ..					Fr. h. and land, St. John's Common.
Marten, John, St. John's Common ..		—			Cp. h. and shop, St. John's Common.
Marten, Stephen, Balcombe ..					Fr. land, Purtens and Inholms farm.
Marten, Henry, New Land ..					Freehold land, Newland farm.
Marten, Fiennes, Wykeham ..					Tithes of Park or lodge farm.
Marris, Thos., St. John's Common ..		—			Land as occupier, St. John's Common.
Norman, William, St. John's Common					Freehold land, St. John's Common.
Pearce, Richard, Stone Rocks ..		—			Land as occupier, Stone Rock farm.
Shaw, William					Freehold land, Kell cottage.
Turner, James, Newland . ..			—		Land as occupier, Newland farm.
Turner, John, Oldland .. , ..	—	—			Ld. as ocp., Old lands and white land

NAMES.	D.	F.	Ch	Cs.	QUALIFICATION AND WHERE SITUATE.
*Wood, James, Ockley ..				—	Freehold farm, Ockley farm.
Wood, John, St. Bartholomew's Hospital, London		—			Freehold land, High chinnies farm.
Woolven, William, Vails Bridge Cm.				—	Land as occupier, Brookland.
LINDFIELD					
Allen, Benjamin				—	Ld. as ocp.,Beadles,& pt. of Gravely fm
*Allen, Wm., Esq., Stoke Newington				—	Copyhold house and land, Beadles fm.
Allin, William, ...				—	Fr. house and land, Cockhaise farm.
Ashby, Robert Avery ..				—	House & ld. as ocp., Woodsland farm.
Beckett, Burrows, Church-row, Aldgate, London				—	Copyhold house and land.
Bryant, William, Church-row, Ditto				—	Freehold manor of Plumpton Boscage.
Burnett, John		—			Land as ocp., Anchor Inn, and land.
Carter, Edward				—	House and land as ocp., Awbrook fm.
Colgate, Charles, High-st., Dorking				—	Copyhold house & land, Skaymes hill.
Comber, Turner				—	Freehold house and ld., Lindfield Town
Compton, Thomas ..		—			Freehold h. and land, Lindfield Town.
Coppard, John				—	Freehold h. and land, Hookland farm.
Copeland, John				—	Freehold house, Lindfield Town.
Dennett, John, Esq., Woodmancote, Newtimber					Freehold house and land, Sünt farm.
Drawbridge, William ..				—	Copyhold house & land, Chapel land.
Godsmark, Thomas, Newick ..				✦	Freehold land.
Grantham, Geo., High-street, Lewes					Freehold h. & ld., Hammon's farm.
*Gurney, S.Esq.,Lombard-st.,London				—	Copyhold land, Scamp's farm.
Hick, William Franklin, Esq., High-street, Lewes ..		—			Fr. h. and land, Little Walsted farm.
Haygarth, Geo. Rev. Henfield ..					Freehold land.
Jowett, Jas., Forbes, Rev., Kingston, Berks		—	—		Freehold house and land.
Jupp, Joseph				—	Cp. house and land, Skaymes hill.
Knight, Joseph				—	Fr. and copyhold land, Finch's farm.
Marchant, Michael, Field-row, Clapham, Surrey ..					Fr. house and land, Burnt house farm.
Mills, Simon				—	Freehold house, Red Lion Inn.
Moase, Richard ..				—	Fr. house and land, Wickham farm.
Morley, Henry					House and land as ocp., Walsted farm.
Noyes, Thomas Herbert ..				—	Freehold house and land, East Mascals
Nye, Thomas				—	Copyhold house and land, Nash farm.
Parker, James					Freehold house, Sloop Inn, Freshfield.
Picknell, William ..				—	Cp. house and land, Wallhouse farm.
Pim, James					Mill, h. & l.d as ocp., Cornmill & lds.
Podmore, Henry, Worth ..					Freehold field.
*Richards, Thomas, Sessions house,		—	—		Fr. house and land, Goddards farm.
Simmons, Samuel					House and land as ocp., Massits farm.
Smith, John, Esq., Dale Park, near Chichester					Fr. land and houses, Graveley farm.
Stamford, John, Lindfield					Copyhold h. and land, Skaymes mill.
Stott, William, 7, St. James's-place, Hatcham, New Cross, Surrey ..					Freehold houses, Lindfield Town.
Tuppen, Richard, Stapely				—	Freehold h. and land, Lindfield Town.
Turner, C. Hampden, Godstone, Surrey					Freehold house and land, Bedalls hill.
Weeler, Jasper					H. and land as ocp., Godenwicke farm
Wood, Robert		—			House and ld. as ocp., Kenwards farm
SLAUGHAM.					
Barry, Timothy, Warninglid ..				— —	Freehold house and land, Warninglid
Blake, R. Dudley, Esq., nr. Handcross					Freehold h. and land, near Handcross

NAMES.	D.	F.	Ch	Cs	QUALIFICATION AND WHERE SITUATE.
Briggs, Henry, Slaugham green				—	Freehold h. and land, Slaugham green.
Easton Richard, Hogshill					Freehold h. and brick yard, Hogshill
Ellison, Rev. Robt., the Rectory		—			House, tithes and glebe of Slaugham.
Haslewood, Wm., Esq., Slaugham Pk.					Lds. & tenmts. as ocp., Slaugham park
Jenner, William, Slaugham green		—			Cp. hs. and buildings, Slaugham green
*Kelsey, John, Handcross		—			Freehold houses and lands, Handcross.
Kensett, William, Slaugham green					Freehold & copyhold houses and lds. adjoining Haywards heath.
*Lewry, William, Old Park farm		—			Lds. and tenmts. as ocp., Old Park fm
Mitchell, Thomas, Slaugham Common				—	Cp. h. and lands Slaugham Common.
John M. Norman, Esq., High Beeches	—				House and land as ocp. near Handcross
Richardson, John, Frydays		—			Cp. house and lands, near Warninglid.
Smith, Richard, Slaugham green		—			Copyhold h. and land, Slaugham green
Sugden, Sir Edward Burtenshaw, Boyle farm, Thames Ditton, Surrey	—				Fr. houses and lands, near Handcross.
*Tully, Thomas, Pontail farm				—	Lds. and tenmts. as ocp., Pontail farm
*Wells, James, Routs farm				—	Lds. & tenmts. as ocp., nr. Warninglid
*Wells, William, Mill Hill farm				—	Lds. & tenmts. as ocp., Mill-hill farm.

TWINEHAM.

NAMES.	D.	F.	Ch	Cs	QUALIFICATION AND WHERE SITUATE.
Botting, John				—	Land as ocp., Twineham place farm.
Broad, James				—	Land as occupier, Windham farm.
Catt, James				—	Land as ocp., Hicksted place farm.
Davey, Edmund				—	Freehold land, Nawes farm.
Gearing, Richard				—	Freehold land, Hurtsfield.
Goring, Charles, Rev.				—	Rectory of Twineham.
Picard, Thomas, Rusper				—	Land as occupier, Groveland farm.
Sharp, William				—	Freehold land, Hunters land.
Stapely, Robert				—	Land as occupier, Hookers farm.
Tuppen, Henry, Market-st., Brighton				—	Freehold land, Herrings farm.
Wood, John, 51, Bedford-st., London					Fr. ld. Hicksted place and other lands.

WIVELSFIELD.

NAMES.	D.	F.	Ch	Cs	QUALIFICATION AND WHERE SITUATE.
Attree, Thomas				—	Land as occupier, Lockstrood, Birth, and Blackmoors.
Bacchus, William Henry, Esq.				—	Fr. and copyhold houses and land, Tile barn, Dartfords, Theabolds & Hanty
Brattle, William, 9, Little Castle-square, Brighton					Freehold and copyhold house and land, Manns and Wilderness farms.
Brattle, John, 9, Little Castle-square, Brighton				—	Freehold and copyhold house and land, Manns and Wilderness farms.
Cook, John, Cleavewaters		—			Land as occupier, Cleavewaters.
Coppard, John, Lindfield		—			Copyhold land, Botches.
Cunningham, Jer., Lunces,					Land as occupier, Lunces.
Denman, Michael		—			Ld. as ocp., Clappers & Rogers & Griggs
Dixon, George, Lindfield		—			Freehold land, Slugwash.
Ellis, Isaac, Slugwash				—	Land as ocp., Slugwash and Moors.
Farncomb, Joseph, Fanhouse		—			Freehold land, Fanhouse farm.
Gosling, Sturt				—	House and shop as ocp., near the Ch.
Homewood, William, Great Oathall, Wivelsfield					Ld. as ocp., Great Oathall & the Strood
*Jones, John, North-street, Lewes				—	Trustee in possession of freehold h.
Knight, Charles, Hawkhurst, Kent				—	Freehold land.
Knight, Frederick, Wivelsfield green	—				Ld. as ocp., Botches, Cheals & Smiths
Tanner, Richard, Esq., Moor House					Fr. house and land, Moore h. and fm.
Tufnell, Rev. John Charles Fowell, Hurstperpoint					Freehold land, Lunces farm.
Wells, Henry, Little Oathall				—	Land as occupier, Little Oathall

NAMES.	D.	F.	Ch Cs.	QUALIFICATION AND WHERE SITUATE.

WEST BLATCHINGTON.

NAMES	QUALIFICATION AND WHERE SITUATE
Dickins, Charles Scrace, West Stoke	Freehold land, Walters Croft.
Wagner,Hy. Mich.,Vicarage, Brighton	Rectorial tithes of West Blatchington.
*William Hodson, ...	Land as occupier, Blatchington farm.

BRIGHTHELMSTON.

NAMES	QUALIFICATION AND WHERE SITUATE
Aaron, Saul Charles, 15, Princes-st..	Freehold land, Rose-hill, Brighton.
Ackerson, Robert, 43, Clarence-place.	Freehold house, London-road.
Ade, James, Kingston, near Lewes ..	Fr. house, 17, Richmond buildings.
Ade, John, 26, Western-street ..	Fr. hs., 38 and 41 New Dorset-street.
Agate, James, Horsham ..	Freehold house, 22, Oriental-place.
Akehurst, Samuel, 109, London-road.	Freehold house, 26, George-street.
Akehurst, Thomas, 9, Charles-street..	Freehold house, 50, Edward-street.
Allcorn, Reuben, 24, Trafalgar-street.	Freehold house, 7, Dean-street.
Allcorn, John, 23, Carlton-street ..	Freehold house, 16, Trafalgar-street.
Allen, Joseph, 5, St. George's-place..	Fr. hs., 8 and 9 Lower-rock gardens
*Allen, John Collins, Brazen Nose College, Oxford	Freehold house, near the Market-place
Alley, William, 89, Chiswell-street, Finsbury-square, London ..	Freehold house, 2, Nelson-street.
*Allfrey, James, 23, Church-street ..	Freehold house, 14, North-lane.
Alliston, Jn. 38, Russell-sq., London.	Fr. hs., 3, 4, & 29 to 34, Crescent-cots.
Anderson, James Stuart Murray, Rev., 12, Arundel-ter., Kemp-town	Freehold Curacy, St. George's Chapel
Anderson,R. Rev. 14, Montpellier-road	Freehold Chapel, Ship-street.
Andrews, William, 134, Western-road	Freehold house, 13, Upper North-st.
Atlee, John Falconer, Wandsworth, Surrey	Freehold land, Atlingworth-street.
*Attree, John, 10, Tidy-street ..	Feeehold messuage and appurtenances, 40, Red-cross-street.
Attree, George Thomas, 22, Francis-st	Freehold house, 21, Oxford-street.
Attree, Thomas, Ship-street ..	Freehold manor, Atlingworth.
Attree, William Wakeford,Ship-street	Copyhold land, Grand Junction-road.
Austin, Lewis Augustus, Pavilion Hotel	Freehold garden, Rose-hill, North.
Aylen, William, 5, Colonnade ..	Freehold house, George-street.
Baber, John James, Knightsbridge, Middlesex	Freehold house, 53, King's-road.
Bacchus, George, Birmingham ..	Freehold house, 11, York-place.
Badger, Edward, Sloane-st., London	Freehold house, Marine-parade.
*Baker, David, 5, Gardener-street ..	Freehold house, 20, Brunswick-place.
Baker, John, 21, New-road ..	One third part of a freehold house, 17, Upper Edward-street.
*Baker, William, 47, Wood-street ..	Freehold house, 3, White-cross-street.
*Baldock, William, 6, Wood-street.	Freehold house, 26, Dean-street.
*Barnard, Nathaniel, 1, King-street	Freehold house, 48, Wood-street.
Barnes, Henry, Horsemonger-lane ..	Freehold house, 27, Laurel-place.
Barnett, William, tendered Cavendish and Curteis. Grenville-place ..	St. James-street.
Barratt, Richard, Falmer ..	Freehold house, 24, Russell-square.
*Bass, Isaac, Black Lion-street ..	Freehold house, 14, Old Steyne.
Bastick, William, 22, St. James's-st.	Freehold stables, Riding School lane, Edward-street.
Batho, Matthew Robert, 31, Dean-st.	Freehold house, 11, St. James-street.
Beal, Richard, 48, Albion-street ..	Freehold house, 47, Albion-street.
Beal, Richard, 31, Camelford-street..	Freehold house, 41, Frederick-street.

NAMES.	D.	F.	Ch	Ca	QUALIFICATION AND WHERE SITUATE.
Beard, Edward, High-st., St. Michael, Lewes					Fr. h., Cavendish Arms, Regent-street
Bedford, George, Lansdowne cottage, Lewes road					Freehold house, 26, Broad-street.
*Bedford, George, 3, Manchester-st.					Freehold house, 4, Manchester-street.
Beedham, William, 93, North-street					Freehold house, 6, Cavendish-place.
*Bell, Henry, 10, Oxford st., London					Freehold brewhouse, Kemp-town.
Bellingham, Charles, 9, Marine-parade					Freehold house, 22, Regency-square.
Bennison, George, Exeter					Freehold houses, 5 to 8, Jackson-row.
*Benson, Thomas, 47, Mighell-street					Freehold house, 42, Mighell-street.
Bentley, William, 16, Edward-street					Freehold houses, Nelson-street.
Betteridge, John, Eastbourne Sussex					Freehold house and grounds, Camden Terrace, in the North lanes.
Beves, Edward, 56, North-lane					Freehold houses, 58 & 59, North lane
*Biggs, William, 45, Lavender-street					Freehold hs.. 100 and 101, Edward-st.
Billinghurst, Edward, 50, King-street					Freehold house, 6, Western-place.
Bishop, John, City of Hereford Inn, Upper St. James's-street					Freehold house, 34, Grenville-place.
*Blaber, Henry, 47, Russell-square					Freehold house, 24, Regency-square.
*Blaber, William, 22, Dorset-gardens					Freehold house, 56, Marine-parade.
Blacklock, William, 32, Old-steyne					Freehold house, 98, St. James-street.
*Blaker, John, 82, Church-street					Freehold house, 4, Regent-street.
Bland, Hy. Daniel, Colchester, Essex					Freehold land, 14, Cavendish-place.
Blicke, Charles Tufton, 15, Regent-street, Westminster					Freehold house, 32, Marine-parade.
Blunt, Chas. Richd., Sir, Heathfield Pk.					Freehold house, Cavendish-place, W.
*Bodle, Richard, Milton Cottage					Freehold house, 17, Grenville-place.
Bollen, Thomas, Stag Inn, Lewes					Freehold house, Clarence-gardens.
Bollen, William, 9, Up. Gardener-st.					Freehold house, 8, Upper Gardener-st.
Boss, George, Edward-street					Fr. hs., 2 houses on Carlton-hill, and the cottages called Boss's gardens.
Boss, Jas., 15, Circus-st., Marylebone					Freehold mews, Carlton-street.
Bowell, Joseph, 48, Waterloo-st., Hove					Freehold house, Camden-terrace.
*Boxall, William, 18, Grand-parade					Freehold stables, Princes-street.
Boyce, Henry Pitches, 22, Upper Wimpole-street, London					Fr. h., Lewes Crescent, Kent-town.
Bradford, Nenyon Masters, Craven cot.					Freehold land, North-level.
Bradshaw, John, 79, Western-road					Freehold house, 78, Western-road.
*Bradshaw, Wm. Auction Mart, London					Freehold house, Marine-view.
*Brake, C., Chapel-house, West-st.					Fr Chapel, the Tabernacle West.-st.
Brigden, Charles, 16, Nelson-street.					Freehold house, 26, John-street.
*Briggs, Charles, 119, North-street.					Fr. hs., at the back 119, North-street.
Briggs, John Thomas, 6, Somerset-place, London					Freehold house, 4, Royal-crescent.
Brightwell, Dobito, 22, Regency-square, London					Freehold land, Regency mews.
Brinton, Rt. Nineham, 26, East-cliff.					Freehold land, Cecil house, Kings-roud
*Bromley, John, 17, Commercial-road, St. George's, East London.					Freehold house, New Inn Yard, Hull.
Brooker, Henry, 14, Hanover Crescent					Freehold house, 2, Hanover crescent.
Brooker, Henry, New Shoreham					Freehold house, Steyne gardens.
*Brookhouse, John, 78, Western-road					Freehold house, 46, Montpellier-road.
Brown, Edward, Steyning					Freehold house, 14, Marshalls-row.
*Brown, Joseph, 17, Hanover crescent					Freehold house, 28, Preston-street.
*Bruton, Edward, Castle-street					Freehold house, 25, Norfolk-square.
Buckman, Richard, 12, Richmond-st.					Fr. hs., 32, 33, and 34, Richmond-bgs.
*Buckwell, George, 35, Mighell-street					Freehold house, 25, George-street.
Budd, H., Grosvenor H., Marine-parade					Fr. h. Rokesley house, Marine-parade.
Burridge, William, Horsham					Fr. hs., 58 and 59, Upper Bedford-'

NAMES.	D.	F.	Ch	Cs	QUALIFICATION AND WHERE SITUATE.
*Burstow, Horace, Westhill cottage, Hampton-place					Freehold house, 32, Upper North-st.
Bury, Robert, Bentley, Hants					Freehold house, 27, Regency-square.
Butcher, Richard, 32, Cavendish-st.					Freehold house, 26, Cumberland-place
Cadbury, James, Ashford, near Hounslow, Middlesex					Freehold house, 54, East-street.
Caffyn, Benjamin, Preston-street					Fr. h., Preston house, Kings-road.
Camp, Wm. Samuel, 28, Bond-street					Fr. h., 1, Little St. James-street.
*Card, Charles, 51, High-street					Freehold house, Grosvenor-street.
Carr, John, 58, West-street					Freehold house, Grenville-place.
*Carter, Friend, 56, Western-road					Freehold house, 33, Grenville-place.
Carter, John, Lord Mayor's Court Office, London					Freehold house, 32, Cannon-place.
Carter, James, Trafalgar-street					Freehold house, Blucher-place.
Carter, Thomas, 120, St. James's-st.					Freehold house, Trafalgar-lodge.
Catt, William, jun., 80, West-street					Fr. h. the Windmill, Upper North-st.
Cazalet, Peter Clement, 19, Lewescrescent, Kemp-town.					Fr h., 18, Lewes Crescent, Kemp-town
Chalk, John, 12, Charlotte-street					Fr. stables, cottage & carpenters shop, leading out of St. James-street, opposite St. Mary's Chapel.
Chandler, John, 117, Edward-street					Fr. houses, 23, 24, Devonshire-place.
Chaplain, William, 44, St. James's-st					Freehold land, East-lane.
Chapman, Henry, 1, Crown-street					Freehold house, 32, Western-road.
Chapman, Richard, 61, North-street					Freehold house, 62, North-street.
Chassereau, George, 21, North-street					Freehold house, 74, North-street.
*Chassereau, James Daniel, 9, Finsbury-square, Middlesex					Freehold house, 71, Marine-parade.
Chatfield, Charles, 61, West-street					Fr. houses, 7 and 8, North gardens.
*Cheesman, Francis, 2, Grovenor-st.					Freehold house, 49, Edward-street.
*Cheesman, George, Kensington-st.					Freehold house, Regent-street.
*Cheesman, Harry, Garden-cottage.					Freehold house, 25, Bread-street.
Cheesman, James, 9, Nelson-street.					Freehold houses, 10 and 11, Nelson-st.
Cheesman, Thomas, 24, York-place.					Freehold house, 16, York-place.
Child, James, 1, Grafton-street					Freehold house, 56, Chesterfield-street
*Childens, John Cheesman, 26, Egremont-place					Freehold house, Ship-street.
*Chitenden, George, Grenville-place.					Freehold ground, 69, North-street.
Choyce, James, 2, Chapel-street.					Freehold house, 8, Charlotte-street.
*Clark, Samuel, 58, Edward-street					Freehold house, 22, Grosvenor-street.
*Clark, Joseph, Maidenhead, Berks.					Fr. houses, 7, 8 and 9, Royal crescent.
*Clark, Somers, 8, Ship-street					Fr. land behind the Royal crescent.
Clay, Wm. 23, Skinner-st., London.					Freehold houses, 37 and 38, West-st.
Clear, Hy., St. Thomas's, Cliffe, Lewes					Freehold houses, Laurel-place.
Cleasby, Richard, 3, Cornwall-terrace, Regent's Park					Freehold house, 42, North-street.
*Cleasby, Stph., Old Broad-st., London					Freehold house, 55, Chesterfield-street
*Clement, Jas. Kinlock, Leytonstone, Essex					Freehold houses, 10 to 13, New-steyne
Clerk, Edward, 22, Camelford-street					Fr. h. and premises, 3, Camelford-street
*Clew, Robert, 41, Up. Russell-street					Fr. hs., 26 & 27, Dean-st., late 23 & 24
Cobb, G., 15, Clement Inn, Middx.					Freehold house, New-road.
*Cobby, Charles, 74, London-road					Freehold house, Ivory-buildings.
Coddrington, Edward, Sir, Western Lodge, Western-road					Freehold house, 1, Western-buildings.
Cohen, Levy Em., 39, Clarence-place.					Fr ground, Burying ground, Rose-hill
Colbatch, Hy., Dublin, Excise-office.					Freehold house, 1, Grand-parade.
Colbatch, John, Rosehill Villa					Freehold house, 5, Grand-parade.

NAMES.	D.	F.	Ch	Ca	QUALIFICATION AND WHERE SITUATE
Colbron, H. Stiles, 28, Devonshire-pl.					Fr. house, 1 to 5, Hanover-terrace.
Colbron, William, 4, Mill-street, Hanover-square, London					Freehold houses, Alfred-place.
Coles, William, 6, Gloucester-place, Hoxton, Middlesex					Freehold Schoolhouse, Paradise-street.
Collins, James, 12, Devonshire-place					Freehold house, 37, Marine-parade.
Colquhoun, Henry, Guildford, Surrey					Freehold hs., 64 and 65, Edward-street
Colwill, Charles, 33, North-street					Freehold house, 29, Bond-street.
Coomber, John, back of Kemp-town					Freehold house, 22, Richmond-street.
Cooke, T., Rev., 12, St. George's-pl.					Perpetual Curacy, St. Peter's Church.
*Cooper, Frederick, 7, Richmond-ter.					Freehold house, 29, Oriental-place.
*Cooper, Isaac, 14, Lr. Rock-gardens					Freehold house, 11, Royal-crescent.
Cooper, Thomas, High-street, Lewes					Freehold house, 25, Bloomsbury-place
Cooper, Thomas Poynton, Upper Clapton, Middlesex					Freehold house, 51, Marine-parade.
Cooper, Wm. Henry, Rev., Washington					Freehold land, third furlong, East lane
Coppard, James, 38, Kensington-gns.					Fr. hs., 18 and 19, Kensington-gardens
*Coppard, Richard, 33, Bread-street					Freehold house, 30, Bread-street.
Coppoch, James, 20, Soley-terrace, Pentonville					Freehold house, 10, Richmond-hill.
Cordy, Charles, 33, North-street					Freehold house, 29, Bond-street.
Cordy, James, 117, London-road					Freehold house, 12, Grand-parade.
Corner, George Richard, 20, Dean-street, Southwark					Freehold house, 18, Richmond-place.
Cornford, Edward, 8, Dorset-garden					Fr. h. Regency cot., Regency-mews.
Cornford, John, 16, Sussex-street					Fr. hs., 39 and 40, Meetinghouse-lane
Costar, William, 51, Edward-street.					Freehold house, 2, Red-cross-street.
Court, John, Lt. 81st In., Birmingham					Freehold house, 5, Charlotte-street.
Cowell, William George Stepney, 5, Marlborough-place					Freehold house, Park, Brighton.
Cox, Stephen, Nottingham-st., London					Freehold house, 1, Burlington-street.
Cosens, Richard, 28, Ship-street					Freehold house, 27, Kensington-gns.
Crawford, Ewd Thos., Sutton, Surrey					Freehold house, 12, Richmond-place.
*Crawford, William, Dorking, Surrey					Freehold house, 20, New-steyne.
Creasy, Albert Thomas, 13, Broad-st.					One third part of a freehold house, 17, Upper Edward-street.
Creasy, Edward Hill, 152, North-street					One third part of a freehold house, 17, Upper Edward-street.
Creswell, Wm., 25, Kensington-place					Fr. house, 9, Mount Sion Place.
Cripps, Robert, 29, New-road					Fr. house, 103 & 104, London-road.
Crookes, Wm., St. Andrew's-hill, London					Freehold house, 41, Ship-street.
Crosweller, Thos., 74, Grand-parade					Freehold house, 122, St. James's-st.
Crouch, James, 100, Edward-street					Freehold house, 18, Mount Sion Pl.
Crowley, Edwd., Lavender-hill, Wandsworth, Surrey					Freehold house, 58, Marine-parade.
Cubitt, T., Clarence-road, Clapham, Surrey					Freehold house, 11, Lewes-crescent, Kemptown
Cubitt, William, 43, Mecklenburgh-square, Middlesex					Freehold house, 3, Chichester-terrace, Kemptown
Cullen, James, , 17, Devonshire-street					Freehold house, Brunswick-place
Cumlidge, Thos., 5, Norfolk-street.					Freehold house, 11, Wood-street
Currie, E., 6, Montague-street, London					Freehold house, 7, Lewes-crescent.
Curtis, Richard, 10, Jew street					Freehold house, 10, North-lane
Dadley, William Pearce, North-lodge, London-road					Freehold house, 81, London-road
Dakins, William Whitfeld, Rev. Dr., Dean's-yard, Westminster					Freehold house, 40, Bloomsbury-pl.

NAMES.	D.	F.	Ch.	Co.	QUALIFICATION and WHERE SITUATE.
*Dale, George, 31, High-st., Lewes					Freehold house, Regent-street.
Doncaster, George, 28, St. James's-st.					Freehold house, 26, St. James's-st.
*Dancey, Stephen, 6, Crown-street.					Freehold house, 52, North-st.-road.
Davey, Richard, 73, Edward-street					Freehold houses, Nelson-street
*Davis, Benjamin, 9, Royal-crescent					Freehold house, Richmond Hill, "Crown and Sceptre."
: Davis, Richard, Anglesea-cottage, London-road					Freehold land, Marlborough-street.
Davies, Wm., 33, North Audley-st.					Freehold house, 7, Bedford-street.
Davison, John, 20, Brunswick-place, North					Freehold house, 8, St. George's-place
*Deacon, Charles Clement, BelleVue, Reigate, Surrey					Freehold house, 26, Marine-square.
Dendy, Samuel, Bream's-buildings, London					Freehold house, 3, White Cross-street
Dew, W. S., 146, Cheapside, London					Freehold houses, 28 to 31, Derby-pl.
Dickens, C. S., Coolhurst, Horsham					Freehold Manor of Brighton.
Dicker, Thomas, High-street, Lewes					Fr. house, Sion-house, Church-street
Dillwyn, Lewis Weston, Penlargon, Glamorganshire					Freehold houses, William-street.
Dennage, Joshua, Southwick					Fr. house, 17 & 18. Cumberland-place
Diplock, John, 53, London-road					Freehold house, 29, Great Russell-st.
Donne, Joseph, 15, York-place					Freehold house, 36, Western-road.
Doubleday, Wm., 2, Burlington-street					Freehold house, 4, Burlington-street.
Drummond, Spencer Rodney, Rev., 11, St. George's-place					Freehold house, 3, German-place.
Du Cane, Henry, Witham, Essex					Freehold house, Bedford-square.
*Duke, Charles, 16, Marlborough-st.					Freehold house, 21, Marlborough-st.
*Duke, Edward, 44, Ship-street					Freehold house, Upper Edward-street
Dumbrell, Charles, 91, St. James's-st.					Freehold house, King-street
Dumbrell, James, 1, Nile-street					Freehold house, 1, Portland-terrace.
Dunstall, William, Falmer					Freehold house, 3, Grand-parade.
Durrant, David, 13, Rotherfield-street, Islington					Freehold house, 34, Hanover-street.
Eastwood, Thos., 129, Edward-street					Freehold tenement, and stable & cow-lodges, Riding-school lane.
Edwards, Charles Wm., George-street, Euston-square, London					Freehold house, Grafton-street.
Edwards, Henry, 165, Western-road					Freehold houses, 25, 26, 27, and 28, Apollo-terrace.
Edwards, James, 8, Brighton-place					Freehold house, 1, Ivory-buildings.
Edwards, James, 8, Windsor-terrace					Freehold chapel, Hanover chapel, Church-street.
Edwards, Richards, 2, Upper N.-st.					Fr. houses, 51 & 52, Up. North-street, and Hampton-cottage, Hampton-pl.
Egles, Gabriel, Lansdowne-pl., Lewes					Fr. houses, 11 to 18, St. John's-place
Eldridge, Charles, 1, Clarence-street.					Freehold houses, 2 & 3, Borough-st.
*Elliott, the Rev. Henry Venn, 31, Brunswick-square, Hove					Freehold house, 12, Cannon-place.
Elliott, John Shearman, Demark-hill, Camberwell					Freehold house, 9, Cannon-place.
*Ellis, Anthony, 56, East-street					Fr. house & land, 14, Montague-st.
*Ellis, Charles, 45, Church-street					Freehold house, 46, Church-street.
*Ellis, Richard, 17, Cavendish-street					Freehold plot of ground, 13 and 14, Mount-pleasant, Edward-street.
Ellis, Samuel, 47, Upper Edward-st.					Freehold house, Upper Edward-street
Ellis, Thomas, 6, Dover-terrace, Walcot, Bath, Somerset					Freehold house, 24, John-street.

NAMES.	D.	P.	Ch.	Co.	QUALIFICATION AND WHERE SITUATE.
*Ellis, William, 3, Preston-street					Freehold house, 11, Cavendish-place
Ellis, William, Rootham, Kent					Freehold house, Rose Hill (North).
*Ellyatt, Hy., 2, Upper Gardener-st.					Freehold house, 1, Upper Gardener-st.
*Elsey, William, Marine Villa					Freehold house, Lower Marine Villa
Evans, C., Kennington-cross, Lambeth					Freehold house, 9, Carlton-street.
Evans, George, Ditchling-terrace					Fr. houses, 4, 5, 6, Ditchling-terrace
Evans, James, Ditchling-terrace					Fr. houses, 4, 5, 6, Ditchling-terrace.
Evans, Wm., Kennington-cross, Lambeth					Freehold house, 8, Carlton-street.
Faithfull, George, 15, Ship-street					Freehold house, Kemp-town.
Faithfull, Henry, Summer-house					Freehold houses, Oxford Court.
Fearon, J. P., 42, Chester-terrace					Mortgagee in possession of fr. mansion
Regent's Park, Middlesex					Portland-house, Portland-place.
Feist, William, 58, St. James-street					Freehold cottage, stable & workshop, 23, Rock-street.
*Field, C., 27, Western Cottages					Freehold houses, Montpellier-road.
*Field, Joseph, 19, Preston-street					Freehold houses, 30 & 31, Bedford-sq.
Field, John, 59, West-street					Freehold house,, coach-houses, and stables, King's-rd. Mews, King's-rd.
Finch, J., 31, Dean-st.,Westminster					Fr. houses, 76, to 81,Egremont-street
Fisher, Henry, Horsted Keynes					Fr house, corner of Lavendar-street.
Flanders, Wm., Upper Hamerton,					Freehold house, 24,Upper Edward-st.
Flanders, William, 8, Upper Woburn-place, Tavistock-square					Freehold house, 15, Upper Edward-st.
Fleeson, William, 85, Church-streeet.					Freehold house, 43, Gardener-street, and 53, 54, & 55, Spring-gardens.
*Flint, J., 17, Brunswick-place, North					Freehold houses, North-lane, Brighton cottage, beer-house, and h. adjoining
Foakes, John, 124, St. James's-street					Freehold house, 19, New-steyne.
Folkard, Daniel, 16, London-road, Southwark					Fr. house, 120 and 121, North-street.
Folker, Samuel Shepherd, 3, Bridge-street, Westminster					Freehold houses, Meetinghouse-lane.
*Foskett, Joseph, Reigate, Surrey					Freehold land, Marine-parade.
Fowle, William, Uckfield					Freehold hs., 8 and 9, Cambridge-st.
Francis, Samuel, 21, St. James s-st.					Fr. houses, 2, 3 and 4, Laurel-place.
Francis, Thos., 8, Charles-street					Fr. hs., 29, 30 & 31, Richmond-place.
Freeman, Thos., 3, Dorset-gardens					Freehold house, 7, Charlotte-street.
Furner, Thomas, Star in the East, Upper Bedford-street					Two freehold ground rents, Gardener-street, Regent-street.
*Furner, William, 1, Pavilion-parade					Fr. h., Orton-house, Marine-parade.
Gallard, George, 32, Norfolk-square					Freehold hs., 30 & 31, Norfolk-square
*Gallard, John, 37, Clarence-place					Freehold house, 36, Russell-street.
Garnham, Stephen. High-st., Lewes					Fr. houses, 12 to 19, Leicester-street.
Gayford, James, 14, Blackman-street					Freehold house, 13, Blackman-street.
Gibbons, Sills, St.Andrews-hill,London					Freehold house, 42, Ship-street.
Gibson, J. Holmes, Laytonstone, Essex					Freehold house,conch-house & stables, 39, Grand-parade.
Gilburd, John, 21, Kensington-place					Freehold house, 26, Kensington-place
Gillam, William, 23, Robert-street					Freehold house, 3, North-lane.
Glaisyer, John, 11, North-street					Freehold house, Princes-street.
Goble, Wm. Hy., Tarrant-st., Arundel					Freehold house, 5, Blackman-street.
Goffe, John, Evesham, Worcestershire					Freehold h., 15, Upper Rock-gardens.
*Godley, Aaron, 9, Edward-street					Freehold house and freehold cottage, 8, Edward-street and Sun-street.
Goldsmith,Edward,St.Michaels,Lewes					Freehold ld., Rock-street, Kemp-town
Goleborn, Thomas Lynch, Picts Hill, Bedfordshire					Fr. houses, 1, 2 and 3, Bedford-squa r

NAMES.	D.	F.	Ch	Ca	QUALIFICATION AND WHERE SITUATE.
Good, John, 18, Great East-street ..					Freehold house, 15, Air-street.
Good, William, Gloucester-lane ..					Freehold house, 4, Brunswick-place.
Goodall, Thomas, 18, Portland-place					Fr. h., 24, Sussex-square, Kemp-town
Goode, Henry, Ryde, Isle of Wight.					Freehold house, 34, Regency-square.
Goodere, Thomas, 54, Edward-street					Ten ls. tenements, Nottingham-street
Goodman, Samuel, Sayers Common, Hurstperpoint					Fr. houses, 37 and 38 Richmond bgs.
Gordon, Alexander, 36, Grand-parade					Freehold house, 1, Temple-street.
*Gotobed, Thomas, 82, Great Russell-street, London					Freehold mews, New-road.
Goulty, J. Nelson, Rev., 16, Western-rd.					Freehold Chapel, Union-street.
Graham, Nathaniel, Primer, Middlesex					Freehold house, 19, Richmond-hill.
Grant, Peter, tendered for Cavendish and Curteis, 109, North-street. ..					34 and 35, Jubilee-street.
Gravely, Joseph, 20, Bond-street					Freehold house, 117, Edward-street.
Green, Henry, 25, George-street ..					Freehold house, 6, Kensington-place.
*Green, Richard, 71, West-street. ..					Freehold house, 45, Western-road.
Green, William, 16, St. James-street..					Freehold house, Steyne Gardens.
*Greene, Anthony Sheppy, Preston, Sussex					Fr. h. York cottage, Trafalgar-street.
*Greethurst, Henry, Hanover-street..					Freehold house, 83, Grand-parade.
Gregory, James, 7, Bond-street ..					Freehold stable, Bond-street row, back of No. 7, Bond-street.
Gregory, Rd. Lemmon, Market-street					Freehold house, 56, Nelson-street.
Grissell, Thomas, York Road, Lambeth					Freehold house, 8, Dean-street.
Guillaume, Thomas, New Shoreham					Fr. houses, 56 and 57 Essex-place.
Gunn, James, 8, Red Cross-street ..					Freehold house, 10, Oxford-street.
Hack, Daniel Pryor, Trafalgar-lodge					Fr. h., Wellington-lodge, Lewes-road.
Haddon, Richard, 1, Richmond gds...					Fr. hs., 5 and 6, Richmond-gardens.
*Haines, Samuel, 1, Sussex-street ..					Freehold house, 21, Grand-parade.
*Hall, Nathaniel, New Hall, Henfield					Freehold house, 49, Russell-square.
Hall, Thomas, 50, Middle-street ..					Freehold house, 16, Regency-square.
Hallett, George, 11, Crown-street ..					Freehold house, 23, Chalybeate-street
Hallett, William, Bristol Hotel ..					Fr. h., 8, Lewes-crescent, Kemp-town
Hamilton, Francis, 130, Jermyn-street, London					Freehold house, Chesterfield-street.
Hamilton, Thos., Trafalgar-street ..					Fr. houses, 2 to 7, North-crescent-st.
Hamlin, Thomas, 5, Clarence-place					Fr. hs., 21 and 22, Clarence-place.
*Hanley, William, Newington-green, Middlesex ..					Fr. hs., 2, 3 and 4, Colebrook-row.
Hanley, W. L., 1, Furnival's Inn, London					Fr. hs., 5, 6 and 7, Colebrook-row.
Hanson, The Rev. Joseph Flesher, Rectory, Backwell, Somersetshire..					Freehold house, Regency-colonnade.
Hanson Wm. Rev., 35, Regency-square					Freehold house, 10, Regency-square.
Hargott, William, Newhaven ..					Freehold house, 14, Oxford-street.
Harley, Wm., Holland-st., Brixton..					Freehold house, 10, Richmond-hill.
Harman, Sargant, 28, Park-street ..					Freehold house, 27, Crown-street.
*Harman, Sargant, 56, Western-road					Freehold house, 9, Grafton-street.
Harper, John, Bond-street ..					Freehold house, 30, New-steyne.
*Harington, George, Old Steyne ..					Freehold house, 36, Bedford-square.
*Harrington, Thos., Esq., Old Steyne					Freehold house, 36, Regency-square.
Harris, James, Prospect-row, Walworth, Surrey					Freehold house, 16, Essex-place.
Harris, W. 50, High Holborn, London					Freehold house, 28, Laurel-place.
Hart, Percival, 9, Upper Bedford-st..					Fr. house, 10, Upper Bedford-street.
Harvey, D. Whittle, Great George-street, Westminster ..					Fr. hs., 19 & 20 Gloucester-place
Harvey, James, 4, Gloster-buildings, Old Kent-road, Surrey ..					Freehold houses, 6 and 7, Duke-street

NAMES.	D.	F.	Ch.	Cs.	QUALIFICATION AND WHERE SITUATE.
Harvey, Thomas, 3, Frederick-street					Freehold house, 15, White-cross-street
*Haslett, Jas., Pier-house, Chain-pier					The Tabernacle, fr. Chapel, West-st.
Havard, Samuel, 63, London-road ..					Freehold stable and coach-house, at the back of 63, London-road.
Haven, John Gordon, 12, Old Steyne					Freehold garden ground, at the back of 12, Old-steyne.
*Hawes, Thomas, Lavender Hill, Wandsworth, Surrey					Freehold h. 10, Marlborough-place.
*Hayward, George, 18, Western-road					Freehold house, 17, Western-road.
*Hawkins, Esau, Park cot., Park-pl.					Freehold land, Carlton lime-kilns, back of Devonshire-terrace.
*Heather, Thomas, 58, Grand-parade					Freehold house, 5, Old-steyne-street.
*Hemsley, Richard, 18, Grenville-place					Freehold house, 30, Grenville-place.
*Hendy, Francis William, 4, Chapel-road, Worthing					Freehold land, Edwards gardens.
Hepworth, Jas., 61, High-st., Gosport					Freehold workshop and dwelling-h. Dorset-street.
Hornon, John, 20, Gloucester-place					Freehold house, 18, Gloucester-place.
Hewitt, Paul, Hampton Cottage ..					Fr. house, 10, Silwood-place or square
*Hicks, William, Twyford, Berks ..					Fr. ld. and buildings, Margaret-street.
Hilder, John, 30, West-street ..					Fr. house and warehouse, North-lane.
Hill, G. Philcox, 29, Western Cottages					Freehold house, 1, Pavilion-parade.
Hill, Nathaniel, 29, Regent-st., London					Freehold house, 15, Cannon-place.
Hoad, Richard, 36, George-street ..					Freehold house, 33, Regency-square.
Hodd, Steph. Tutt, White Horse Hotel					Freehold stables, Marlborough-mews.
Hodgson, John, 35, Seething-lane, London					Fr. houses, 17 and 27, Frederick-place
Hodgson, Thomas, Mill Cottage ..					Freehold land, Francis-street.
*Holbrook, Richard, Southwick-lodge, near Shoreham					Fr. stbs. Hampton stbs. Hampton-place
Holden, J. Douglas, 78, London-road					Freehold house, 40, Grand-parade.
*Holford, Chas, Hampstead, Middlesex					Fr. h. 4, Lewes Crescent, Kemp-town.
Holford, Ed. 17, Marlborough-place.					Fr. hs., 38, 39 and 40, Church-street.
Holford, John, 14, Waterloo-place.					Fr. land, back of Union-street, North.
*Hollingdale, William, Poynings ..					Freehold house, Chesterfield-street.
Hope, William, 133, North-street ..					Freehold house, King-street.
Hoper, John, jun., Esq., Southover, near Lewes..					Fr. h. and land, back of Nelson-street.
*Hopps, John, Weymouth, Dorsetshire					Freehold house, 13, York-place.
*Howard, Edmund, Brecon					Freehold stables, Royal-mews.
*Howard, Geo., Manchester, Lancashire					Freehold stables, Royal-mews.
*Howard, Richard, Brecon.. ..					Freehold stables, Royal-mews.
*Howell, Charles, Hove ..					Freehold house, 22, Old-steyne.
*Hughes, David, 4, Park Cottages ..					Freehold houses, 3, Park cottages.
*Humphrey, Richard, 15, Brighton-place					Freehold house, 14, Brighton-place.
*Humphrey, Wm., 15, Brighton-place					Freehold house, 16, Brighton-place.
Humphreys, William, 55, Old Steyne					The Tabernacle, fr. Chapel, West-st.
*Humphrey, Wm., 17, Brighton-place					Three fr. hs., behind 17, Brighton-place
Hunter, John, Cheapside, corner of Red Cross-street					Fr. hs., 39 and 57, Chesterfield-street.
Hunter, Thomas, Richmond-terrace..					Freehold house, 8, Richmond-terrace.
Hussey, William, tendered for Cavendish, Marine-square					8, Marine-square.
*Ingram, Hugh, Steyning.. ..					Freehold house, Hanover-street.
Inman, Richard, 40, St. James's-street					Freehold house, 10, Derby-place.
*Inman, T. Atkins, 10, Black Lion-st.					Freehold house, Upper Bedford-street.
Isaacson, Thomas, Regent Cottage, Western-road..					Fr. house, " the Castle," Castle-street

NAMES.	D.	F.	Ch.	Cs.	QUALIFICATION AND WHERE SITUATE.
Izard, John, 18, St. James's-street ..					Freehold house, 12, Broad-street.
*James, Thomas, 114, North-street..					Freehold house, 44, Grenville-place.
Johnson, Rev. Henry Luttman, Tillington, Petworth					Fr. buildings and ground, Nelson-row.
*Johnson, N., Free Butt, Albion-st.					4th part of four freehold houses, 147 to 150, North-street.
Jones, George, Jermyn-street, London.					Freehold house, 7, Red Cross-street.
Jones, James, 21, Upper St. James's-st					Freehold houses, 2 and 3, Foundry-st.
*Judson, Henry, Richmond-villa.					Freehold house, 8, Old-steyne.
Kay, John, 19, Upper Rock-gardens..					Freehold house, Apollo-terrace.
Keeping, John, Steyning ..					Fr. h. stables and garden, Round-hill.
Kemp, Grover, 12, North-street ..					Freehold house, 44, Gardener-street.
Kemp, Thomas Read, Kemp-town .					Freehold farm, Scabbs-castle.
Kendall, Henry Edward, 17, Suffolk-street, Pall Mall East, London ..					Fr.h. 2, Chichester-terrace, Kemp-town
Kent, Richard, 7, Brunswick-row ..					Freehold house, 9, Clarence-place.
Kent, Edward, tendered Darby & Fuller					Centurion-pl., Mighell-st., Windmill.
Kent, Samuel, 14, Spring-gardens ..					Freehold house, 31, Oxford-street.
Kentfield, Jonathan, 15, Manchester-st.					Fr. Billiard rooms, 14, Manchester-st.
Kine, Thomas, Nelson Cot., Nelson-pl.					Freehold houses, 20 & 21, Carlton-st.
*King, George, 3, Upper St. James's-st					Freehold house, 92, St. James'-street.
King, John, 23, Brunswick-sq., Hove					Freehold house, 33, Montpellier-road.
King, John, Norbiton Lodge, Kingston, Surrey					Freehold hs., 21 and 22, Mighell-street
*King, William, 2, Regency-square..					Freehold house, 1, Oriental-terrace.
*Kipping, William, 18, Russell-square					Freehold house, West-street.
*Knapp, John, Duke-street ..					Freehold house, 51, King's-road.
Knight, Christopher, Southwick ..					Freehold house, 13, Bond-street.
Knight, Wm., tendered for Cavendish & Curteis, Upper North-street					Castle-street.
Kymer, Maximilian Richard, Fair Mead Lodge, Loughton, Essex ..					Freehold house, 17, Crescent-cottages
Laker, Benjamin, West-st., Horsham					Freehold dwelling-house, 50, Wood-st
Lambert, Charles, 186, Western-road					Freehold house, Regents-row.
Lambert, Richard, 13, Crown-street					Freehold house, 12, Crown-street.
Lambert, William, 92, Western-road					Freehold house, 90, Western-road.
Lamprell, Abraham J., Baths, East-st.					Freehold stables, Church-street.
*Lane, Henry, King & Queen, Brighton					Freehold hs., 2, 3 and 4, Carlton-row.
Langdon, Gilbert Henry, Rev., Upper St. James's-street					Perpetual Curacy of All Souls Church, Upper Edward-street.
Langley, George, 3, Stone End, Newington, Surrey					Freehold house, 46 & 47, Carlton-row.
*Langley, William, 32, Brighton-place					Freehold house, 25, Upper Edward-st.
Langridge, Joseph, 31, Meeting-h. lane					The Tabernacle f. chapel, West-street.
*Lansdell, John, 11, Richmond-place					Freehold house, 16, St. James's-street
*Lashmar, George, Chesterfield-street					Freehold house, 91, St. James'-street.
*Lashmar, John, 25, Ship-street ..					Freehold house, 39, Gardener-street.
Lashmar, Richard, 28, North-street..					Freehold house, 75, Western-road.
Latter, Edward Aday, 51, Ship-street					Freehold house, 26, North-street road.
Leach, Charles, 9, Pavement, Finsbury					Freehold house, 18, Richmond-place.
Lebright, Geo., 4, Brunswick-row N.					Freehold house, 20, Oxford-street.
*Lee, Henry, Royal Sovereign ..					Freehold houses, 3, 4 & 11, Grafton-st
Legg, James, 146, North-street ..					Freehold house, 23, Oriental-place.
Lewis, Hyam, 31 & 32, Ship-street..					3 copyhold houses, 1, 2 and 3, Lewes-bridge, North-street.
*Lewis, Thomas, Union Assurance Office, London					Freehold house, West-street.
*Linn, Richard, Derby-place . ..					Fr.h. Bloomsbury cot. St. George's-road

NAMES.	D.	F.	Ch.	Co.	QUALIFICATION AND WHERE SITUATE.
*Lloyd, Benjamin, 44, King's-road ..					Freehold house, 11, Dean-street.
*Locke, Richard, 6, St. George's-place					Two eight parts of the freehold of the Chapel-royal,Princes-place, North-st.
Lomer, Wilson, Reading, Berks ..					Freehold house, 27, Regency-square.
*Lower, George, 16, Little Russell-st.					Freehold house, 4, Ivory-buildings.
Lower, Henry, 10, Manchester-street					Freehold house, 10, Chapel-street.
*Lulham, Thomas, 150, North-street					Freehold land, Guildford-terrace.
Lyal, John, 11, Bedford-square ..					Freehold house, 12, Bedford-square.
Lyon, William Joseph, 27, Claremont square, Pentonville, Middlesex ..					Fr. houses, 60 to 65 Hereford-street.
Mackie, William, 2, Charlotte-street, Surrey road, London					Freehold house, 68, Regency-square.
*Mc Whinnie, John Sidney, Ship-street, Brighton					Freehold ground, Park-place.
Malleston, John Philip, Rev., Hove..					Freehold Chapel, New-road.
*Manfield,Wm., Denmark Hill, Surrey					Fr. house, Bedford hotel, King's-road.
Mancer, Francis, 17, Crescent-street					Freehold house, 7, Burlington-street.
*Mantle, Joseph, 27, Bond-street ..					Freehold house, Carlton-hill.
*Mantle, Thos., Wheat Sheaf, Bond-st.					Freehold house, back 21, New-road.
*Marshall, Edmund, 17, York-place..					Freehold house, 20, York-place.
Marshall, George, 22, Marshall's-row					Freehold house, 27, Gardener-street.
Marshall, John, 25, Preston-street ..					Freehold house, 42, Preston-street.
*Marshall, Richard, Hurstperpoint ..					Freehold house, London-road.
*Marshall, Thomas, Arundel ..					Freehold house, 3, Temple-street.
Marsham,R.,D.D.,MortonCol.,Oxford					Fr.h., 14, Lewes-crescent, Kemp-town
Marten, George, 8, Carlton-row ..					2 freehold houses, Edward-street-gns.
Marten, Henry, 136, North-street ..					Freehold house, 78, King's-road.
Masquerier, John Jas.,8,Western cots.					Freehold house, 21, Regency-square.
Maynard, George, 52, Preston-street					Freehold house, 9, Stone-street
*Meakin, Thomas, 10, Norton Falgate, London..					Freehold house, 17, Oriental-place.
Medcalf, Thomas, 19, Grove Hill terrace, Camberwell, Surrey ..					Freehold house, 9, Western-cottages.
*Mellish, Thomas, 24, Crown-street..					Freehold house, 10, Crown-street.
Michell, James Charles, 68, East-st.					Fr. ld., second furlong, Hilly-lane.
*Miles, Aron Robert, 11, Regent-row					Freehold house, 7, Regent-row.
Miller, James Francis, Croydon ..					Freehold house, New-steyne-street.
Miller, Wm. Oliver, High-st., Croydon					Freehold house, New-steyne-street.
Mills, John, St. George's-place ..					Freehold house, 12, Marine-square.
*Mills, James Henry, 58, High-street					Freehold house, 1, Chesterfield-court.
Mollineux, Edward, 77, Edward-street					Freehold house, 20, Gardener-street.
Monk, Thomas, 33, Bond-street ..					Windsor-terrace.
Montagu, David, Paddington, Midx.					Freehold house, 18, Oriental-place.
Moore, John, Lincolns Inn, London					Freehold house, 5, Montpellier-road.
*Morley, Francis, 40, Grosvenor-street					Fr. houses, 11 and 19, Apollo-terrace.
*Morley, George, 35, Michael's place, Brompton, Middlesex ..					Freehold house, 21, Oriental-place.
*Morley, H. 25, Upper St. James-st.					Freehold house, 35, Warwick-street.
*Morling, Edward, 22, Albion-street.					Freehold house, 25, Brunswick-place.
Morling, Robert, 9, Camelford-street.					Freehold house, 7, Cambridge-street.
Morris, Arthur, Cliffe, near Lewes ..					Freehold house, Nelson-street.
Morris, David Edward, 18, Suffolk-street, Pall Mall, London ..					Freehold house, 57, Marine-parade.
Morrison, Wm.Ogilvie,Linndore-villa.					Fr.h,Bloomsbury-villa,St.George's-rd.
Mott, Robert, 12, Crescent-street ..					Freehold house, 6, Royal-crescent.
Munn, Thomas, 33, Bond-street ..					Freehold house, 5, Windsor-terrace.
*Murrell, George, 72, London-road..					Freehold house, Church-street.
Neale, William, tendered for Cavendish and Curteis, 5, Regent-hill ..					Western-road.

NAMES.	D.	F.	Ch.	Cx.	QUALIFICATION AND WHERE SITUATE.
Neale, James, tendered for Cavendish and Curteis, Steyning					Clarence-place.
Newman, W. High-street, Lewes					Freehold house, Russell-street.
Newnham Richard, Steyne-lane					Fr.house, Wright's library, Colonnade.
Norman, James, Rocdale, Patcham					Freehold house, 14, Camelford-street.
Norman, Jn. Hy., Deale, Kent					Fr.ground,Borough-street,Western-rd.
North, John, Montague-place					Freehold houses, Edwin-place.
Nugee, Francis James, 2, Albany, Piccadilly, London					Freehold house and land, Eastern-terrace, Marine-parade.
Nutley, Thomas, 48, Regent-street					Freehold house, 6, King-street.
Oak, Thomas, Greenwich					Freehold house, 2, Sloane-street.
*Ockendon, Reed, 51, Up. Bedford-st.					Fr. h., 22 and 23, Upper-Bedford-st.
Oddy, Henry, 11, Burlington-street					Fr. houses, 17 and 18, Marine-square.
Olive, John, 97, London-road					Fr. house, Branch-house, London-road
Olliver, George, 13, St. George's-st.					Freehold house, Frederick-street.
*Ormond, James Cowle, 4, Charles-street, Queen's Elms, Brompton					Freehold stables, John-street.
Orphin, Thomas, 5, Temple-street					Freehold house, 33, Norfolk-square.
*Over, Thomas, 18, Wood-street					Freehold house, 22, Wood-street.
Packer, John, near Woolwich, Kent					Freehold house, 20, Clarence-place.
Packham, Thomas, 90, Western-road					Freehold house, Western-road.
Page, John, 31, North-lane					Freehold house, 19, Mighell-street.
Paine, Thomas, 36, John-street					Freehold house, Edward-street.
Palmer, George, 12, Upper Woburn-place, London					Freehold house, 3, Regency-square.
*Palmer, Philip, 118, St. Martin's-lane, London					Fr, h., 22, Lewes-crescent, Kemp-town
*Palmer, Thomas, 129, North-street					Freehold house, 44, Western-road.
Pannett, Richard, Chailey					Freehold house, 91, St. James'-street.
Pannett, Stephen, 2, St. George's-rd.					Freehold house, 5, Old-steyne.
*Parker, Christopher, 54, Church-st.					Freehold house, 55, Church-street.
*Parker, Geo. Lucas, 17, Trafalgar-st.					Fr.h. s. & cow-lodge,St.Georges-mews
Parker, George, Shoreham, Sussex					Fr. h., Trafalgar-gns. Trafalgar-street
*Parker, John, 20, Wood-street					Freehold house, 8, Wood-street.
*Parker, William, 12, Cheapside					Freehold house, 20, White-cross-street
Parsons, George, York Hotel					Freehold house, 37, Crescent-street.
Parsons, Henry, 1, St. George's-st.					Freehold house, 2, St. Georges'-street
Parsons, Jonathan, Isleworth, Midx.					Freehold house, 23, Hanover-crescent.
Parsons, Joseph, 24, Marine-parade.					Freehold house, 20, Union-street.
Parsons, William, 35, Mighel-street.					Freehold house, 7, George's-street.
Paskins, Robert, 45, Cavendish-street					Freehold house, 19, Cumberland-place
*Patching, John, 26, Duke-street					Freehold land and stable, Chalybeate-street and Duke-street.
Patching, James, 12, Ship-street					Freehold house, 13, Kensington-street
*Patching, Robert, 20, Calthorpe-place, Gray's Inn-lane-road, London					Freehold house, 40, Portland-street.
Patching, Richard, Duke-street					Freehold house, 41, Portland-street.
Patching, Richard, jun., 8, Duke-st.					Freehold house, 10, Duke-street.
Payne, Richard Kent, 12, Brunswick-pl.					Freehold house, 17, Red-cross-street.
Payne, George, 3, Edward-gardens					Freehold land, Edward-gardens.
Peachy, J., 39, Brunswick-sq., London					Freehold house,12, Marlborough-place
Peel, Laurence, Esq., 32, Sussex-square, Kemp-town					Freehold garden, Kemp-town.
*Pell, Christopher, Camelford-street.					Freehold houses, Jubilee-street.
Penfold, Wm., North-street.					Freehold house, Richmond-buildings.
Pentecost, Dennis, 92, North-street.					Fr. hs., 13, 14 & 15, Mount Sion-place
Pentecost, Thomas, 75, North-street.					Freehold house, 10, Bond-street.
Penton, Thomas, Castle-street					Freehold house, 7, Clarence-gardens.

NAMES.	D.	F.	Ch	Cs	QUALIFICATION AND WHERE SITUATE.
Perkins, Frederick, Chipstead-pl., Kent					Freehold house, 5, Royal-crescent.
Perkins, John, Bletchingly, Surrey ..					Freehold land and 4 houses, East-mill-place, near the windmill, Kemp-town.
Perkins, Charles, South-ends Sydenham, Kent					Freehold house, 13, Royal-crescent.
Phillips, J. Francis, 19, Camelford-st.					Freehold house, 91, St. James's-street
Phillipson, J. B., 118, London-road..					Freehold house, 10, Gloucester-place.
*Philp, Robert James, 13, North-street					Freehold house, 41, Regent-street.
Pickford, James, 1, Cavendish-place					Freehold houses, Hereford-street.
Pike, James, 19, Dean-street ..					Freehold house, 32, Dean-street.
*Pilbeam, John, 16, Mount Sion-place					Freehold house, 17, Mount Sion-place
Pilcher, J. Giles, Morgan's-lane, London					Freehold house, Chesterfield-street.
Pilcher, Jer., 56, Russell sq., London.					Freehold house, East-cliffe.
Pilcher, Wm. Humphrey, 18, New-Broad-street, London ..					Fr. hs., 62 and 65, Chesterfield-street
*Pitt, George, 16, Carlton-street ..					Fr. houses, 26 and 27, Jubilee-street.
Pocknell, Wm., Westow-hill, Norwood					Freehold house, 57, Ship-street.
Pocock, John, 21, Grenville-place ..					Freehold house, 20, Russell-square.
Pocock, John, 45, Gardener-street ..					Parish clerk of St. Nicholas Church.
*Pocock, John, Montpellier-road					Freehold house, King's-road.
Pocock, J. Blagrave, 110, London-road					Freehold stable, Essex-street.
Pocock, Thomas, 65, Western-road..					Freehold house, 64, Western-road.
*Pocock, William, 2, Ship-street ..					Freehold house, 32, Middle-street
Pollard, Francis, 32, West-street ..					Freehold house, Brighton-place, Mrs. Russell, tenant.
Pollard, John, 8, Gloucester-place ..					Freehold house, 80, Grand-parade.
Pollard, Philip, White Lion Yard ..					Freehold hs., 5 and 6, Upper North-st.
Potts, Thomas, Clapham, Surrey ..					Freehold house, 9, Charlotte-street.
Poune, John, 31, New-road ..					Freehold house, 59, King's-road.
Powell, G., jun., 1, York bgs., Islington					Freehold house, 24, Regent's-street.
Preece, James, tendered for Cavendish and Curteis, Lindfield ..					Princes buildings.
Price, Barrington, Portland-place ..					Freehold land, St. George's-road.
*Price, Charles, 3, Old-steyne					Freehold house, 22, Princes-street.
Prosser, Wm., tendered for Cavendish and Curteis, St. James's-place ..					Jubilee-street.
*Pullinger, Arthur, 63, William-street					Freehold house, 31, George-street.
Pullinger, William, Cheapside .					Freehold hs., 10 and 11, Gardener-st.
*Ranger, George Thomas, 45, George-street, Devonport					Fr. house and land, 13, Montague-st.
*Ranger, Richard, Grafton Cottage..					Fr. house and land, 20, St. James's-st
*Ranger, William, 11, Great Dean's-yard, Westminster					Freehold h. and land, 27, New-steyne
Raphael, Alexander, Great Stanhope-street, London					Fr. h, 120, London-road, Canton-house
Reason, William, 57, High-street ..					Freehold house, 28, King-street.
Reed, Richard, 63, Edward-street ..					Freehold h. 10, Devonshire-terrace.
*Reynolds, Charles, 6, Clarence-place					Fr. houses, 22 and 23, Blucher-place
*Reynolds, John, 6, Clarence-place..					Freehold house, 27, Old-steyne.
Ricardo, Moses, Montpellier-road ..					Freehold house, in the road leading from Upper North-street, to Wick.
Rich, I. T., High-st., Guildford, Surrey					Freehold house, 10, Richmond-place.
Richardson, Hy., Kingstone, nr. Lewes					Fr. hs., 1, 2 and 3, Richmond-buildings
*Ridley, Samuel, 138, North-street..					Fr.h., Hilly-house, Richmond-buildings
Roberts, Nathl. Wood-st., Barnet, Herts					Freehold house, George-street.
Roberts, Hemmings Thos., tendered for Cavendish & Curteis, 19, Grand-pd.					Freehold house, 29, Regency-square.
Roberts, John, 11, London-road ..					Freehold house, 12, York-place.

NAMES.	D.	F.	Ch	Cs.	QUALIFICATION AND WHERE SITUATE.
Robertson, Archibald, 34, Gardener-st.					Freehold house, 35, Gardener-street.
Rogers, Edward, 17, North-street ..					Freehold house, 22, Kensington-gns.
Rogers, John, 24, Western-road ..					Freehold house, 23, Marlborough-st.
Roper, John Riddall, 15, New-steyne					Freehold Chapel, St. Margaret's, Cannon-place.
Rolfe, Thomas, Clifton Cottage, Hove					Freehold house, 47, Regent-street.
*Rowland, Joshua, 6, Belmont-place					Freehold houses, Belmont-place.
*Sanders, S. Farncombe, 5, Waterloo-pl.					Freehold house, 35, Albion-street.
Sandham, Benjamin, King-st., Arundel					Freehold houses, King-street.
Sattin, Edward, 17, Edward-street ..					Fr. h., Edward-gardens, Edward-st.
Saunders, John, 119, St. James's-street					Freehold house, 79, King's-road.
Saunders, John, jun., 8, Grand-parade					Freehold house, 59, Western-road.
Saunders, William, 112, St. James's-st.					Freehold house, 9, Pavilion-parade.
*Savage, Edmund, Pavilion Hotel ..					Fr. h., Anglesea-cottage, London-road
Sawyer, George William, tendered for Cavendish and Curteis, Up. North-st.					
Sawyer, George, 36, Middle-street ..					Clerk of fr. Chapel, Chapel-royal.
*Sawyer, John, 5, Little Castle-square					Freehold house, 25, Gardener-street.
Scott, Sir David, Sillwood ..					Freehold house, Oriental-place.
Scott, Jas. Sibbald David, Esq., Sillwood					Freehold house, 31, Western-cottages
Scutt, Thomas, Rev., West-street ..					Freehold houses, Montpellier-terrace.
Shallcross, Moses, Whitecross-street					Freehold house, Tidy-street.
*Sharood, C., Brighton Horse Barracks					Freehold building, 28, Jubilee-street.
Sharood, Charles, Harstperpoint ..					Freehold house, Oxford-street.
Sharp, Ebenezer, 16, Black Lion-street					Freehold house, 39, Bond-street.
Sharp, William, Union-street (South)					Freehold house, Great Russell-street.
Sharp, William, 11, Rose-hill, North					Freehold house, 10, Rose-hill.
Shaw, Benjamin, 72, Cornhill, London					Freehold house, 20, Norfolk-square.
Shaw, George, Mosely-st., Manchester					Freehold house, 30, Oriental-place.
Shaw, W. Kentish-town, near London					Freehold house, 8, Colebrook-row.
Shelley, William, 3, Mount Sion-place					Freehold house, 5, Mount Sion-place.
Sheppard, Charles, 37, Wood-street					Freehold house, 35, Wood-street.
Sheppard, Hards, 75, Pimlico ..					Freehold house, 9, Wood-street.
Shrivell, Cornelius, 10, Mighell-street					Freehold house, 6, Mighell-street.
Shrivell, Thomas, 1, Upper Russell-st.					Freehold house, 4, Blucher-place.
Sickelmore, William, 19, Tralfalgar-st.					Freehold house, 48, London-road.
Simpson, J. C., 1, St. George's-place					Freehold house, 72, Western-road.
*Simpson, William B., 38, Edward-st.					Freehold land, Edward-gardens.
Skilbeck, John Joseph, 15, Highbury-place, Islington					Freehold house, 28, Russell-square.
*Slater, William, 9, Portland-street..					Freehold hs., 1 and 2, Kensington-st.
Slee, John, Western-road ..					Freehold house, Western-road.
Slight, Lewis, 34, West-street ..					Freehold house, Upper North-street.
*Smith, C., Waterloo-pl., St. James's					Freehold house, 14, Western-cottages
Smith, Horatio, 10, Hanover Crescent					Freehold house, 5, Hanover-crescent.
*Smith, John, 24, St. James's-street					Freehold house, Western-road.
Smith, John, tendered for Cavendish and Curteis, Hanover-place ..					Freehold house, Rock-house.
*Smith, John, Unicorn-yard ..					Freehold house, 117, North-street.
Smith, O. Hy., Thames Bank, Chelsea					Freehold house, Crescent, Kemp-town
Smith, Samuel, 37, Grand-parade .					Freehold house, 38, Grand-parade.
Smith, Stephen, E. J., Horsham ..					Freehold house, 10, York-place.
Smith, Thomas, 4, Union-street (South)					Freehold house, 9, Blackman-street.
Smith, William, Dorset Arms, 29, Gardener-street					Freehold house, 21, Kensington-gns.
*Smith, William, 36, George-street					Freehold house, 15, Lower Rock-gns.
Smith, William, 9, Camelford-street					Freehold house, 10, Lower Rock-gns.
*Smith, Wm., 40, George-street ; ..					Fr. house, 10, Lower Rock-gardens.

NAMES.	D.	F.	Ch.	Cs.	QUALIFICATION AND WHERE SITUATE.
*Smithers, Henry, 83, North-street					Freehold h., the " Nelson" Russell-st.
Solly, Hollis, Albany Crescent, Kent-road, Surrey					Fr. h., 6, Lewes Crescent, Kemp-town
*Solomon, Henry, 23, Little Castle-sq.		—			Freehold land, Rose-hill, used as a Burying-ground.
Soper, James, 25, Wood-street ..		—			Freehold house, 7, Wood-street.
Spyring, John Samuel Shepheard, 8, St. Peter's-place					Freehold h., 9, St. Peter's-place.
Stacey, Thomas, Grosvenor-street ..		—			Freehold house, 6, Providence-place.
Stammers, Edward, 99, Strand, London					Fr. h. and stable, 2, Queensbury-place
*Standen, John, 3, St. Peter's place					Freehold house, Whitecross-street.
Stanford, Richard, Preston ..					Freehold house, Oxford-street.
Stephens, George, Hove Lodge .					Freehold h., 8, Brunswick-place, North
Stephens, Robert, Henfield .					Freehold house, 12, Richmond-hill.
Sterry, Rd., Hoddlesden, Hertfordshire		—			Four freehold houses, Nile-street.
Stevens, William, 25, North-street ..				—	Freehold house, 31, Bond-street
Stewart, Charles, 28, Oriental-place		—			Freehold house, 31, Oriental-place.
*Still, Francis, 4, Russell-square ..				—	Freehold house, 70, King's-road.
Stilwell, Joseph, 58, North-street ..					Freehold house, 5, St. Peter's-street.
Stocks, Matthew, 14, Waterloo-place					Freehold house, 2, Clarence-street.
*Stone, Benjamin Jeremiah, 2, St. James's-place				—	Freehold hs., 102 and 103, Edward-st.
*Stone, John, 51, East-street ..				—	Freehold house, 25, Dorset-gardens.
Stone, Thomas, Newhaven :				—	Freehold house, 20, George-street.
Stonham, George Alex., 26, Ship-st.				—	Freehold house, 40, Middle-street.
*Storrer, Thomas, 31, Preston-street				—	Freehold house, 30, Preston-street.
Story, P. Laycock, Tusmore H., Oxford					Fr. h., 25, Sussex-square, Kemp-town.
Street, George, Warnham.. ..				—	Fr. houses, 31 to 33, New Dorset-st.
Streeter, Edward, 1, Steyne-place ..				—	Freehold house, 71, North-street.
Streeter, Jonathan, 40, Clarence-place					Freehold house, 71, North-street.
Strivens, Edmund, 23, Mighell-place		—			Freehold house, 24, Mighell-street.
*Stuckey, Richard, 67, London-road				—	Freehold house, 69, London-road.
Stunt, John, Strand, London ..					Freehold house, 7, Hampton-place.
*Suggers, G. King's Arms, George-st. .				—	Freehold house, 8, Montague-street.
Sully, C. 149, Fenchurch-st. London. .		—			Fr. hs., End of Apollo-terrace, Rose-hill cottages and the one adjoining.
Sutton, A. White, Teddington, Middx.					Freehold house, 44, Paradise-street.
Swaysland, Stephen, 18, Nile-street..		—			Freehold houses, Portland-street.
*Tamplin, H. Pagden, 1, Lennox-place					Fr. h., White Hart Inn, Russell-street.
Tamplin, Richard, Lennox-place ..					Fr. h., Golden Cross, Princes-street.
*Taylor, Robert, 27, Old-steyne ..				—	Freehold stables, Princes-street.
Taylor, John, East Mill House ..				—	Freehold house, 9, Brunswick-place.
Taylor, Thomas, Tunbridge Wells, Kent				—	Freehold house, 9, Dean-street.
*Tester, Richard, 31, Lavender-street					Freehold house, 16, Dean-street.
Thomas, George, Chapel End, Walthamstow, Essex					Freehold house, 10, Devonshire-place
Thomas, John, 14, Up. Russell-street				—	Freehold house, 20, Bedford-square.
Thomson, Denzil Ibbetson, Kilburn Priory, Middlesex					Freehold house, 7, Marine-parade.
Thorby, Thomas, 35, North-street ..				—	Freehold house, 32, Oriental-place.
*Thorncroft, Saml., 6, Windsor-terrace		—			Freehold house, 9, Queen-street.
*Thornton, Thomas, Horsham ..					Freehold house, 15, Devonshire-place
Thorp, John, sen., Horsham ..					Freehold house, 42, Gardener-street.
Thunder, Carter, 2, Castle-square ..		—			Freehold house, Lower Rock-gardens.
*Ticehurst, James, 18, Devonshire-st.				—	Freehold house, 36, Devonshire-street
Ticehurst, Joseph, Cumberland-place				—	Freehold house, 33, Devonshire-place
*Tickner, Charles, Mount Pleasant..				—	Fr. houses, 21, 22 and 23, Derby-place
Tidy, William, 31, Brunswick-place				—	Freehold house, 32, Brunswick-place

NAMES.	D.	F.	Ch	Cs.	QUALIFICATION AND WHERE SITUATE.
Tilbury, Edward, 1, Patriot-place ..					Freehold house, 2, Patriot-place.
Tipping, William, 14, Gloucester-pl.					Freehold house, 22, New-road.
Towner, William, 41, Western-road					Freehold house, 38, Ship-street.
Trangmar, Anthony, 30, London-road				—	Freehold houses, 94 & 95, London-rd.
*Trangmar, JohnTanner, 8,Boyce's-st.				—	Freehold house, 29, London-road.
Trangmar, Wm., 37, Great Russell-st.				—	Freehold house, 7, Guildford-terrace.
Trench, George, Angmering, Sussex					Fr. stable, at the top of North-street.
Trist, John, 1, Upper Rock-gardens					Freehold house, 28, Old-steyne.
Trist, William, 59, St. James's-street					Fr. house, 53, Upper Edward-street.
Trocke, Thos., Rev., 17, Duke-street					Perpetual Curacy of Chapel Royal, Princes-place.
Trocke, William, 2, Norfolk-square.					Freehold house, 4, Marine-square.
Troup, James, 120, Cheapside, London					Fr. houses, 9, 10 & 11, Oriental-place
Tugwell, William, Crescent Cottage				—	Freehold house, 30, Union-street, East
Tulley, William, 64, Russell-street ..					Freehold house, Russell-street.
*Tuppen, Benj., Bedford-square road				—	Freehold h., 32, Montpellier-place.
Tuppen, Jno.,30, Richmond-buildings				—	Freehold warehouse, workshop and yard, 42, Meetinghouse-lane.
Tuppen, Richard, 93, St. James's-st.				—	Freehold house, 8, Upper Edward-st.
Tuppen, Thomas, 43, North-lane ..					Freehold house, 44, North-lane.
Turner, Edward, Bell-street, Reigate					Freehold house,33, Marlborough-place
Turner, George Matthias, Lambeth-green, Surrey					Fr. h., stables and yard, Sussex-street.
Turner, John, Paddington, Middlesex					Freehold house, 18, Oriental-place.
Turner, Philip, Leigh-street, Red Lion-square, London					Freehold house, Upper Bedford-street.
Turner, Richard, All Saints, Lewes					Freehold house, 20, Dorset-gardens.
Turner, Robert, New Park, Lyndhurst, Hants					Freehold house,34, Marlborough-place
*Turner, Thomas, Tunbridge Wells..				—	Fr. houses, 28 and 29, Bedford-square
Turner, William, Eastbourne ..					Freehold house, 30, Devonshire-street
Turpin, Thomas, Bennett-street, Blackfriars-road, Surrey ..				—	Freehold house, 7, Norfolk-square.
Twine, Henry, 8, Marlborough-street				—	Freehold house, 7, Marlborough-street
*Upton, John, 131, North-street ..				—	Freehold house, Temple-street.
Usborne, Thomas, Gilwell House, Sewardstone, Essex					Freehold house, 13, Bedford-square.
Vallance, Charles, Chippenham, Wilts.					One fifth part of a freehold house, Gun-hotel, East-cliffe.
Vallance, Edmund, West-street ..				—	One fifth part of a freehold house, Gun-hotel, East-cliffe.
Vallance, George, 45, Ship-street ..					Freehold house, 3, Blackman-street.
Vallance, Henry, Bristol ..					One fifth part of a freehold house, Gun-hotel, East-cliffe.
Vallance, James, jun., Hurstperpoint, Sussex					One fifth part of a freehold house, Gun-hotel, East-cliffe.
Venner, Ambrose, Middle-street ..				—	Freehold house, 2, Duke-street.
Verrall, Esau, All Saints, Lewes ..				—	Fr. house, Little St. George's-street.
*Vick, C. Wren, 132, North-street ..				—	Freehold house, Norfolk-square.
Virgo, Samuel, 18, Cheltenham-place				—	Freehold houses, 1 and 2, Egremont-st
Wagner, Henry Michell, Rev.,Vicarage					Freehold Vicarage of Brighton.
Waite, Thomas, 1, St. George's road				—	Freehold house, St. George's-road, Burlington-arms.
*Walker, Jas. Kinlock, 40, Drury-lane, London				—	Freehold land, Chesterfield-street.
*Walker, Matthew Clement, 48, Skinner-street, London				—	Fr. h., St. James'-street, the Royal Oak
*Walker, Thos., Denmark-hill, Surrey				—	Freehold house, 4, Regency-square.
Walls, Joseph, 11, Up. North-street				—	Freehold house, Western-road.

NAMES.	D.	F.	Ch	Cs.	QUALIFICATION AND WHERE SITUATE.
*Walls, William, 11, Up. North-street					Freehold house, 63, King's-road.
*Walpoles, Edward, Saville-row, London					Fr h., Albion-lodge, Preston-street.
*Walton, Charles, 37, Western-street					Freehold house, 97, King's-road.
Walton, William, 29, Western-street					Freehold house, 25, Bedford-square.
Warn, John, 39, Hanover-street, Portsea, Hants					Freehold house, 10, Dean-street.
Warner, John, 5, North-street ..					Fr. hs., 39 and 40, Frederick-street.
*Warren, Robert, 30, Strand, London					Freehold houses, New Dorset-street.
*Weatherly, Samuel, 5, Bridge-street, Westminster					Freehold houses, 26 & 27, Derby-place
Weaver, Joseph, 26, Up. Edward-st.					Fr. hs., 9 and 10, New Steyne-street.
Weller, Charles, Cheapside ..					Freehold house, 36, Francis-street.
Weller, Samuel, 134, North-street ..					Freehold house, Western-road.
West, Thomas, 3, Lewes Crescent ..					Freehold house, 6, St. George's-place.
West, Thos. Paine, 49, Frederick-st.					Freehold house, 48, Frederick-street.
Whichelo, J., East Teignmouth, Devon					Fr. land, part of the tenantry down.
*Whiteman, Charles, 14, North-street					Fr. house and warehouse, Ship-street.
Whiteman, Randall, High-st., Lewes					Freehold dwelling-house, 8, King-st.
Whitmarsh, Thos. Webb, 8, Bruns-wick-place, Hove					Freehold house, 46, Russell-square.
Whitington, Peter, Paper Court House, near Ripley, Surrey					Freehold house, 47, Nelson-street.
Whitworth, William, 25, Bond-street					Freehold slaughterhouse, Vine-street.
Wigney, I. N., Esq., 21, Brunswick-sq.					Freehold house, 62, East-street.
Wigney, Wm., 60, Great East-street.					Freehold house, 17, Cannon-place.
*Wigney, William, jun., Marten Lodge, Henfield					Freehold house, Brunswick-place.
Wilds, Amon Hy., 8, Western-terrace					Freehold house, 6, Western-terrace.
Wilkins, John, 25, Richmond-place..					Nine freehold tenements, Vine-street.
Wilkins, Richard, Falmer					Fr. house, 27 and 28, Oxford-street.
Wilks, Jos. Brown, 4, Sussex-square.					Fr. h., 6, Sussex-square, Kemp-town.
Williams, R. Stroud-green, Hornsey.					Freehold house, 18, Frederick-place.
Williams, Wm., 21, Richmond-place.					Freehold house, 17, Richmond-place.
Williams William, 12, Bond-street ..					Freehold house, 6, Old-steyne.
Williamson, Joseph, Compton, Guild-ford, Surrey					Freehold house, 1, Dean-street.
Willis, Benjamin, 6, William-street..					Freehold houses, 7 to 10, Grosvenor-st.
*Wilson, E. Webb, 2, Egremont-place					Freehold house, 24, Old-steyne.
Wingham, Barak W., 25, West-street					Freehold house, 16, New-steyne.
Wingham, Thomas, 25, West-street..					Freehold house, 97, Western-road
Wisden, George, tendered Cavendish and Curteis, Upper North-street ..					Freehold house, Upper North-street.
Wisden, Thomas, 2, Hampton-place..					Freehold house, 113, Western-road.
*Wood, Benjamin, 41, Clarence-place					Freehold hs., 4 and 5, Crown-street.
Wood, David, 4, Richmond-street ..					Freehold house, 28, Tidy-street.
*Wood, Frederick, 5, Ship-street-gns.					Freehold house, 12, Kensington-street
Wood, George Edward, Broad-street					Freehold house, 12, Regency-square.
*Wood, John B., Clapham-road, Surrey					Freehold house, 33, Cannon-place.
Wood, James, 20, Dean-street ..					Freehold house, 32, Dean-street.
Wood, R. Waterbeach, nr. Chichester					Freehold house, 2, Mount-pleasant.
Woodhams, Wm., 22, George-street..					Freehold house, 29, George-street.
Woodin, Joseph Stewart, 35, Gerrard-street, Soho, London ..					Fr. houses, 10 to 18, Spring-street.
Woolger, Josias, Steyning ..					Fr. h., 22, Brunswick-place, North.
Woolgar, Richard, Newhaven ..					Freehold house, 14, Oxford-street.
Wren, Thomas, 27, Cumberland-place					Freehold house, 4, George-street.
*Wright, T. Henry, 31, Cannon-place					Freehold house, 108, London-road.
Wright, Wm. Consett, Springfield Cottage, Upper Clapton ..					Freehold house, 12, Pavilion-parade.

NAMES.	D.	F.	Ch	Cs.	QUALIFICATION AND WHERE SITUATE.
Yeates, John, 18, York-place					Freehold house, 8, Grand-parade
*Younger, Thos., 8, Richmond-place					Fr. houses, 20 and 21, St. George's-st.
FULKING.					
Blaker, Nathaniel, Perching					Land as occupier, Perching.
Howell, Charles, Hove					Land as occupier, Paythorne.
Marchant, William,					Copyhold house and land, Fulking.
Schomberg, Alex. W. Rev., Edburton.					Rectorial tithes of Fulking.
Strivens, James					Land as occupier, Fulking.
Stephens, James					Land as occupier, Fulking.
HOVE.					
Adams, Charles Marsh, Devonshire..					Freehold house, 2, Lansdown-place.
Baker, George Leeke, 7, Up. Woburn-place, Tavistock-square, London ..					Freehold house, 33, Brunswick-square
Boys, Jacob, 60, Grand-pr., Brighton					Freehold house, 4, Stanhope-place.
Boys, John, 6, Albion-street, Lewes					Freehold house, 35, Brunswick-square
*Bransbury, George, Littlehampton..					Freehold buildings and land, Little Western-street, and Cross-street.
*Capon, Samuel, Leominster, Sussex					Cp. h. and stable, 2, Marine-villa.
Dowson, Joseph, Denmark Hill, Camberberwell, Surrey					Freehold house, 30, Brunswick-square
Dumbrell, James, Nile-st., Brighton					Freehold house, 18, Brunswick-square
Dalrymple, Sir A. J., 5, Brunswick-ter.					Fr. stable, Chapel-mews, Waterloo-st.
Egan, John, 58, Guildford-st., London					Fr. houses, 2 and 3, Brunswick-terrace
Elliott, Edward Bishop, Tuxford, Notts					Freehold house, 30, Brunswick-terrace
Everard, Rev. Edwd., D.D., Wick H.					Perpetual Curacy of St. Andrews-Chapel, Waterloo-street.
Elliott, Henry Venn, 31, Brunswick-sq.					Freehold house, 11, Cannon-place.
Goldsmid, Isaac Lyon, Dulwich House, Camberwell ..					Freehold house and land, Hove.
Green, Philip, Buxton, Surrey					Freehold house, 27, Brunswick-square
*Lambert, William, Waterloo-street..					Freehold house, 49, Brunswick-square
*Long, Charles, New Bond-street, Fitzroy-square, London					Freehold house, 12, Lansdowne-place
Murray, Wm., Grosvenor-st., London					Freehold house, 29, Brunswick-terrace
*Mills, James, Mills's-terrace, Hove					Freehold house, 40, Brunswick-square
Michelson, D., 10, Grand-pr., Brighton					Freehold house, Western-road.
Maxse, James, Woolbeding, Midhurst					Fr. stables, Brunswick-mews, West.
Parkin, Hugh, Ashurst Lodge, East Grinstead ..					Freehold house, 52, Brunswick-square
Power, Nicholas, Gifford's Hall, Stoke Nayland, Suffolk					Fr. hs., 34 and 35, Brunswick-square.
Polhill, Edward, 17, Brunswick-square					Freehold house, 17, Brunswick-square
*Round, John, Danbury-hall, Essex					Freehold house, 15, Brunswick-terrace
Schofield, J., 11, Trafalgar-st., Brighton					Freehold house, 13, Brunswick-square
Sawyer, Geo. William, Upper North-street, Brighton ..					Freehold house, 6, Stanhope-place.
Soames, Henry, Broadfield, Herts ..					Freehold house, Brunswick-place.
*Strange, John, Hove Villa					Freehold house, Brunswick-square.
*Saunders, Thos., 34, York-ter., London					Freehold house, 27, Brunswick-terrace
Stanford, Richard, Preston-pl., Preston					H. & land, as ocp., Long Barn-farm.
Stephens, George, Old Hove					Freehold house and land, Old Hove.
Smith, Edmund, Horsham					Freehold houses, Wick-road.
Stone, J. Benj. St. James's-pl, Brighton					Freehold houses, 49, Waterloo-street.
Williams, Robert, Brighton					Freehold house, 9, Lansdown-place.
Webb, Samuel, 6, Lansdowne-place..					Freehold house, 5, Lansdown-place.

NAMES.	D.	F.	Ch.	Cs.	QUALIFICATION AND WHERE SITUATE.

NEWTIMBER.

Gordon, C. Esq., Newtimber-place ..					Freehold land, Newtimber-estate.
Gordon, William, Rev.					Rectorial tithes of Newtimber.
Tapsell, Francis . ..					Land as occupier, Newtimber-farm.

OVINGDEAN.

Kemp, Nathaniel, Esq.					Freehold house and land.
Marshall, The Rev. John W. Henry,					Freehold tythes of Ovingdean.

PATCHAM.

*Atkins, John Rev., Albourne ..					Vicarage of Patcham.
Ayling, John, Withdean ..					Ld. as ocp., pt. of Withdean, Eastern fm.
Ballard, Richard..					Freehold mill, Patcham-mill.
Blaker, George					Leasehold house, in the village.
Botting, William, Withdean ..					H. & ld. as ocp., Withdean Eastern-fm
Gorringe, James, Grand-pr., Brighton					House and land as occupier, part of Withdean, and Eastern-farm.
Newman, Charles					H. & ld. as ocp., Withdean Western-fm.
Paine, John, Esq.					Fr. house and land, Patcham-place.
Scrace, Thomas					Freehold house, in the village.
Tanner, William					House and ld. as ocp., Gatehouse-farm
*Tillstone, Rd. M., Esq., Moulscomb					H. and land as ocp., Moulscomb-place

PIECOMBE.

Brown, William					Cp. house and land, in the street.
Blaker, Nathaniel					Land as occupier, Pangdean-farm.
Blaker, George					Land as occupier, Pangdean-farm.
*Carter, Thomas					Copyhold house and land, Hobbes.
Dench, James					Copyhold house, in the street.
Penfold, The Rev. J., Steyning ..					Freehold land, the Glebe.

PORTSLADE.

Arnold, John					Copyhold house and shop, in the street
Ayres, James					Copyhold h. and garden, in the street.
Barnett, William, Wilderness Park, Sevenoaks, Kent					Freehold house and ld., Copperas-gap
Blaker, Thomas					Land as occupier, in the street.
Blaker, Harry, West-street, Brighton					Freehold house and land, in the street
Borrer, John					Freehold house and land, Manor-farm
Butcher, Rev. Edw. Rt., Northampton					Copyhold house and land, the Stonery
Cooper, Thomas					House and land as ocp., the Stonery.
Fuller, Hugh					Freehold land, little Gothards.
Goddard, Thomas					Cp. stable and garden, in the street.
*Hall, John					Freehold and copyhold house and land, Portslade-house.
Hardwick, John, Hangleton ..					Freehold house and shop, Copperas-gap
Hoper, Rev. Henry, Vicarage ..					Victorial tithes of Portslade.
Huggett, William, Copperas-gap ..					Freehold house, Copperas-gap.
Mott, Luke					Cp. house and garden, in the street.
Peters, Thomas					Fr. h. mill and land, Portslade-mill.
Reed, Reuben					H. and land as occupier, in the street.
Seymour, Wm., Dorset-gns., Brighton					Land tax of £20. per annum, on Red-house farm, and other lands.
Wallis, John					Freehold house, near the Church.

H

NAMES.	D.	F.	Ch.	Ca.	QUALIFICATION AND WHERE SITUATE.

POYNINGS.

Graimes, James					Ls. buildings and land, Poynings-mill.
Gumbrell, Samuel					Copyhold houses, in the street.
Gallop, Edward, Amberly					Copyhold houses, near the mill.
Hardwick, William					Copyhold house and land, in the street
Hardwick, Wm. H., jun.					Land as occupier, in the street.
Holland, Samuel, Rev.					Rectory of Poynings.

PRESTON.

Chatfield, John, Wick Farm, Hove					Ld. as ocp., adjoining the Dyke-road.
Green, Anthony Sheppey					House and land as occupier, Preston.
Kelly, Walter, Rev.					Vicarage of Preston cum Hove.
Streeter, J., 30, Grenville-pl., Brighton					Leasehold land and windmill, adjoining the Dyke-road.
Stanford, William Esq.					Freehold land, Preston-place.
Stanford, William, jun.					Land as occupier, Preston-place farm.
Smithers, Bartholomew					Land as occupier, Preston.

EASTGRINSTEAD POLLING DISTRICT.

EAST GRINSTEAD.

Akehurst, Stephen					Freehold house and gn., Ashurst-wood
Aldridge, William, Rev.					Freehold house, Chapel-lane.
Arnold, William					Land as occupier, Stone-farm.
Ayshford, Robert, Ifield					Cp. hs. & ld., East Grinstead-common
*Bankin, George					Freehold houses, Rock-gardens.
Barber, Henry					House as occupier, Ship Inn, Town.
Betchley, Richard					Land as occupier, Goodwins-farm.
Betchley, Thomas, jun.					Ld. as ocp., Burnthouse-fm. Forest-row
Betchley, Thomas					Copyhold house, Ashurst-wood.
Belton, William, Hedge Court					Copyhold house, Hedge-court.
Blackstone, Henry					Copyhold house and land, Forest-row.
Blackstone, John					Copyhold house and land, Forest-row.
Blunt, Joseph					Freehold land, Blawhatch.
Bond, Thomas					Fr. house and land, Ashurst-wood.
Born, Moses, Smithfield, London					Cp. house and land, near Cuttons-hill.
Bowrah, John					Freehold house, Forest-row.
Brook, Richard, Chiddingstone, Kent					Freehold house, Forest-row.
Brooker, Benjamin					Copyhold ld. and house, Ashurst-wood
Budgen, Thomas					Freehold houses, near the town.
*Burchett, Charles					Fr. h. and gn., nr. East Grinstead-com.
Burt, Wm. Curtis, Reigate, Surrey					Copyhold house and land, Horncastle-lodge, Ashdown-forest.
*Byrne, Patrick, Lingfield, Surrey					Freehold land, Packhills.
Caffin, Thomas					House and land as ocp., Mill-place-fm.
Capes, John, Walworth, Surrey					Freehold house and ld., near the Town

NAMES.	D.	F.	Ch.	Co.	QUALIFICATION AND WHERE SITUATE.
Chapman, Benjamin					Freehold house, near the Town.
Chapman, James					Copyhold house and land, Coomb-farm
Chapman, Thomas					Copyhold house and land, Coomb-fm.
Chapman, John, Hartfield					Freehold land, Cook's mead, East-Grinstead-common.
Chapman, William					Freehold houses, near the Town.
*Charlwood, Thomas					Fr. houses, East Grinstead-common.
Colling, John					Land as occupier, Claypits-farm.
*Collins, Miles Bailey					Copyhold house and land, Forest-row
Coomber, James					Houses and land, as occupier., the Roebuck at Wychross.
Coomber, William, Cowden, Kent					Land as occupier, Busses-farm.
Coomber, William, jun.					Freehold house and land, near Busseu.
Cotton, Abraham					House and land as occupier, Swan-Inn, and Ashurst-wood.
Couchman, James, Leigh, Kent					Freehold and copyhold land, Thompsetts Bank-farm, Forest-row.
Cranston, Edward, Esq.					Freehold house and land, East-court.
Crawfurd, Robert, Esq.					Freehold land, Saint-hill.
Crowley, Abraham, Alton, Hampshire					Freehold house, Ship-Inn.
Crowley, Chas. S., Croydon, Surrey					Freehold house, Ship Inn.
Crowley, Henry, Alton, Hampshire					Freehold house, Ship Inn.
*Curling, Jesse, Bermondsey, Surrey					Freehold house, in the Town.
Dempster, James					House & ld. as ocp., the Dorset-hotel
Donovan, Alexander, Esq., Framfield					Freehold land, Homestall-farm.
*Edgar, John, Esq.					Freehold house and land, Pickstones.
Ellis, George					Freehold houses, in the Town.
Ellis, Thomas, Catterham, Surrey					Freehold house, in the Town.
*Elphick, Edward					Land as occupier, Moats-farm.
*Figg, William, High-street, Lewes					Freehold land, Forest-row.
Finch, Thomas					Copyhold house and land, Forest-row.
Foster, Richard					Land as occupier, Boyles-farm.
Foster, William					Cp. house and land, Ashurst-wood.
*Fowle, Richard					Freehold house, in the Town.
*Fuller, Augustus Elliott, Esq., Clifford-street, St. James's					Fr. house and land, near Forest-row.
Gardner, John					Land as occupier, Mudbrooks-farm.
Gardner, Thomas Champion					Land as occupier, Ridge-hill farm.
Gerritt, William, Godstone, Surrey					Copyhold house and ld., Ashurst-wood
Gibb, Thomas					Fr. house and garden, in the Town.
Goodrick, George, Forest-row					Freehold house, Forest-row-green.
Goodwin, Sawyer					Cp. house and garden, Ashurst-wood.
Gosling, John					H. as ocp. in the Town & Ashurst-wood
Gourd, William					Cp. houses and land, Ashurst-wood.
Harcourt, G. Simon, Ankerwycke, Bucks					Freehold house and land, Shovelstrode
Hastie, Charles Nairn, Esq.					Fr. house and land, Ashurst-wood.
Head, Benjamin, Horley, Surrey					Freehold house and garden, the wood.
Head, George					Copyhold land, near the Town.
Head, John, Lewes					Freehold house, Old-mill
*Head, William Alston, Esq.,					Freehold house, in the Town.
Heasman, Edward Whitby					Cp. house and land, Ashdown-forest.
Heaver, Edward					House and land as ocp., Tablehurst-fm
Hills, Henry					Copyhold house, Ashurst-wood.
Histed, John					Freehold house and land, Forest-row.
*Holford, Henry					House and land as occupier, Lags-heath
Hone, James, Brixton, Surrey					Copyhold houses and land as mortgagee in possession, East Grinstead-com.
Hounsome, Abraham					Land as occupier, Harley-farm.

NAMES.	D.	F.	Ch	Cs	QUALIFICATION AND WHERE SITUATE.
Huggett, John					Freehold house and gn., Ashurst-wood
Jewell, James, Godstone, Surrey					Copyhold house and land, Lynns.
*Kell, W. Polhill, St. Michael's, Lewes					Freehold house and land.
*Kelsey, Robert, Lingfield, Surrey					Freehold house and land, nr. the Town
Knight, Robert					Freehold house, in the Town.
Lambert, George					Freehold house, in the Town.
*Lambert, James					Freehold house, in the Town.
Lane, Thomas, Russell-sq., London					Freehold house and land, Busses-farm.
*Lowcock, George					Freehold house and land, Cuttons-hill.
Lowdell, G., Esq., Middle-st., Brighton					Freehold house and land, Dallinridge.
Lynn, James					Freehold house, in the Town.
Magens, John Dorrien, Esq.					Fr. house and land, near Brooklands.
*Magens, Magens Dorrien, Esq.					Freehold house and land, Hammerwood
Martin, Benjamin					Freehold houses, Forest-row.
Martin, Frederick					Copyhold house and land, Forest-row.
*Martin, William					Freehold houses, near the Town.
*Maynard, Robert					Cp. h. & ld. Cold-harbour, nr. Plawhatch
Mills, Robert					Copyhold house and ld., Ashurst-wood
Michell, John					Copyhold h. and land, Tomsetts-bank.
Morris, Thomas					Freehold house, in the Town.
Morphew, Christopher					Freehold houses, in the Town.
*Nevill, Christopher, Rev.					Vicarage of East Grinstead.
Newman, Ralph					Freehold house and land, Forest-row.
Norman, Wm. Geo., Bromley, Kent					Freehold house and land, Harley-farm.
Parrott, William Jackson					House and ld. as ocp., Ashurst-wood.
*Pattenden, Edward, Copthorne					Freehold house, East Grinstead-com.
Pattenden, Henry, Hedge Court					Copyhold house, Hedge-court.
Pattenden, William					Freehold house and land, self occupier
Paul, William, Bucklersbury, London					Freehold house, East-Grinstead.
Payne, John					House and land as oep., Bugdens-barn
Payne, Robert					Freehold house, in the Town.
Pocock, Henry					Cp. house and land, Ashurst-wood.
Pollington, Stephen					Land as occupier, Cansiron-farm.
Prentice, John					Copyhold house and ld., Ashurst-wood
*Ray, John					Land as occupier, Worsteds-farm.
Ready, John, Chichester					Freehold house and land, Tan-yard.
Relf, Samuel					Fr. house and ld., East Grinstead-com.
Riddle, James					Land as occupier, Hoskins-farm.
*Roupell, Geo. Boone, Lingfield, Surrey					Freehold house, workshop and garden, East Grinstead-common.
Sanders, Carew					Land as occupier, Gulledge-farm.
*Sawyer, Charles					Freehold house, in the Town.
Schrader, C. F., East Grinstead-com.					House and land as occupier, Chandlers
*Shearman, James					Land as occupier, Fairleigh-farm.
Simmonds, John					Fr. h. and gn., East Grinstead-common
Sisley, Richard					Land and mill as occupier, Brambletye farm and mill.
Smead, William					Land as occupier, Brooklands farm.
Soper, Thomas					Copyhold house, Forest-row.
Southey, William					Fr. house and land, Felbridge-water.
*Stanbridge, John					Ld. and mill as ocp., Fenn-place-mill.
Stanford, James, Lingfield, Surrey					Freehold land, Goodwins-farm.
Stenning, George, Tunbridge					Freehold houses, near the Town.
Stenning, John					Fr. h. and land, East Grinstead-com.
Stenning, William					Freehold houses, near the Town.
Stoner, Stoner Thomas, Pyrton, Oxon					Moiety of freehold land, Brambletye, and Court Inholmes.
Taylor, Henry Thomas					Copyhold house and land, Charlwoods

NAMES.	D.	F.	Ch	Cs	QUALIFICATION AND WHERE SITUATE.
Taylor, Thomas ..					Cp. h. & ld., East Grinstead-common.
Trego, James, York-place, Brighton					Freehold houses, in the Town.
*Trill, Thomas, Greenwich, Kent ..					Freehold house and lands.
Turley, John .					Freehold house and ld., near the Town
*Turner, John					Hs. and land as ocp., Ashurst-wood, and in the Town.
Underwood, John					Land as occupier, Luxfords farm, and Old Tan-yard.
Vallance, John, Hedge Court					Freehold house, Hedge-court.
Waghorn, Daniel					Cp. house and land, Ashurst-wood.
Walder, William					Freehold house, in the Town.
Walls, John ..					Land as occupier, Walesbeach-farm
Waters, John..					Copyhold house and land, Forest-row.
Wells, William					Copyhold houses and land, Forest-row
Whyte, John ..					Copyhold house and lands, Forest-row
Wicks, Richard ..					Fr. house and gn.,East Grinstead-com.
Wood, George ..					Copyhold house and land, Forest-row.
Woodman, James, Withyham					Freehold house and land, nr. Ridgehill.
Worrell, Jonathan					Freehold house and land, Framepost.
Wren, James ..					Land as occupier, South-park-farm.
Wright, John, Hampstead, Middlesex					Freehold house and land, the Priory.

FLETCHING.

NAMES.	D.	F.	Ch	Cs	QUALIFICATION AND WHERE SITUATE.
Awcock, George, Barcombe					Copyhold house, near Danehill.
Awcock, William					Land as occupier, Mill farm.
Adams, John ..					Freehold house and land, Fletching-st.
Ashby, Thomas, Sheffield mill					Mill and farm as ocp., Sheffield-mill.
Bannister, William					Copyhold h. and land, Splaynes-green.
Bennett, James					Copyhold house and land, Chelwood.
Budd, Henry, Folly House, near Lip-hooks, Hants					Mortgagee in possession of freehold and copyhold lands, Woolpack's, Luxfords light-row & Wilmshurst.
Browning, William, Danehill					Freehold house and land, Danehill.
Carr, Henry					Freehold house and land, Fords-green
*Cave, William ..					Freehold h. and land, Fletching-street.
Coatsworth, David					Land as ocp., Colin Godman's-farm.
Coleman, James..					Copyhold house, Fletching-common.
Davis, Francis John, Lieut.-Colonel					Freehold house and land, Danehurst.
Davies, Warburton, Esq.					Freehold house and land, Woodgate.
Diplock, William					Fr. ld.. Argules, Groslings-common.
Durrant, Stephen					Land as occupier, Downstreet-farm.
Fleet, Benjamin					Freehold house and land, Shortbridge.
Friend, David ..					Cp. house and ld., Chelwood-common.
Fuller, James ..					Freehold house and gn., Fletching-st.
Fry, John					Land as occupier, Northland-farm.
Gilbert, Daniel					Ld. as ocp., East-park-farm, Sheffield.
Gibert, Edward					Copyhold house and land, Piltdown.
Gilbert, William					Land as occupier, Barkham, Piltdown.
Goord, William					Cp. house and land, Chelwood-gate.
Gilham, John ..					Cp. house and land, Chelwood-gate.
Greenfield, Zephaniah, 55, Devonshire Mews, Portland-place, London ..					Cp. h. and land, Chelwood-common.
*Hemsley, George					Freehold house and land, Shortbridge.
Kell, Christopher, St. Michael, Lewes					Fr. h. and land, Grislings-common.
Kember, John..					Land as occupier, Pound farm.
Kenward, James					Freehold house & land, Portsmansford. Sheffield Green.
Langridge, James					Copyhold house and land, Danehill.

NAMES.	D.	F.	Ch	Cs.	QUALIFICATION AND WHERE SITUATE.
Luckings, Thomas					Copyhold house and land, Chelwood.
Marten, Benjamin					Copyhold house and land, Danehill.
Osborn, James					Freehold house & garden, Shortbridge.
Osborn, Thomas					Land as occupier, Woodcock farm.
Parker, William					Fr. h. & ld., Turner's Green Cottage.
Pratt, John					Land as occupier, Athralls farm.
Penfold, Peter					Copyhold house, Danewood.
Rogars, Daniel					Copyhold h. & ld., Chelwood Common
*Reay, John, 75, Mark Lane, London					Copyhold h. & ld., Netherhall farm.
Stevenson, George					Cp. h. & ld., near Piltdown brick-kiln.
Stevenson, George, jun.					Cp. h. & ld., School House, Piltdown.
Stevenson, James					Fr. house & land, Fletching Street.
Stevenson, Henry					Fr. house and land, Fletching Street.
Turner, George					Land as occupier, Church farm.
Turner, Jethro					Copyhold h. & ld., Chelwood Common
*Taylor, William					Cp. fm., h. & ld., Pond fm., Piltdown.
Uridge, Isaac					Fr. house and land, Hillwood farm.
Vinall, William					Fr. house & land, near Fletching Street
Webb, John					Cp. house & land, Fletching Common.
*Weston, Edward					Cp. h. & ld., Bandswick, nr. Netherhall
Wheeler, William					Ld. as oc., Spring & Homedales farms
Wilson, Sir Thoms Maryon, Bart. Charlton House, Kent					Freehold manors Tarring, Camois, Barkham and Netherhall.
Wood, Charles					Fr. house & garden, Fletching Street.
Wheeler, Charles					Cp. house & land, Chelwood Common
*Wood, John					Copyhold house and land, Danehill.
Young, Richard					H. & ld. as ocp., Sheffield Arms Inn.

HARTFIELD.

NAMES.	D.	F.	Ch	Cs.	QUALIFICATION AND WHERE SITUATE.
Bridger, James, Coleman's Hatch					Cp. messuage & land, Furnace farm.
Brooker, Ambrose, Perry Hill					Land as occupier, Perry Hill farm.
Brooker, James, near Coleman's Hatch					Cp. house & land, nr. Colman's Hatch.
Bashford, Wm., Quabrook Common.					Copyhold house and land, Quabrook.
Chapman, William, in the Forest, near Chuck-hatch					Fr. house & land, near Chuck-hatch.
Elliott, Augustus George					Freehold house & land, Newbridge.
Elliott, Abraham, nr. Coleman's Hatch					Fr. house & land, Little Shepherds.
Edwards, Robert, in the 500 acres.					Fr. messuage & land, Andrews Bank.
Edwards, William, Withyham					Copyhold house & lands, Quabrook.
Edwards, Thomas, Chuck-hatch					Cp. h. & gn., near Colman's Hatch.
Edwards, Richard, Chuck-hatch					Freehold house & land, Little Reeds.
Everest, James					Fr. house and garden, in the village.
*Fry, John, Harts farm, Hartfield					Land as ocp., Harts & Hurstlands fms.
Foster, Thomas, Clay pits					Fr. & cp. h. and land, Clay-pits farm.
Fillery, James, Newbridge Mill					Freehold garden, Newbridge green.
Fitness, George, near Colman's Hatch.					Cp. h. & ld., near Colman's Hatch.
*Gainsford, Joseph, Cowden, Kent.					Fr. house and land, Gallants or Kitford
Greenland, G. T., Esq., Hartfield Grove					Freehold house, Hartfield grove.
Godly, Luke					Land as occupier, Cotsford farm.
Gardner, William, Old Lodge					Land as occupier, Old Lodge farm.
Henniker, M. J., Hon., Ashdown Park.					Freehold h. and ld., Ashdown park.
Hill, John, Beeches					House and land as ocp., Beeches farm.
Hooker, John, Callinghurst					Land as occupier, Callinghurst farm.
Heasman, Saml., near Grinstead brook.					Cp. house & land, Quabrook Common.
Horne, George					Land as occupier, Stairs farm.
Hollomby, William, Whitehouse					Ld. as ocp., Whitehouse & Scray's fms.
Harvey, Thos., jun., Rev., Cowden, Kent					Freehold land, Island mead.

NAMES.	D.	F.	Ch.	Co.	QUALIFICATION AND WHERE SITUATE.
*Jackson, Henry H., Esq., Holly Hill					Freehold house and land, Holly-hill.
Jowett, John, Rev., Rectory House ..					Rectory, Hartfield.
Jackson, Joseph, Quabrook Common					Cp. house and land, Quabrook-com.
Kenward, William, Holtye ..					House and land as occupier, White-horse Inn, and Broxhill farm
Killick, Henry					Fr. house and garden, Laurel-cottage.
Kinnard, Thomas, Church-street					Freehold house & garden, Church-st.
Maitland, F., Lieut.-Gen., Hollywish					Fr. house and lands, Hollywish-farm.
Marchant, Charles, Heath-place ..					Freehold land, Heath-place.
Newton, John, sen.					Freehold messuage, Newtons-terrace.
Nye, Henry, London-road, Tunbridge Wells					Freehold h. and land, Paradise-place.
Philcox, George, Lower Parrock ..					Land as occupier, St. Ives, and Lower Parrock-farms.
Philcox, Thomas, St. Ives, Hartfield					Copyhold house and land, Portobello, at Newbridge-green.
Payne, Henry, Bolebrook ..					Land as occupier, Bolebrook-farm.
Paine, William, Chartness ..					Land as occupier, Chartness-farm.
Richards, Thomas					Copyhold house, Green-cottage.
Spencer, Abraham, Bassetts ..					Freehold house and land, Puxties.
Shoesmith, John, Gallypot town ..					Copyhold houses, Turks.
Tasker, John, near Coleman's Hatch					Cp. house and land Mount-Pleasant.
Turner, William, Frogs hole					Cp. house and land, near Chuck-hatch
Trice, George, Tunbridge Wells ..					Copyhold h. and land, Golden-castle.
Taylor, Jesse, Horsmonden, Kent ..					Copyhold houses & ld., Rogers-town
*Woodhams, Wm., Gallypot town ..					Copyhold house and garden, Turks.
Wallis, William					House & land as occupier, Church-st.
Wallis, James, Kitford					Fr. house and land, Holtye-common.
Willsworth, Henry, 17, White Hart-street, Kennington, Surrey ..					Cp. h. and ld., Jefferys in the forest.
Weeding, Thomas, Alone Oak Hall..					Cp. house and land, Alone Oak-hall.
Welfare, William					Copyhold house and land, House-plot.
Young, Henry, Fincham					Fr. house and land, Fincham-farm.

HORSTEDKEYNES.

NAMES.	D.	F.	Ch.	Co.	QUALIFICATION AND WHERE SITUATE.
Austin, William, Rev.					Rectory of Horstedkeynes.
Arnold, Thomas					Freehold h. and land, Horsted-house.
Assender, Joseph, No. 30, New-road, St. George's east, London ..					Freehold house, Dane-hill.
Brigden, James					Freehold h. and land, Horsted-green.
Buttenshaw, John : ..					Ld. as ocp., Freshfield and Inholms-fm.
Comber, John					Land and mill as ocp., Horsted-mill.
Coppard, Samuel					Land as occupier, Latchetts-lane.
Flint, Benjamin					Land as occupier, Town-house-farm.
Flint, Benjamin					Ld. as ocp., Old Tan-yard & Aldgates
Faulconer, R. H., Esq., High-st., Lewes					Freehold houses, Freshfield-lane.
Guy, William .. .					Land as occupier, late Marchants-farm
Holman, Thomas					Freehold house and land, Cheeleys.
Hoadley, John					Land as occupier, Oddens-farm.
Hilton, John, Dane·Hill ..					Copyhold house and land.
Jenner, Robert					Freehold house and ld., Horsted-green
Lucas, William, 9, Butcher Hall-lane, Newgate-street, London ..					Freehold house.
*Martin, Thomas					Land as occupier, Deans-land.
Obbard, George					Cp. house and land, Medhurst-land.
Obbard, William.. ..					Land as occupier, Town-place-farm.
Roser, John					Freehold house and land, Freshfield.

NAMES.	D.	F.	Ch	Co.	QUALIFICATION AND WHERE SITUATE.
Stone, John					Freehold house and land.
*Turner, R., Chafford, Penshurst, Kent					Freehold house and land.
Warnett, William					Copyhold farm, Burghurst.
Wright, John, King's-road, Fulham, Middlesex					Copyhold farm.

MARESFIELD.

NAMES.	D.	F.	Ch	Co.	QUALIFICATION AND WHERE SITUATE.
Attree, Samuel					Freehold land, in the street.
Barnes, William					Land as occupier, Dairyhouse-farm.
Bourner, James					Land as occupier, near the street.
Cameron, James, Uckfield					Copyhold land, Nutley Nursery.
*Draper, Henry, Southampton					Freehold land, Pickbones-farm.
Hick, William Franklin, Lewes					Freehold land, Nutley-mill, Coppice.
Hill, Joseph					Ld. and mill as ocp., Maresfield-mill.
Holford, R., Esq., Niton, Isle of Wight					Freehold land, Marshalls-farm.
Hobbs, Isaac					Copyhold house and ld., Foards-green
Huggett, William					Copyhold house and land, But-place.
Knight, Thomas					Copyhold house and land, Butletts.
Knight, James					Land as occupier, Masketts-farm.
Laurance, John					Fr. h and land, near the Old-forge.
Mannington, Richard					Land as occupier, Marshalls-farm.
Marten, Joseph					Land as occupier, Maresfield-end.
Mitchell, James					Freehold land, Piltdown.
Page, Edward					Copyhold land, Maresfield-forest.
Pierce, Henry					Copyhold house and land, Piltdown.
Richardson, Thomas					Copyhold land, Little-clay-lands.
Shelley, John Villiers, Esq.					Fr. house and land, Maresfield-park.
Standing, Ambrose					Copyhold house and land, Dodsbank.
Stanford, Charles					Freehold house and land, Street.
Stevenson, William					Freehold house, Gardeners' Arms.
*Shirley, Henry, Esq.					Freehold land, Pippingford.
Tyler, John					Copyhold house and land, White-house
Tyler, Jacob					Copyhold land, White-house.
Turner, William					Cp. house and ld., Mill-brook, Nutley.
Tunks, William					Freehold h. and land, near Dudleswell
Woodward, Rev. George					Rectory of Maresfield.
Weller, David					Land as occupier, Park-farm.
Warner, George					Copyhold h. and land, Maresfield-end.
Walter, John					Freehold land, Maresfield-end.
Wood, William					Copyhold land, Woodlands Nursery.
Wood, James					Copyhold house and land, Maresfield, Old-brick-kiln.
Wood, Daniel Lewery, Streatfields					Copyhold house and land.

WESTHOATHLY.

NAMES.	D.	F.	Ch	Co.	QUALIFICATION AND WHERE SITUATE.
Arnold, John					Freehold house and land, Hudds-farm.
*Bostock, Ellis, 41, Hunter-st., London					Fr. h. and land, Great-house-farm.
Bingham, William					Cp. h. & land, at Stumblewood-com.
Baker, Thomas					Cp. house and garden, in North-lane.
Clifford, Thomas					Freehold house and ld., Pickridge-fm.
Comber, John					Lands as occupier, Hoathly-hill, Newlands and tyes.
Coppard, George, Brighton					Fr. house and garden, in the village.
Finch, Edward					Freehold house and garden, Cobwebs.
Goord, Thomas					Cp. house and garden, at Birchgrove.
Gibson, James					Land as ocp., Upper Sheriff-farm.
Hollands, Henry, Cowden, Kent					Cp. windmill & ld., at Selsfield-com.

NAMES.	D.	F.	Ch	Cs.	QUALIFICATION AND WHERE SITUATE.
Hobbs, Obadiah					Land as occupier, Greathouse-farm.
Hudson, Thomas					Freehold house and land, near Selsfield-common.
*King, Richard					Freehold house and land, Sopers-ride.
Pollard, Philip					Freehold h. and garden, in North-lane
Patterson, Charles John, the Rev.					Vicarage of Westhoathly.
*Pollard, Thomas, Nutfield, Surrey.					Freehold house and shop.
Payne, William, Chevening, Kent					Freehold land, Lucas-land.
Poile, John					Fr. h. and lds., Bakers Gravetye, Wildgoose, Midgates and Park-farm.
Rose, James					Land as occupier, Riceland.
Roberts, William, Horstedkeynes					Freehold house and gn., in North-lane
Riddle, John					Land as occupier, Gravetye.
Simmonds, Thomas					Fr. houses and garden, in North-lane.
Streater, Richard					Windmill and land as occupier, at Selsfield-common.
Turner, John					Lds. as ocp., Langridge & Smeeds-fms
Turner, Richard					Lds. as ocp., Ludwell & Barmland-fms.
Wheeler, Jasper					Freehold h. & land, Lower Sheriff-fm.
Wheeler, William					Watermill and land as occupier, Burstow-bridge.
Wood, William.					Land as occupier, Hamingden and Brookhouse-farms.

WITHYHAM.

NAMES.	D.	F.	Ch	Cs.	QUALIFICATION AND WHERE SITUATE.
Avis, Peter					Land as occupier, Hunts-farm.
Bannister, Richard, Hever, Kent					Copyhold house and land, Blackham.
Bennett, Edmund, Tunbridge Wells.					Cp. h. and land as trustee, Blackham.
Blackstone, John					Land as occupier, Cook's-corner.
Box, Francis					Freehold house and land, Rugsmith.
Britt, John, 2, Upper Sussex-place, Old Kent-road, Southwark					Freehold land, Florence-farm.
*Chappell, Frederick Cooley, Abindon-place, Camberwell					Freehold farm, Grubs-farm.
Chewter, William					Fr. house and garden, Little-Alksford.
Constable, Henry, Penshurst, Kent					Fr. cottages and land, Blackham-com.
Cowhurst, William					Ld. as ocp., Hilders-farm, Blackham.
Crowhurst, William					Fr. h. and land, Stephens Blackham.
Dives, James					Land as occupier, Blackham-court.
Doggett, George					Land as occupier, Buckhurst.
*Gillam, William					Freehold land, Maynards Blackham.
Hale, Abraham					Land as occupier, Hale.
Hall, Abraham					Land as occupier, Duckings.
Hall, Joseph					Fr. house and garden, Mots-mill.
Hall, Obadiah					Land as occupier, Kendal-farm.
Heasman, Samuel					Freehold house and land, Friers-gate
Heath, Adam					Copyhold house and garden, Mots-hill
Henniker, John, Lord, Great Thornham, Suffolk					Fr. h. and land, Crowborough-warren
Hoath, James					Freehold house and land, Old-moor.
Jenner, James					Fr. house and land, near Leigh-green.
Kember, Michael					Freehold house and land, Leigh-green.
*Marden, William					Cp. h. and ld., near Crowborough-mill
Neve, Robert, Ringmer					Copyhold house and land.
Neve, William					Freehold house and land, near Fryers.
Parris, John					Land as occupier, Ham.
Patching, James, Battle					Freehold house and land, Lutmar
Patching, Thomas					Fr. house and land, Great-Alks'

NAMES.	D.	F.	Ch	Cs.	QUALIFICATION AND WHERE SITUATE.
Price, Richard, Duke-st., Westminster					Freehold house and land, Highfields.
Richardson, Daniel					Freehold lands, Stephens-farm.
*Sale, Thomas, Penshurst, Kent					Fr. house and land, near Ashurst-mill.
*Shoesmith, Edward Sears					Freehold land, Blackham.
Tasker, Philip					Cp. and pt. fr. ld., Crowborough-Town
Tomsett, James					Copyhold houses & ld., Crowborough.
*Turner, Jno., Summerford, Withyham					Land as occupier, Summerford.
Yeats, Grant David, Tunbridge Wells					Freehold house and land, Willets.
Young, Samuel, Frant					Copyhold house and ld., Crowborough.

WORTH.

NAMES.	D.	F.	Ch	Cs.	QUALIFICATION AND WHERE SITUATE.
Akehurst, Samuel, Copthorne, Worth					Copyhold house and land, Copthorne.
Alcorn, John, Poundhill, Worth					Fr. house and land, Black-corner.
*Allingham, Richard, Croydon					Freehold house and land, Copthorne.
Bethune, Rev. G. M., Worth Rectory					Fr. house and land, Parsonage-house.
Blunt, Francis Scawen, Crabbett, Worth					Freehold house and lands, Crabbott-h.
*Burt, Thomas Robert, East Grinstead					Freehold land, Copthorne.
*Boorer, Joseph, Turner's Hill					Freehold house and land, Turners-hill
Boorer, Thomas, Hedge Court, Godstone, Surrey					Leasehold house and land, Copthorne.
*Boorer, Wm., Crawley Down, Worth					Freehold house and land, Turners-hill.
Borer, William, Copthorne					Freehold h. and lands, Little-frenches.
*Brace, John, Turner's Hill					Copyhold house and land, Copthorn.
Brigden, James, Crawley Down					Fr. house and land, Crawley-down.
Bristow, Henry, Furnace, Worth					Land as occupier, Furnace-farm.
*Brown, Joseph, Copthorne					Copyhold house and land, Copthorne.
Brown, Richard, Nutfield, Surrey					Copyhold house and land, Copthorne.
Caffin, Peter, Woolborough					Land as occupier, Woolborough-farm.
Chandler, Benjamin, Crawley Down					Leasehold h. and land, Crawley-down.
*Chandler, Richard, Turners Hill					Freehold house, Lion-Inn.
Chart, William, Godstone, Surrey					Copyhold house and land, and freehold land, Copthorne.
*Commerell, Jno. Wm., Strood, Sussex					Freehold house and lands.
*Compton, Thomas, Reigate, Surrey					Freehold house.
Creasy, Edward, Gibsaven farm, Worth					Copyhold house and land, Copthorne.
Duncy, Josiah, Buckswood, Beeding.					Leasehold h. and land, Turners-hill.
Davis, James, High heath, Worth					Freehold house, High-heath.
*Elgar, Thomas, Reigate, Surrey					Freehold and copyhold houses and ld.
Field, John, Merton-road, Mitcham, Surrey					Freehold farm and land, Turners-hill.
Fieldwick, Thomas, Turners hill					Copyhold house and land, Turners-hill
*Flint, Benjamin, Turners hill					Freehold house and land, Turners-hill.
Franks, George, Crawley down					Freehold h. and land, Crawley-down.
*Franks, Wm., Wallidge house, Worth					Freehold house and land.
Fuller, John, Turners hill					Freehold house and land, Turners-hill.
*Garraway, Abel, Durham-place, Hackney-road, Middlesex					Freehold land.
Grayham, Edward, Hall, Worth					Freehold house and land, Hall.
Hains, Henry, Copthorne					Copyhold house and land, Copthorne.
*Hains, Philip John, Copthorne					Freehold house and land, Copthorne.
Harbour, Fenner, Copthorne					Copyhold house and land, Copthorne.
Harbour, Henry, Copthorne					Copyhold house and land, Copthorne.
Hardy, William Robert, Horne, Surrey					Freehold land.
Hewetson, Henry, Turnham-green, Middlesex					Freehold house and land.
Holland, Richard, Hedgecourt					Copyhold house and land, Hedgecourt.
Hooker, John, Rowfant, Worth					Ld. as ocp., Rowfant-mill and land.
~~, Thomas, Old Rowfant					Land as occupier, Old Rowfant.

NAMES.	D.	F.	Ch.	Cs.	QUALIFICATION AND WHERE SITUATE.
Humphrey, Thomas, Turners hill					Freehold house, Turners-hill.
*Hurst, Robert Henry, Horsham					Freehold land, Three-bridges.
*Hurst, John, Thakeham					Freehold land, Three-bridges.
Illman, Richard, Copthorne					Freehold land.
Jeal, William, Three-bridges					Freehold house, Three-bridges.
Jenner, Jas., Woodcock mill, Godstone					Freehold house and land.
Jewell, John, Lingfield, Surrey					Freehold land, The Rushets.
Johnson, John, Hogshill, Worth					Land as occupier, Hogs-hill-farm.
King, William, Turners hill					Copyhold house and land, Turners-hill
Knight, John, Ifield					Freehold house and land, Crossways.
Langridge, John, Turners hill					Copyhold house and ld., Crawley-down
*Leggatt, Horatio, Pound hill					Copyhold house and land, self-occupier
Lidbetter, Richard, Copthorne					Copyhold house and land, Copthorne.
*Lundie, John S., East-lodge, Worth					Copyhold house and land, Copthorne.
*Michell, Henry, Horsham					Fr. h., the Plough-Inn, in the Town.
Miller, Martin, Turners hill					Freehold house and land, Turners-hill.
Milligon, Charles, Woolwich, Kent					Freehold house and ld., Crawley-down
*Milner, Ralph, 4, Prospect-place, St. George's-road, Southwark					Freehold house and land.
Neale, Thomas, Reigate, Surrey					Freehold house and land.
Nickalls, George, Turners hill					Freehold house and land, Reedings-fm.
Orwry, John, Paddock-hurst, Worth					Freehold h. and land, Paddock-hurst.
Padwick, Henry, Horsham					Freehold house and ld , Three-bridges.
Parker, Joseph, Turners hill					Freehold house and ld., Crawley-down
Parsons, James, Copthorne					Copyhold house and land, Copthorne.
*Parsons, Robert, Edenbridge, Kent					Fr. house and land, Copthorne-bank.
Payne, Jeremiah, Copthorne					Copyhold house and land, Copthorne.
*Perkins, William, Reigate, Surrey					Freehold house and ld., Tinsley-green.
Podmore, Henry, Turners-hill					Freehold house and land, Turners-hill.
Potter, John, Copthorne					Freehold house and land, Copthorne.
Prevett, G. Hophurst-fm., this parish					Land as occupier, Hophurst-farm.
Prevett, William, Copthorne					Copyhold house and land, Copthorne.
Rose, William, Worth-lodge					Farm as occupier, Worth-lodge.
Shelley, Sir Thimothy, bart., Field-place at Warnham					Freehold land.
Shepherd, John, Crawley-down					Freehold house and land, Walnut-tree.
Silvester, Edward, Pound-hill					Ls. house and land, The King's-head.
Squire, William, Copthorne					Freehold land, Copthorne.
Stanbridge, J. Fen-place in this parish					Land as occupier, Fen-place-farm.
Starley, Walter, Turners-hill					Freehold house, Woodgates.
Stening, Stephen, Copthorne					Copyhold house and land, Copthorne.
Stone, H., Hook, near Epsom, Surrey.					Fr. and Cp. house and land, Copthorne
Sanders, John, Furnace-mill					Freehold land, Turners-hill.
Tester, William, Copthorne					Freehold house and land, Dukes-Head.
Uridge, John Alexander, Copthorne					Copyhold house and land, Copthorne.
Vardon, Samuel Arthur, Pound hill					Copyhold house and land.
Vigar, Robert, Copthorne					Freehold house and land, Copthorne.
Wells, Moses, Turners hill					Freehold house and land, Turners-hill.
Walker, Charles, Hunts land					Freehold land, Hunts-land.
West, William, Pound hill					Copyhold house and land.
*Walker, Frederick, Huntland					Copyhold and land, Huntland.
*Woodman, William, Westhoathly					Freehold house and land, Turners-hill.
Young, Henry, Burleigh arches					Land as ocp., Burleigh, Arches-farm.

NAMES.	D.	F.	Ch	Cs.	QUALIFICATION and WHERE SITUATE.
BURWASH.					
Appleyard, R. S., Bedford-sq., London					Freehold house & land, Batemans-fm.
Appleyard, Fredk. Newman, Cursitor's Office, London					Cp. house and land, Burnthouse-farm.
Button, Richard					House and land, the Bear-Inn.
Briggs, George, 54, Wigmore-street, Cavendish-square, London ..					Freehold house and land, Browings-fm.
Baker, Edward					Freehold house.
Baker, Anthony					Freehold house.
*Baldock, John					Freehold house and land, in the Town
Bunden, John . ..					Land as occupier, Southovers-farm.
Brook, John Charles, Bexhill ..					Freehold houses.
Brown, Stephen					Freehold house, in the Town.
Cane, James					Freehold house.
Cheeseman, Thomas					Fr. house and ld., Willards-hill-farm.
Crowhurst, Robert					Freehold house, in the Town.
Cruttenden, Samuel					Copyhold land, Platts-farm.
Cruttenden, John					Freehold house and land, Tott-farm.
Carman, Edmund, Tunbridge, Kent					Copyhold house and land, Bear-Inn.
Dann, Jesse					Copyhold lands, Burwash-wheel.
Ellis, James, Barming, Kent . ..					Freehold house and land, Southovers-fm
Ellis, Thomas					Lds. as ocp., Burnthouse & Clements-fm
Evans, Thomas Abel					Houses and land as ocp., in the Town.
Fleming, James					Freehold house, in the Town.
Gilbert, George Fagg					Fr. house and land, Witherest-farm.
Gould, Rev. Joseph					Land and tenements as ocp., Rectory house and Glebe-land.
Gillett, Thomas					House and land as occupier, part of Willards-hill-farm.
Henty, John . ..					Freehold house and land, Frys-farm.
Haviland, Henry Hone ..					Fr. hs. and ld., Frenches and Newhouse
Honeysett, John					Copyhold watermill, house and freehold land, Dudwell-mill.
Hyland, Joseph					Land as occupier, Lodge-farm.
Hyland, David					Fr. house and land, in Burwash Town.
Lade, James					Land as occupier, Brickhouse-farm.
Langridge, Stephen, tendered for Darby and Fuller					Land as occupier, Mottingsden-farm.
Leaney, James					Freehold-house.
Leney, Abraham, Wrotham, Kent ..					Copyhold land, Keylands.
Lucas, H. 20, Bridge-st., Westminster					Freehold farm, Mottingsden-farm.
Mackensie William, tendered for Darby and Fuller					
Manwaring, William ..					Freehold house, in the town.
Manktelow, Richard . ..					Freehold house, in the town.
Newington, Joseph					Houses, mills and land, as occupier, Withernden hill & the Green farm.
Newington, Samuel					Freehold house, in the town.
Newington, John					Land as occupier, Bines-farm.
Noakes, John					Freehold house, in Burwash-town.
Noakes, James					Land as occupier, Square-farm.
Noakes, James					Fr. h. and copyhold land as trustee in possession, Bell Alley and Daws.

NAMES.	D.	p.	Ch.	Cs.	QUALIFICATION AND WHERE SITUATE.
Oliver, William					Land as occupier, Goadsoal-farm.
Park, John					Freehold house, in Burwash-town.
Parsons, William					Copyhold land, Little Daws.
Parkinson, J., Wal.-c.,Cheshunt,Herts					Freehold land, Witherhurst-farm.
Payne, Thomas					Freehold house, in the town.
*Philcox, James					Freehold house and land, nr. the town
Pilbeam, James					Freehold house, in the town.
Pilbeam, Edmund					Freehold house, in the town.
Press, John, Heathfield					Bg. and ld. as trustee in possession, Chapel in the town and Crowhurst bridge-farm.
Russell, James					Cp. h. and ld., Pound fm. at the Wheel
Roakes, Edward, sen.					Land as occupier, Perimans-farm.
Relf, James					Fr. h. & gn., adjoining the Ch.-yard.
Russell, Francis, jun.					Freehold h. mill and land, Park-mill.
Russell, Thomas					Land as occupier, Rye green-farm.
Reeves, Richard					Freehold h. and land, in Batemans-lane
Sawyer, Joseph					Freehold house, in the town.
Simes, Edward					Land as occupier, Pounceford-farm.
Smith, John, Lewes					Freehold h. and land,Grandtwizzle-fm.
Sone, George, Burwash					Freehold house, in the town.
Sutton, John					Freehold house, in the town.
Thompson, William					Freehold house, in the town.
Veness, Samuel					Freehold house and land, Budds-farm.
Vigor, John					House and land as occupier, in the town, and the Ships-land.
Weston, Phillip					Freehold houses, in the town.
Westall, W.,Love-lane, Aldermanbury					Freehold land, Mill-field.
Winchester, William					House and land as occupier, the Rose and Crown-Inn, and Swan-meadows
Wood, Benjamin					Freehold houses, in the town.
Wood, Richard					Freehold house, in Bell Alley.
BUXTED.					
Allchorn, Thomas					Copyhold farm, Highhurst-wood.
Allchorn, Samuel					Copyhold house and ld, Potters-green.
Baldock, E. H , Hanway-st., Oxford-st.					Copyhold h. and land, Pound-green.
Baldock, William					Cp. hs. & ld., Gatehouse & Buckwell.
Batchelor, Henry					Copyhold house, Pound-green.
*Benham, George Spencer					Freehold house and land, Puckstye.
Berwick, Thomas, Uckfield					Copyhold house, Pound-green.
Best, James					Copyhold land, Popes-wood.
Balcomb, Thomas, Withyham					Copyhold land, Pound-green.
Brumsden, William					Freehold house, Manor-house.
Booker, Richard					Cp. house and land, Highhurst-wood.
Coe, James					Freehold house and land, Great Totease
Cottingham, John					Freehold houses and land, Burghill.
*Dadswell, Nicholas					Cp. house and land, Highhurst-wood.
Dodswell, William					Land as occupier, Stone-farm.
Duvall, John					Land as occupier, Highhurst-wood.
Edwards, William Reid					Minister of St. Marks chapel, Hadlow-down.
Ewen, William					Freehold house and land, Packhurst.
*Firth, James Francis, No. 3, York-place, Walworth, Surrey					Freehold house and gn., Buxted-street
Gilbert, Isaac					Land as occupier, Claygate-farm.
Gorringe, William					Freehold house and ld , Five-chimneys
Hall, Benjamin, Esq.,					Freehold house and ld., Buxted-lodge.

NAMES.	D.	F.	Ch.	Cs.	QUALIFICATION AND WHERE SITUATE.
Holland, John					Freehold house, Buxted-bridge.
Holman, John					Copyhold farm, Burnt-house.
Herriott, Thomas					Land as occupier, Wilderness-farm.
James, Joseph, Hascomb-place, Surrey					Fr. ld. Howbourne-fm.,
Luck, Thomas					Curtains-hill.
Muddle, John					Copyhold h. and land, Highhurst-wood
Nash, William					Fr. ld., Five Chimnies or Middles.
Norman, James ..					Land as occupier, Hole-farm.
Olive, John					Freehold house and land, New-house.
Pierce, George					Copyhold house and land, Buxted-hill
Piper, Robert					Land as occupier, Upper Totease.
Parris, John					Land as occupier, Chillies.
Parris, John, jun.					Land as occupier, Chillies.
Pratt, James					Copyhold h. and ld., Highhurst-wood.
Richardson, Joseph, Withyham ..					Cp. house and land, Buxted-wood.
Rogers, Edward, Uckfield ..					Copyhold house, Coopers-green.
Starr, Thomas.. ..					Copyhold land, Barnsden.
Susans, Thomas					Cp. house and land, Roses-common.
*Stapley, Joseph, Albourne ..					Cp. house and land, Highhurst-wood.
Taylor, William					Copyhold houses, Five Ash Down.
Tanner, John Olive ..					Copyhold house and land, Totease.
Wordsworth, Rev. Dr. Christopher..					The Rectory, Buxted.
Watson, Edmund					Cp. house and land, Highhurst-wood.
Wickens, Samuel					Freehold house and land, Tan-yard.
Winter, James					Copyhold house and land, Buxted-wood
Winter, James, jun.					Land as occupier, Shadwell and Glebe.
Wildish, William					Freehold land, Tibbs-mill.
Wren, Thomas					Copyhold house and land, Pounsley.
Willet, Edward					Freehold h. and land, Upper Totease.
*Wheatley, William					Land as occupier, Hendall.

FRANT.

	D.	F.	Ch.	Cs.	
Budgen, William					Freehold house, Snagshole.
Blackwell, George					Leasehold houses, Rumbers-street.
Bennett, Edmund, Tunbridge Wells.					Leasehold houses, Nevill-place.
Bennett, James, Tunbridge Wells ..					Land as occupier, Frant-forest.
Carr, John					Copyhold house, Frant-street.
Cheesman, Charles					Land as occupier, Sunningly-farm.
Carruthus, John, Esq., Speldhurst, Kent					Copyhold land, Waggons-gate-farm.
Caire, William, Eridge-road ..					Land as occupier, Flying-horse.
Clarke, William					Land as occupier, Bearlands-farm.
Carr, John					Freehold house, Frant-green.
Delves, Thomas, Esq., Tunbridge Wells					Freehold land, Tuttys-farm.
Delves, William, Tunbridge Wells ..					Land as occupier, Frant-forest.
Eastland, William, Tunbridge Wells					Land as occupier, Strawberry-hill.
Fulljames, Richard					Copyhold house, Slow-hall.
Field, William					Freehold, Frant-green.
Field, Edward					Land as occupier, Lightlands-farm.
Grace, Sheffield, Esq.					Freehold house and land, Knole-farm.
Gillett, Richard, Tunbridge Wells ..					Land as occupier, Sussex-cottage.
Hebden, Robert, Esq.					Fr. house and land, Ely-house, Frant.
Homewood, W., Abergavenny Arms Inn					House as occupier, Frant-green.
*Hickmott, Timothy, Eridge Park ..					Land as occupier, Ramsly-farm.
Jones, Richard, Rev., Brasted, Kent					Freehold house, Tunbridge Wells.
Jones, Stephen					Land as ocp., Benhall mill and farm.
Jones, Richard, sen.					Freehold houses, Bellsewe-green.
Jacob, Adam					Freehold house, Frant-green.
Jeffery, William, Portland House ..					Leasehold house, Tunbridge Wells.

NAMES.	D.	F.	Ch	Cs.	QUALIFICATION AND WHERE SITUATE.
Jacob, Nathaniel					H. and land as occupier, High-rocks.
Kine, Edward..					Land as occupier, Newhouse-farm.
Knell, Benjamin, Tunbridge Wells .					H. and land as occupier, Nevill-cottage
Killick, Anthony, Sunbridge, Kent ..					Freehold land, Mayfield-road.
Macfarlane, James, Major,					Freehold house, Frant-street.
Minet, George Lewis, Captain					Freehold house and land, Delvidere-h.
Moon, Thomas					Freehold land, Courtlodge-farm.
Montier, John, jun., Tunbridge Wells					Leasehold houses, Tunbridge Wells.
Nevill, the Hon. Wm., Birling, Kent					Vicarial tithes of Frant.
*Neal, Edward, Tunbridge Wells ..					Leasehold house, Frant-road.
Powell, James..					Mill and ld. as occupier, Bartley-mill.
Pegg, Harry, Tunbridge Wells					Leasehold house, Sussex Hotel.
Rowland, Daniel, Esq., .					Fr. house and land, Saxonbury-lodge.
Roper, William, Esq., Bayham, Frant					Land as occupier, Higham-farm.
Rogers, Robert ..					Copyhold house, Frant-street.
Rabson, John ..					H. and land as ocp., Little Shoesmiths
Sartin, George ..					Freehold house, Little Forking.
Solomon, L., Esq., 4, Crosby-sq., London					Freehold house and land, Riverhall.
Sloman, John, Tunbridge Wells ..					Bg. as ocp., Theatre, Tunbridge Wells.
Stone, John, Esq., Tunbridge Wells ..					Copyhold house, Frant-street.
Spratt, Water, Esq., tendered for Darby and Fuller ..					
Stringer, John, Tunbridge Wells ..					Ls. brewery, Tunbridge Wells, brewery
Wickins, Obid					Land as occupier, Frant-green.
West, Samuel, Tunbridge Wells ..					Leasehold house, Nevill Arms.
HEATHFIELD.					
Baker, T., 31, Trinity-sq., Southwark					Freehold houses and land.
Baker, John ..					Freehold messuages and land, Heathfield, and part in Waldron.
Baker, John, jun.					Freehold messuage and tan-yard.
Balcomb, John, sen.					Freehold house and land, Walnuts-fm.
Barrow, William					Freehold house and land, Haffendens and Funnells-farms.
Barton, Thomas ..					Three freehold houses.
Blunt, Sir C. R., bart., Heathfield Park					Freehold h. and land, Heathfield-Park
Burford, Thomas, Minster Abbey, Sheppey, Kent ..					Half part of freehold farm, Stonehurst
Burton, Mark ..					Freehold house and land, Clappers-fm.
Chrismas, George					Fr. ld., Cade-street and Brown-down.
Chrismas, Henry					Land as ocp., Fords and Baldocks.
Collens, Joseph					Freehold house and land, Pumets-town
Cornwall, Robert, Mayfield					Fr. h. and ld., Little Bignknowle-farm.
Dallaway, Samuel					Cp. land and mill, Cherryclack-mill.
Dray, William ..					Freehold messuage, Cade-street.
Daw, Samuel					Cp. house and land, near the Chapel.
Errey, William ..					Freehold h. and land, Pigstrood-farm.
Featherstone, John					Freehold messuage and land, Mugread
Fuller, George, Major					Land as ocp., near Heathfield Church.
Fuller, John Thomas, Esq., Wartling					Freehold house and land.
Gosling, William					Freehold house and land, Cade-street.
Gilbert, Thomas					Cp. house and land, Little Saperton.
Goble, Theophelus					Freehold house and lands.
Gorringe, William, Kingston-by-sea					Fr. house and land, Marlegreen-farm.
Gorringe, Wm. Pennington, Southwick					Freehold farm.
Haffenden, George					Freehold messuage, Cade-street.
Haffenden, James, jun. ..					Freehold house and land.
Haffenden, Richard					Freehold farms, West-street.

NAMES.	D.	F.	Ch	Cs.	QUALIFICATION AND WHERE SITUATE.
Haffenden, Robert, sen.					Freehold farms, Steel-yards and Pigs-trood farms.
Harmer, Henry					Lands as occupier, Bignowle Nursements and Taylors farms.
Huggett, John					Land as occupier, Deerings-farm.
Haffenden, John					Cp. messuage and land, Lovers-park.
Harmer, Jonathan					Cp. messuages & shop, Portland-place.
Harmer, Joseph					Freehold messuage and land.
Hayward, John					Freehold house and land, Cold Harbour
Hayward, Michael					Freehold messuage and ld., Streetend.
Hebden, John					Land as occupier, Saperton-farm.
Howell, John					Freehold house, Crown Inn.
Huggett, James					Land as occupier, Marlegreen-farm.
Kemp, Peter					Freehold messuage and shop, Cade-st.
Kemp, Henry					Fr. & cp. hs. and ld., Punnets town.
Knight, Thomas, jun.					Freehold mill and ld., Theobolds-green.
Lulham, Benjamin					Land as occupier, Tottingworth farm.
Lovell, George					Freehold messuage and land, Streetend.
Mepham, Thomas					Freehold messuage and land.
Miles, William, Tunbridge, Kent					Freehold messuage and land, Fairplace and Southben-farms.
*Mortimer, Keith					Freehold & copyhold farm, Brigknowl.
Overy, William					Ld. as ocp., Cowden & Marlegreen-fms.
Oxley, William, jun.					Land as occupier, Cade-street-farm.
Oliver, John					Freehold messuage and land.
*Pain, William					Fr. messuage and land, Street-end.
Pettitt, John					Freehold h. and land, Stonehurst-farm.
Press, John, the Rev.					Freehold Chapel, messuages and lds., by the common.
Porter, Henry					Freehold house and land, Streetend.
Relf, James					Three copyhold messuages.
Skinner, William					Lds. as ocp., Mill and Brownham-fms.
*Steer, Humphrey					Fr. messuage and land, Oulsbury-farm.
Stone, William					Cp. messuage & land, near the Church
Tapley, William, Fort House, Gravesend, Kent					Half-part of fr. farm, Stonehurst.
*Thomson, Jonathan Smith					Cp. messuage and land, Runtington.
Thomson, Samuel					Two copyhold messuages and land.
Thomson, Joseph					Copyhold farm, Milkhurst toll.
Upfield, Thomas					Freehold messuage, near the Church.
Upfield, William					Fr. messuage and land, Mutton hall.
Valentine, John					Freehold messuage, Cade-street.
Waters, Stephen					Freehold h. and land, Burnthouse-fm.
Weller, William					Land as occupier, Hugletts-farm.
White, Samuel					Land as occupier, Nettlesford-farm.
Winchester, Henry					Freehold messuage, near the Church.
Woodward, Henry, Esq., 4, Little George street, Westminster					Freehold land, Tottingworth-farm.
Young, James, the Rev.					Fr house, land and tithes of Heathfield

LAMBERHURST.

NAMES.	D.	F.	Ch	Cs.	QUALIFICATION AND WHERE SITUATE.
Ballard, Joseph					Freehold house, Lamberhurst town.
Ballard, Isaac					House and land as occupier, Down-fm.
Barton, Thomas					H. & ld. as ocp., Lamberhurst-town.
Beeching, Thomas, Tunbridge, Kent					Freehold houses, Lamberhurst town.
Boorman, James					Fr. h. & ld., Yew Tree, Green-farm.
Boorman, Thos. Hugh, Brixton, Surrey					Freehold houses, Lamberhurst town.
Cutbearth, John, Lamberhurst, Kent					Freehold houses, Lamberhurst-town.

NAMES.	D.	F.	Cb	Cc	QUALIFICATION and WHERE SITUATE.
Eastland, Thomas, Lamberhurst, Sussex					House and land as ocp., Lamberhurst.
*Filmer, Sir Edmund, East Sutton, Kent		—			Freehold land, Hoathly-farm.
*Geary, Sir William Richard Powlet, bart., West Packham		—			Freehold wood and ld., Whisketts-wood
Hawkens, Rev. R., Lamberhurst, Kent		—			Vicarial tithes of Lamberhurst.
Hussey, E., Esq., Lamberhurst, Sussex		—			Freehold house and land, Down-house
Jones, John, Goudhurst		—			Freehold houses, Lamberhurst-town.
Lansdell, Thos., Lamberhurst, Sussex		—			House and land, Lindridge-lodge.
Lashmar, J. L., Lamberhurst, Sussex		—			House as occupier, Lamberhurst.
Marchant, Thos. B., Brenchley, Kent			—		Freehold houses and ld., Lamberhurst
Morland, William Alexander Esq., Lamberhurst, Kent ..		—			Freehold houses and ld., Lamberhurst
Noakes, John, Lamberhurst, Sussex		—			Freehold house, Lamberhurst-town.
Noakes, Joseph Elias, Salehurst ..		—			Freehold house, Lamberhurst.
Prickett, Charles, Lamberhurst, Kent		—			H. & ld. as ocp., Lamberhurst, Sussex
Prickett, Thomas, Lamberhurst, Sussex		—			Fr. h. and land, Hook-green-farm.
Sale, George, Lamberhurst, Sussex ..		—			H and land as ocp., Spray-hill-farm.
Shepherd, Robert, Hastings, Sussex		—			Freehold houses, Lamberhurst-town.
*Springate, Richard, Goudhurst, Kent		—			Fr. houses and land, Cophall-farm.
White, John, Lamberhurst, Sussex ..		—			H. and land as ocp., Bewlbridge-farm.
*Wilmshurst, Adam, Brenchley, Kent		—			Freehold houses, Lamberhurst.

MAYFIELD.

NAMES.	D.	F.	Cb	Cc	QUALIFICATION and WHERE SITUATE.
Avery, Thomas				—	House & land as ocp., Hampdens-lodge
Blackford, Thomas, Stockland, Mayfield	—				House & land as ocp., Stockland farm.
Bryant, John, Dartford, Kent ..		—			Ls. house for 99 years, Fletching-st.
Bridger, Thomas		—			Fr. farm, Horleigh-green, Mayfield.
*Buss, Benjamin		—			Freehold land, Hoopers land.
Boarer, John		—			Fr. house & land, Town & fair fields.
*Baker, Samuel		—			Freehold farm, Meer's farm.
Bridger, John, jun.		—			Freehold house & land, Leed's farm.
Bridger, Thomas		—			Freehold house and land.
Beney, Benjamin		—			F. h. & ld., Hams & Holstons farm.
Bassett, John		—			Freehold house & land, Wallis's farm.
Briss, John		—			Freehold house & land, Hadlow Down.
Bryant, John		—			Freehold house, Back lane.
Baker, Michael		—			Freehold h. and land, Style Reed-fm.
Brook, Samuel		—			H. and land as ocp., Great Brodhurst
Baker, John			—		Freehold house and land, Crab-hill.
Bridger, John..			—		Copyhold land, part in Mayfield, and part in Waldron.
*Barclay, Donald, village of Mayfield			—		Freehold house and land, the Pound-house and Longs-farm.
Brooker, Michael, near Dudsland-gate, Mayfield		—			Freehold cottage and land.
Bones, Thos., nr. Five Ashes, Mayfield		—			Fr. house and land, near five Ashes.
Chatfield, Nicholas		—			Freehold house and land, Downford.
*Corter, William, Fletching ..		—			Freehold house & land, Chequers-fm.
Cottingham, Charles, Hadlow Down, Mayfield		—			Fr. h., Mount Pleasant, Hadlow Down
Cottingham, James, Hadlow Down, Mayfield		—			Freehold house, Hadlow Down.
Cottingham, William, Hadlow Down, Mayfield		—			Freehold house, Hadlow Down.
Carter, Robert, Littlehampton, Sussex			—		Fr. house and land, Chequers-farm.
Dudlow, John, West Malling, Kent .	—				Fr. h. & ld., Lower-h.-farm, Mayfield.
*Day, John, 28, Montagu-st., London	—				Freehold farm.
Damper, James					Freehold house, town.

K

NAMES.	D.	F.	Ch	Cs	QUALIFICATION AND WHERE SITUATE.
Durrant, Thomas Parker					H. & ld. as ocp., Froghole & Barns-ld.
Dadswell, Edward Okill, Huggett's Furnace Mill, Mayfield					Copyhold land in Rotherfield.
Dudney, Henry					Fr. house and cottage, Mayfield-town.
Errey, Joseph, Hellingly					Freehold house and garden.
Field, Benjamin					Freehold house, Fletching-street.
Fry, John					Freehold house and land, Skippers-hill
Field, William					H. and land as ocp., New Pin-farm.
Fry, Richard					Freehold h. and land, Butchers-cross.
Field, William					H. and land as ocp., High-fields-farm.
*Fry, John					Freehold house and shop, High-street, and Pound-hill.
Fry, Robert					Fr. house and land, Hodges-farm, &c.
Forth, George Eyre					Fr. h. mill and land, Househule-mill.
Foard, Thomas					Freehold house, High-street.
Frost, James, Hadlow Down, Mayfield					Fr. cottage and ld., Hadlow Down.
*Gilbert, William					House and shop as occupier, house and shop, High-street.
Gates, James, South Malling-street, Cliffe, Lewes					Freehold house, Hadlow Down.
*Hosman, George					Freehold house, Back-lane.
*Hurssell, Jonathan					Freehold lane, High-street.
Hall, Henry					Freehold land, Cadswell.
Homewood, George					House and land as occupier, part of Mayfield-place-farm.
*Holmes, Bright					H. and ld. as ocp., Homestalls-farm.
Holland, Wm. B., Cloisters, Chichester					Lease for three lives of Manor of Sherrenden.
Jenner, John					H. and land as ocp., Herrings-farm.
Kirby, Henry, Oakley-eye, Suffolk					Fr. hs. and lds., Place Old-mill, Knowle, Pococks, and common-land-farms.
Kemp, William					Copyhold houses, High-street.
Kirby, Rev. John					Glebe h. and Vicarial tithes of Mayfield
Kell, Christopher, High-street, St. Michael's parish, Lewes					Freehold h. and lands, Hadlow Down.
Knight, A., tendered for Darby & Fuller					H. and land as ocp., Inwoods-farm.
King, Zachariah					Freehold house, Fletching-street.
Lateward, James Frederick, No. 52, Notting-hill-square, Kensington					Fr. hs. & ld., Place Old-mill, Knowle, Pococks, and common-land-farms.
Lawrence, George					Freehold house, High-street.
Lade, Luke					Copyhold house, Pack-lane.
Medhurst, J., Fletching-st., Mayfield					Two cp, hs. and gns., Fletching-street
Maxfield, Joseph, jun., High-st., Lewes					Fr. h. near Hadlow Down, Mayfield.
Marchant, William					Freehold house and land, Streel-farm.
Marchant, John					Freehold house and land, Beedings-fm.
Marchant, Thomas					Fr. house and land, Great Freemans.
Mann, William					H. & ld. as ocp., Dudsland & other fms.
Miller, Thomas, Whites farm, Goudhurst, Kent					Freehold land.
Martin, N., Huggetts Furnace, Mayfield					H. & ld. as ocp., Huggetts Furnace-fm.
Martin, John, Hastingford, Mayfield					H. and land as ocp., Hastingford-farm
Moon, Richd., Hadlow Down, Mayfield					Cp. hs. and ld., near Hadlow Down.
Martin, James					Freehold land, Walters-farm.
*Noaks, John					H. and land as occupier, Great Bainden
*Noakes, John, jun.					House and land as occupier, Gillhope and Little Bainden.
Norman, Thomas					Freehold cottage and garden, in a lane belonging to the brick-kilns.

NAMES.	D.	F.	Ch	Co	QUALIFICATION AND WHERE SITUATE.
Olive, John		—			Freehold house, Mayfield-town.
Piper, Joseph		—			Freehold house, Fletching-street.
Packham, Richard		—			Freehold house, High-street.
Packham, Samuel					House and ld. as ocp., Cranesdens-fm.
*Piper, Thomas		—			Copyhold houses, High-street.
Piper, William		—			Freehold house, Fletching-street.
Packham, John		—			House and land as ocp., Turks-farm.
Piper, James		—			Freehold house, Fletching-street.
Pursglove, Henry		—			H. and land as ocp., Bunglehurst-fm.
Paine, John		—			Freehold house, High-street.
*Packham, William				—	House, mills and land as occupier, Merryweathers farm and two mills.
Penfold, John				—	Freehold house and land, Encotts, Coggins-mill-street.
Phillips, William, Cliffe, near Lewes				—	Two fr. houses, at Hadlow Down.
*Rose, Alexander		—			Freehold house, High-street.
*Rochester, David .. . Ȼ		—			House and land as ocp., Forge-farm.
Rose, John		—			House and land as ocp., Allens-farm.
Rabson, Henry				—	H. and land as ocp , Mousehale-farm.
*Richardson, Samuel		—			Freehold house and land, Bassetts-fm.
Russell, Thomas		—			Freehold farm, Croust.
Russell, William		—			H. and ld. as ocp., New Inn and land.
Russell, Francis		—			H. and land as ocp., Claytons-farm.
Richardson, William		—			Copyhold house and gn., High-street.
Stone, Nicholas		—			Freehold house and land, High-street, Miss and Piccadelly.
*Stone, Wm. Owen				—	Fr. fms., Wellbrook and other farms.
Shoebridge, Richard				—	Freehold h. and land, Little Trodgers.
*Smith, Henry				—	Freehold h. and land, Hadlow Down.
Stevenson, Thomas		—			Houses and land as occupier, Pennybridge farm and Trodgers farm.
Thomas, Morgan, Esq.		—			Fr. hs. and ld., Gatehouse & other fms.
*Tooth, William		—			Fr. h. and ld., Crabb & Wellbrook-fms.
Tompsett, Benjamin		—			Freehold house and land, Moat-hill.
Turk, John		—			Freehold house and land, Cryers-farm.
Tompsett, John		—			Freehold house and land, Fletching-st.
Tompsett, James		—			Freehold h. and land, Cinderhill-farm.
Tompsett, William, Bollering, East Peckham, Kent				—	Freehold h. and land, Cinderhill-farm.
Tompsett, Benj., Heathfield, Sussex				—	Freehold h. and land, Cinderhill-farm.
Tompsett, Henry				—	Freehold h. and land, Cinderhill-farm.
Weston, William		—			Freehold house, North-street.
*Wallis, Michael				—	Fr. houses, High-street and Back-lane.
Walter, Thomas				—	Freehold house, Fletching-street.
Weston, Thomas				—	House and land as occupier, Broomfields and other farms.
Weston, Joel				—	Copyhold houses, Back-lane.
*Weston, Aaron, North-st., Mayfield		—			Freehold land and mill, Argos-hill.

ROTHERFIELD.

Allchorn, Richard, Eastbourne ..				—	Part of fr. land, Sweet Haws-farms.
Allchorn, William					House and land as occupier, Hall-farm.
Avery, William					H. and land as occupier, Dengate-farm
Arnold, George		—			Copyhold house and ld., Crowborough.
Avery, John		—			Freehold house and land, Steep.
Aitchison, Edward		—			H. and ld. as ocp., Old Tan-yard-farm
Babington, Thomas					Freehold land, High-gate.
Bennett, George, Tunbridge Wells ..					Freehold land, Great Hart-farm.

NAMES.	D.	F.	Ch	Cs.	QUALIFICATION AND WHERE SITUATE.
Bryant, *Wm.*, tendered for Curteis					Freehold house, Crowborough.
*Bryant, William					Copyhold house, in the village
Blunden, James					H and land as ocp., Gravel Hill-farm.
Bridger, Joseph					Freehold land, Townrow-green.
Bassett, Joseph					Copyhold hs. and ld., Crowborough.
Best, George					Freehold house and land, Boars Head.
Best, Joseph, Ashurst, Kent					Fr. and copyhold tenements, Pales-gate
Camfield, George					Cp. hs. and land, Crowborough-cross.
Cochrane, John, Esq.					Freehold land, Brownings-farm.
Cole, William					Freehold houses, in the village.
Cork, Benjamin					House and land as occupier, Maynards-gate and Marlings.
Corke, William					H. and ld. as ocp., Bletchingly-farm.
Crawley, Rev. Richard					Freehold house and land, Glebe-land.
Crittall, Robert					House and land as occupier, Spout, Great Hart and Argots-hill.
Cole, Silas					Freehold house and land.
Card, William					Two copyhold houses and land.
Dadswell, Alfred Taylor					Freehold land, Boarshead.
Dadswell, David Taylor					Fr. ld., Homestall and Luxfords-fms.
Dadswell, Robert					Cp. land, Beeches and Pellings-farms.
Dadswell, Edward Ohill					
Day, William, Esq., Maresfield					Freehold land, Inch Reed-farm.
Delves, J., Esq., Tunbridge Wells					Fr. ld., Dengate, Motts & Hodges-fms.
Delves, Thos., Esq., Tunbridge Wells					Freehold land, Renbys-farm.
Dadswell, John					Cp. houses and land, Crowborough.
Dadswell, Nicholas					Part of fr. farms, Sweet Haws-farm.
Damper, William					Freehold houses, Townrow.
Edlin, Ewd. Colsill, Bond-st., London					Freehold house, at the Church-gate.
*Field, Thomas					H. and land as ocp., Walshe's-farm.
Field, William					H. and ld. as ocp., Townrow-green.
*Foreman, Robert, Tunbridge Wells					Copyhold land, Steel-cross.
Fenner, George					Copyhold house, in the village.
Fermor, William					Copyhold h., High-cross, Rotherfield
Jenner, William					Rotherfield.
Hider, William					Copyhold house, in the village.
Harling, George					Cp. h. and land, near Jarvis-brook.
Hallett, Thomas					Copyhold h. and land, Townrow-green
Isard, John, Bromley, Kent					Fr. land, near Crowborough-cross.
*Jarvis, William					Cp. house and land, White Hart Inn.
Kenward, Henry					Freehold house and land, Stone-cross-rocks, and Moses-farms.
Killick, John					Freehold land, Boarshead.
Langridge, John					Copyhold houses, in the village.
Leonard, Thomas					Fr. ld., Orch, Reed, & Walkers-farms.
Lockyer, John					Freehold land, Boarshead.
Lockyer, Thomas					Freehold house, Boars-head.
Maplesden, William					Freehold land, Ham farm.
*Miles, Michael					Fr. house and land, King's Arms Inn.
Moon, John, Tunbridge Wells					Trustee of freehold land, Dengate.
Moon, William					Fr. ld., Mottens hill & Clackhams farm
Moon, William					Cp. house & land, Porters green.
*Miller, Giles, Goudhurst, Kent					Freehold house and land, cottage-fm.
*Miles, Thomas					Fr. h. and land, near Jarvis-brook.
Marchant, Thomas					Cp. h and land, near Jarvis-brook.
Maplesden, Ezra					Cp. hs. shop & warehouse, in the village
Newnham, John					Freehold land, Rumden-farm.
*Newnham, William Henry					House and land as ocp., Walshes.
*Newnham, James					H. & l. as ocp., Cp. & Duddles-farms

NAMES.	D.	F.	Ch. Cs.	QUALIFICATION AND WHERE SITUATE.
Paige, Edward				Freehold house and land, Townrow.
Paine, Henry				Freehold house and land, Minns.
Peckham, Edward, Withyham				Freehold house and land, Sandhill.
Peerless, William				Freehold and copyhold land, Argots-hill, and Loose-farms.
Penfold, Rev. G. Saxby, D.D., Goring				Freehold house and land, Hall-farm.
Pratt, James				Fr. h. and ld., near Crowborough-cross
Pratt, Richard				H. & ld. as ocp., Benhurst & Hole-fms.
Peerless, William				Cy. h. & ld., near Crowborough-beacon
Rogers, William				Copyhold land, Halfords-farm.
Sales, Samuel				Freehold house and land, Park-corner.
Salter, James				Freehold h. and land, Alfreys-farm.
Savage, Chas. A., Fetter-lane, London				Freehold land, Perrymans-farm.
Smith, Abel, Esq., Portland-pl., London				Fr. house and land, in the village.
Stapley, John Baker				Freehold h. and land, Hamsell-farm.
Smith, Samuel				Freehold and land, Mottons-hill.
Thwaites, Henry, Esq.				Freehold land, Hamsell-farm.
Turner, Rev. John Jarvis William				Freehold house and land, Charity-land
Taylor, John Hider				Copyhold h. and land, Crowborough.
Taylor, William				Cp. h. and ld., Steep & Crowborough
Taylor, John				Cp. house and land, near Steel-cross.
Taylor, John				Cp. house and fr. land, Crowborough.
Tickner, Samuel				Freehold house and land, Mark-cross.
Vinall, John				House and land as occupier, Bidden-don-hole-farm.
Walter, William				Copyhold land, Castle-hill.
Whitewood, John				House and land as occupier, Pound-field, Tubwell, and Ivyhouse-farms.
Wickenden, William				Freehold house and land, Meads-farm.
Wickenden, William				Freehold house and land, Renly-farm.
Wickens, Benjamin				Copyhold house, in the village.
Wickens, George				H. and ld. as ocp., Mark and Catts.
Wickens, James				Freehold house and land, Smiths-farm.
Wickens, John				Freehold houses, in the village.
Wickens, Joseph				Freehold house and land, Garden-h.
Wickens, Joseph				Freehold land, Townrow.
Wickens, Joseph				H. and land as ocp., Brookhouse-farm.
Wickens, Samuel				House, mill and land as occupier, Rud-gate mill and Woodside.
Wickens, Thomas				House and land as occupier, Pinehurst
Wickens, Thomas				Freehold house and land, Boarshead
Wilson, John				Freehold land, Boarshead.
*Wickens, James				Freehold h. and land, Townrow-green
*Wickens, James				Freehold house and land.
Waters, William				H. and land as ocp., Ford-brook-farm.
Wood, William				H. & ld. as ocp., Rumden & Jarvis-brook
Wimble, William, Hull, Yorkshire				Freehold h. and land, Owlsbury-farm.

TICEHURST.

NAMES.	D.	F.	Ch. Cs.	QUALIFICATION AND WHERE SITUATE.
Adams, John				Freehold cottage, Dale-hill.
Austin, James				Freehold house and land, Burners-hill, near Flimwell.
*Boscawen, the Rev. John Evelyn, Wooton Rectory, nr. Dorking, Surrey				Vicarial tithes & glebe l. of Ticehurst.
Buss, Benjamin				Freehold houses, Cottenden.
Barden, Thomas				Land as occupier, Coopers-farm.
Barrow, Richard				Land as occupier, Briggs-farm.

NAMES.	D.	F.	Ch.	Cs.	QUALIFICATION AND WHERE SITUATE.
*Barren, Wm., Troytown, Rochester, Kent					Freehold houses, Burners-hill.
Blackman, John, Lamberhurst					Freehold land, Bolsters-gate.
Buckland, John					Land as occupier, Walters-farm.
Boorman, Samuel					Land as occupier, Bearhurst.
Baker, John					Copyhold land, Bardown.
Bussenden, William					Freehold land, Broomden.
Bull, John					Fr. h. and gn., three legged-cross.
Clapson, Francis					Copyhold house, Ticehurst.
Courthope, Geo. Campion					Freehold house and land, Whiligh.
Child, Joseph					Freehold house, Ticehurst.
Carrick, Richard					Fr. h. and gn., three legged-cross.
Ditch, John					Copyhold land, Tolhurst-farm.
Elliott, William					Copyhold farm, Ticehurst.
Field, Benjamin					Freehold house.
Field, Thomas					Land as ocp., Hazle Ash-farm.
*French, James					Freehold house, Gravel-pit.
Farrance, John					Land as occupier, Borzell.
Forward, Thomas					Ld. as joint ocp., Mompumps-farm.
Forward, Thomas, jun.					Land as joint ocp., Mompumps-farm.
Glanvil, Thomas William, No. 5, Cambridge terrace, Edgware-rd., London					Fr. and copyhold land, Pickford.
Golding, James					Freehold house and land, nr. Flimwell
Hyland, William					Freehold school house, Ticehurst.
Huntly, Thomas					Freehold house and mill, Dunsters-mill
Hodge, George					Freehold house, Ticehurst-village.
Harris, William					Freehold house, Ticehurst-village.
Jarvis, Gibeon					Freehold house, Dale-hill.
Jarvis, Thomas					Land as occupier, Dale-hill.
Kemp, George					Copyhold house, Ticehurst-village.
Kemp, Henry					Freehold house, Dale-hill.
Marchant, Jesse					Land as ocp., Bricklehurst-farm.
Moren, Joseph					Land as occupier, Dale Hill-farm.
Martin, Jesse					Freehold house and garden, High-st.
Nokes, William					Copyhold house, Ticehurst-village.
*Nokes, Henry					Freehold land, Gravel-pit-farm.
Newington, George					Land as occupier, Beaumans-farm.
Newington, Charles					Freehold house, Highlands.
Newington, Joel					Freehold house, Witherden.
Newington, Thomas					Land as occupier, Hazlehurst-farm.
Nokes, George					Copyhold farm, Ticehurst-village.
Oyler, George					Land as occupier, Bardown-farm.
Penfold, Peter					Fr. h. and garden, three legged cross.
Petitt, Joseph					Shop and warehouse as joint occupier, Ticehurst-village
Pullinger, John					Fr. h., near Lower-gate, Ticehurst.
Powell, Thomas					Ld. as ocp., Claphatch & Welches-fms.
Pinyon, Aaron, Sandhurst					Freehold h. and garden, near Flimwell
Read, Peter					Land as occupier, Stone-gate.
Rogers, James					Land as occupier, High-street.
Smith, Henry, Goudhurst, Kent					Chapel as joint trustee, Wesleyan Chapel.
Smith, William					Chapel as joint trustee, Wesleyan Chapel
Stanbridge, Benjamin					Freehold houses, Flimwell.
Smith, Robert					Copyhold land, Wishdown.
Standen, Stephen					Land as occupier, Wardsbrook-farm.
Siggs, Samuel					Freehold houses, Burners-hill.

NAMES.	D.	F.	Ch.	Cs.	QUALIFICATION AND WHERE SITUATE.
Stevenson, Stephen					Freehold land, Overies-farm.
Sievyer, John ..					Copyhold houses, Ticehurst-village.
Standen, John					Copyhold house, Ticehurst-village
Sale, William ..					Copyhold house, Ticehurst-village.
Stapley, Henry ..					Freehold house and garden, High-st.
Tapsell, Richard					Freehold house, Ticehurst-village.
Tomsett, James					Freehold land, Holbeam-wood.
Tomsett, S. 98, Fenchurch-st., London					Freehold land, Holbeam-wood.
Taylor, Charles					Copyhold house, Ticehurst-village.
Vidler, William					Land as occupier, Battenhurst-farm.
Walker, Joseph					Land and house as occupier, Flimwell
White, Stephen					Land as occupier, Hammerden-farm.
Wetherell, the Rev. Richard					Freehold land, Pashley.
Waghorn, Thomas					Land as occupier, Wedds-farm.
Winch, John ..					Freehold house, Flimwell.
West, Daniel, Goudhurst, Kent					Freehold house and land, near Flimwell
Willsher, Thomas					Ld. as joint ocp., Gibscead-farm.

WADHURST.

NAMES.	D.	F.	Ch.	Cs.	QUALIFICATION AND WHERE SITUATE.
Ashby, William					House, mill and land as occupier, Riverhall-mill.
Austen, Henry					House and land as ocp., Durgates.
*Austen, Thomas					House and land as ocp., Couseleywood
Avard, Edward					Freehold land, Pell-green.
*Baldwin, Samuel					Freehold house, town.
Baldwin, Samuel, jun.					House and land as occupier, town.
Barton, Thomas					House and ld. as occupier, Little-pell.
Bassett, Thomas					Freehold house and land, town.
Bellamy, J., Wisbeach, Cambridgeshire					Freehold land, Frankham-wood.
Benge, Wm. Henry					Freehold land, Cousley-wood.
Brissenden, Thomas					H. and land as occupier, Little Butts.
Barham, Eastman					Freehold house, Sparrows-green.
Ballard, Thomas					Freehold house, Cousley-wood.
Carr, John					Freehold land, Gatehouse.
Crismas, Joseph ..					House and ld. as occupier, Newnhams
Crowhurst, William, Penbury					Leasehold houses, Cousley-wood.
Chittenden, William					Freehold house, town.
Dadswell, Edward					Freehold house, town.
David, Jonathan					Freehold house, town.
Down, George					Freehold house, town.
Eveleigh, James, River, near Dover					Freehold house and land, Cousleywood Pettitt, tenant.
Field, Joseph ..					Freehold land, Clarks.
*Farrant, John, Maidstone					Freehold land, Beggars-bush.
French, William					House and land as occupier, Snape.
Field, Samuel, Tonbridge Wells					Freehold house.
Fairbrother, William					Freehold house, Cousleywood.
Gardiner, the Rev. Robert, Barlow					Vicarage of Wadhurst.
Gibb, James					H. and land as ocp., Buckhurst-wood.
Gridlestone, S., Wisbeach, Cambridgsh.					Freehold land, Frankham.
Haly, Aylmer, Esq.					Freehold land, Wadhurst Castle.
Hammond, Thomas					Freehold house, town.
Harmer, James					H. and land as occupier, Walland.
Hilder, John ..					H. and land as occupier, Shoesmiths.
Holman, Jasper					House and land as occupier, Watleys.
Hickmott, John, Lamberhurst					H. and land as occupier, Crabby-wood
Hiscock, Evenden					H. and land as occupier, Whitegates.
Harman, Anthony, Tonbridge					Part freehold house, Red Lion Inn.

NAMES.	D.	F.	Ch	Cs.	QUALIFICATION AND WHERE SITUATE.
Harman, Henry, Tonbridge					Part freehold house, Red Lion Inn.
Harman, Thos., Oakfield-lodge, Berks					Part freehold house, Red Lion Inn.
Kine, Joseph					Freehold land, Skinners.
*Kine, Matthew, Frant					Freehold land, Bestbeech-hill.
*Kemp, Thomas.					Copyhold houses, Pell-green.
Latter, Lawrence					House and land as occupier, Earls.
Lowles, John					H. and land as occupier, Frankham.
Moren, William					H. and land as occupier, Wickhurst.
Maryon, John					Freehold house, town.
Newington, John, Esq.					Freehold land, Towngate.
Newington, John Baker, Northiam					Freehold land, Flattenden.
Noakes, J. T., St. Saviours, Southwark					Part freehold house, Wadhurst-town
Noakes, William, jun., Ticehurst					Part freehold house, Wadhurst-town
Noakes, William					Freehold house, Stone-cross.
Pierson, Thomas					House and land as ocp., Ladymeads.
*Playstead, Alfred					Freehold land, Buttons.
Playsted, Geo. Luck					Freehold land, Smiths.
Playsted, Henry, jun.					House and land as occupier, Hightown
Packham, John					House and land as occupier, Bassetts.
Playsted, Alfred Baker					H. and land as occupier, Churchsettle.
Rogers, Henry					Freehold land, Little Faircrouch.
Roberts, Samuel					H. and land as occupier, Chittenhurst.
Smith, George					House and land as occupier, Newhouse
Smith, Richard					Freehold house, Sparrows-green.
Smith, Samuel					Freehold house, town.
Springett, John					House and ld. as occupier, Riverhall.
Stone, John, Tunbridge Wells					Freehold land, Maitland.
Stunt, Joseph					Freehold house, town.
*Smith, William					Freehold land, Three Oaks.
Smith, John					H. & ld. as ocp., Durgates & Tapsals.
Smith, Samuel, Lamberhurst					H. & ld. as ocp., Durgates & Tapsals.
Stone, William, Tunbridge Wells					Freehold land, Maitlands.
Tompsett, John					Freehold land, Scragoak.
*Tompsett, Jesse					House and land as occupier, Coomb.
Vigor, Richard					Freehold house, town.
Wace, Thomas, Esq.					Freehold land, town.
Waghorn, John					House and land as occupier, Perrins.
Wallis, John					Freehold house, town.
Wallis, Samuel					Freehold house, Sparrows-green.
Walter, Edward, Rotherfield					Freehold land, Bestbeech-hill.
Worsley, John					Freehold house, town.

WALDRON.

Adkins, Harry, Warwick Goal					Freehold house and land, Belle-vue.
Avery, Thomas, Mayfield					Copyhold house and land.
Apps, James					Copyhold house and land.
Bonnick, Josias					Fr. houses and land, Burgh and green.
Colman, James					Fr. h. ld. and mill, Cross in hand, &c.
Cornwell, Thomas					Cp. h. and land, near Cross in hand.
Cornwell, William, Framfield					Copyhold houses and land.
Carey, John					House and land as ocp., Cross in hand
Dyke, G. H., Esq., Tonbridge, Kent					Freehold houses & land, Horeham, &c.
Davis, William, 106, Borough, London					Freehold house and land.
Dawes, Alexander					Cp. house and garden, Waldron-street
Durrant, Jesse					Copyhold house and land.
Durrant, Henry					Cp. house and land, Waldron Down.
*Fuller, Joseph, Laughton					Fr. h. & ld., White-h. & New-barn-fms

NAMES.	D.	F.	Ch.	Cs.	QUALIFICATION AND WHERE SITUATE.
Flint, Samuel, Lewes					Freehold house and garden.
Fuller, John ..					Freehold house, land and mill.
Garrett, John, Brighton ..					Freehold house and land.
Goldsmith, Benjamin					Freehold house and land, New-house.
Gosling, Peter					Leasehold h. and land, Cross-in-hand.
Gilbert, William					Freehold house and ld., Little London
Gosling, William					Cp. house and land, Waldron Down.
Gallup, Edward					Copyhold house and land, Lyons-green
Gyles, Thomas					Cp. h. and land, near Cross-in-hand.
Heathfield, John					Fr. house and land, Cross-in-hand.
Hassell, Thomas					Houses and ld. as ocp., Waldron-street.
Hendly, William					Cp. house and land, near New-pond.
Jenner, Thomas					Hs. and ld. as occupier, Possingworth
Jenner, James					Cp. houses and land, Waldron Down.
Johnson, Henry					Houses and land as ocp., Rock-hill.
Kennard, John					Freehold house and land, Pooks.
Mannington, Isaac					Hs. and land as occupier, Horeham.
Moon, William, Buxted					Freehold house and land.
Moore, Joseph, Mayfield					Leasehold land.
Page, Henry ..					Freehold house and land, Thorns.
Raynes, Rev. Thomas					Rectory, Waldron.
Russell, William					Fr. h. & ld., near the Hanging Birch.
*Russell, John					Freehold land, Little London.
Reeves, John ..					Freehold houses and land, Burnt-oak.
Starr, John, Eastbourne					Freehold house and land.
Snashall, John					Cp. h. and land, near Cross-in-hand.
Tommas, William					Freehold house and land, Harpers.
Unstead, John					Leasehold house and wheelwrights-shop, Waldron-street.
Wood, James					Freehold house and land, Brailsham.
Waters, John ..					Cp. house and land, Thorns-common.
Waters, Benjamin					Freehold house and land, Pook Reed.
Woodgate, Henry					Copyhold house and land.
Westgate, Peter					Copyhold houses and land.

WARBLETON.

NAMES.	D.	F.	Ch.	Cs.	QUALIFICATION AND WHERE SITUATE.
Avard, George ..					Freehold house and land, Favifoots-fm.
Blackman, John					Freehold houses and land, Fowl-mill.
Buckland, Thomas					Copyhold house and land, Avery-farm
Baitup, Richard					Mill and land as ocp., near Rushlake.
Balcomb, Thomas					Freehold h. and shop, Rushlake-green
Barton, John					Fr. h. and garden, Bodle-street-green.
Bennett, Henry					Freehold h. and shop, Rushlake-green
Blackman, Henry					Freehold house and land, Mill-land.
Booth, John ..					Freehold house and land, self-occupier
Burgess, James					Fr. house and land, nr. Rushlake-green
Burgess, Jeremiah					Fr. house and ld., Horse & Groom Inn
Burgess, Michael					Fr. h. and garden, Bodle-street-green.
Crowe, William					Copyhold houses and ld., late Fenners
Chapman, John					Freehold house and land, Lade-farm.
Cole, Benjamin, Rev.					Rectory and glebe of Warbleton.
Cornford, Samuel					Freehold house and land, Turners-farm.
Crowhurst, James					Freehold house and land, Pleydells.
*Crutenden, Edmund					Land as occupier, Crawl-farm.
Dallaway, Stephen					H. and land as ocp., Downgate-farm.
*Darby, George, Esq.					Freehold houses and land, Priory-farm
Darby, H., Esq., Leap Castle, Ireland					Freehold houses and land, Grovely.
Easton, Peter					Fr. h. and garden, Bodle-street-green.

L

NAMES.	D.	F.	Ch	Cs.	QUALIFICATION and WHERE SITUATE.
Errey, Edward					Fr. house and land, near Three Cups.
Errey, Joseph, jun.					Copyhold h. and land, Rigfords-farm.
Farrance, William					H. and land as ocp., Little Bucksteep
Goldsmith, James					Freehold house and land, Brick-kiln.
Goldsmith, William					Fr. hs. and land, Bodle-street-green.
Green, Richard, Henfield					Rectorial land tax, Rectory.
Griffiths, John, Lewes					Freehold house and shop.
Hart, Edward, Wartling					Freehold house and garden.
*Hunt, Samuel					Fr. h. and garden, Rushlake-green.
Isted, William					H. and land as ocp., Sandhill-farm.
Keely, John					Freehold house and land, Hooks Down
Keely, Richard					Fr. house and land, near Blackdown.
*Lade, Thomas, Wartling					Freehold h. and land, Churches-green
Lade, Vincett					H. & ld. as ocp., Grovely & Cripp-fms.
Lavender, John					Freehold house and land, Little Rigford
Longhurst, Thomas					Fr. h. and garden, Bodle-street-green.
Martin, Stephen					House and land as ocp., Court-lodge.
Martin, John					House and land as occupier, Beestons.
Message, Thomas					Freehold house and land, Horeham.
Noakes, John					House and land as ocp., Priory-farm.
Oliver, Jesse					Freehold h. and land, near Stone-house
Pattenden, John					House and land as ocp., Egypt-farm.
*Pattenden, Robert					Freehold h. and land, Rushlake-green
Pettit, Thomas					Fr. h. and garden, Bodle-street-green.
Potter, Henry					H.& ld.as ocp.,Chantry fm.& common.
Potter, Thomas					Cp. mill & ld., John Saunders, tenant
*Smith, Jesse					Mills and land as occupier,Bodle-street and Bucksteep.
Saunders, John					Mill and land as ocp.,part of Horeham.
Shorter, Richard					Freehold house and land, Flitter-brook
Simmons, Thomas					H. & ld. as ocp., Parris's & Fords-fm.
Starr, Thomas					Freehold houses and land,Deane-farm.
Symes, William, West Grinstead					Freehold land, Wm. Isted, tenant.
Trill, James, Dallington					Freehold house and land, Three Cups.
Waters, John, Lewes					Copyhold land.
Wenham, James					H. and land as ocp., Stonehouse-farm.
*Whiteman, John					H. and land as ocp., Great Bucksteep.
Wilmshurst, Stephen					Freeehold h. and land, Punnetts town.
Wisram, John					Fr. house and garden, near Red Pale.
Wood, William					Fr. h. and garden, Bodle-street-green.

BATTLE POLLING DISTRICT.

ASHBURNHAM.

NAMES.					QUALIFICATION and WHERE SITUATE.
Beeney, Samuel					Copyhold windmill and house.
Dorset, Henry, Hurstmonceux					Fr. house and land, Frankwell-farm.
Golden, Joseph					Freehold house and land.
*Gutteridge, William, 68, London-road, Brighton					Moiety of freehold buildings and land, Wilsons-farm.

NAMES.	D.	F.	Ch	Cs.	QUALIFICATION AND WHERE SITUATE.
Lemmon, William					Copyhold house and shop.
Maker, Charles Martin, Woodlands, Taunton, Somerset					Moiety of freehold buildings and land, Wilsons-farm.
*Martin, John					Land as occupier, Wilsons-farm.*
Noakes, Thomas					Land as occupier, Lattendens-farm.
Pennington, William					Land as occupier, Linghams-farm.
Pinyon, James					Land as occupier, Frankwell-farm.
Pilbeam, Francis, Dallington					Copyhold house and garden.
*Smith, Henry					Land as occupier, Kitchenham-farm.
Syms, William, West Grinstead					Freehold farm.
Veness, John					Land as occupier, Courtlodge-farm.
Warneford, Rev. Edward					Vicarage of Ashburnham.

BATTLE.

NAMES.	D.	F.	Ch	Cs.	QUALIFICATION AND WHERE SITUATE.
Ackland, Sir Peregrine Palmer Fuller Palmer, Bart., Fairfield, near Bridgewater					Copyhold farm.
Alderton, Henry					Freehold house, Star-Inn.
Bryant, Richard					Copyhold house.
Bellingham Thomas Charles					Freehold house.
Barton, Thomas					Freehold house.
Badcock, Thomas, sen.,					Freehold house.
*Burgess, John					Freehold house.
*Burgess, James					Freehold house.
Burgoyne, T.J.160, Oxford-st., London					Fr. hs., Richardson and others tenants.
Beney, George					Freehold house.
Bourner, Charles					Ld. as ocp., Telham farm and lands.
Badcock, Thomas, jun., Cranbrook					Copyhold house.
Birch, Nicholas					Freehold house and land.
Bourner, Thomas					Land as ocp., Brick-kilns and land.
Beney, John. Westfield.					Freehold house and land.
Christmas, Robert					Land as occupier, Beanford-farm.
Crisford, Robert					Land as occupier, Ringletts-farm.
Cocket, Richard					Freehold house.
Clarke, William					Freehold house and garden.
Duke, Wm., George street, Hastings					Freehold land.
Donne, Edward, New Inn, London					Freehold land, Netherfield Toll-farm
Eldridge, Robert					Land as ocp., part of Almoney-farm.
Eldridge, Thomas					Freehold house, Half Moon Inn.
Emary, Charles					H. and land as ocp., Fullers land and h.
Elliott, John					H. & ld. as ocp., Wellington Inn & ld.
Franks, John					Copyhold house.
*Ferris, the Rev. Thomas, Dallington					Copyhold house.
Flood, L. T., Esq., Fairlight & Chelsea					Freehold house and land, Rose-green.
*Funnell, Henry.					Freehold house.
*Goodwin, Charles Augustus					Copyhold house.
Gibbs, William, sen.					Freehold house.
Gower, James					Freehold house.
Gausden, Charles					H. & ld. as ocp., North-trade, ld. & h.
*Griffin, George, Tenterden					Copyhold house.
Gibbs, William, jun.					Land as ocp., Great Heminfold-farm.
Glaizyer, James					Freehold house.
Hammond, Charles Sampson					Freehold house and land.
*Hobbs, Edward, Brighton					Freehold house.
Hunt, Thomas					Land as occupier, Great Beach-farm.
Habgood, James, Loughton, Essex					Freehold house.
Hobbs, William					Freehold house.
Kenward, John					Freehold land, Darvel-hole-farm.

NAMES.	D.	F.	Ch	Cs	QUALIFICATION AND WHERE SITUATE.
Kell, Nathaniel Polhill, Esq.					Freehold land.
Knight, William					Fr. h. and land, North-trade Nursery.
*Lansdell, James					Freehold house.
Laurence, Charles					Freehold house.
Ludlam, Thomas, Sandhurst					Fr. land and building, Wesleyan chapel
Laurence, James					Copyhold Smith's shop.
Litler, the Rev. John					The Deanery of Battle.
Lukin, John, Nutshalling, nr. Romsey, Hants					Freehold and copyhold farm, Ringlets
Mathis, Thomas					Copyhold house.
Morris, George, Gosfield					Freehold house.
*Martin, James					Copyhold house.
Metcalf, William					Copyhold house.
Metcalf, George ..					Copyhold house.
Mann, Thomas, Netherfield					Fr. h. and ld., formerly the Gun Inn
Middlemas, Richar, Hastings					Copyhold house.
Mills, George, Dover					Freehold house.
Mercer, Joseph, Mountfield					Copyhold house.
Mitchell, William					Copyhold house.
Neve, William					Freehold house and mill.
*Noakes, William					Freehold house.
Pain, Daniel, Deptford					Freehold house.
Patching, James					Land as occupier, Beech-farm.
Quaife, T., Somerset House, London.					Half part of freehold houses.
Quaife, W., Somerset House, London.					Half part of freehold houses.
Spray, James					Land as occupier.
Sargeant, George					Freehold house.
Shaw, John					Freehold house and land.
*Slatter, George					Freehold house.
Smith, James					Freehold house and land.
Smith, Walter ..					Freehold house and land.
Sellins, Samuel					Land as occupier.
Taylor, Stephen ..					Freehold house.
Ticehurst, William					Freehold and copyhold land.
*Thorpe, George					Freehold house.
Ticehurst, F., High-street, Hastings					Freehold house.
Ticehurst, William, Jun., Haverstock-hill, Middlesex..					Freehold house and stabling.
Walker, Adam					Copyhold house.
Worge, John					Copyhold house.
Weller, William					Freehold house.
Watts, Robert					Freehold house.
Watts, James ..					Freehold houses.
Watts, Francis					Freehold house.
Wickham, Thomas					Freehold house.
White, William, sen.					Freehold house.
Weller, Ebenezer					Mill and land as occupier.
BODIAM.					
Body, John					Freehold h. and land, Kitchenham-fm.
Buckland, James					264 acres of ld. as ocp. Northlands-fm.
Bishop, John					200 acres of ld. as ocp., New-h.-farm.
Cawston, Thomas, Turweston, Bucks					Fr. h. and land, Court-lodge-farm.
Collingwood, George Lewis Newnham, Hawkhurst, Kent					Fr. house and ld., Northlands-farm.
Levett, William, Wittersham, Kent					Fr. h. and land, Little Northlands-fm.
Paine, Samuel, Sandhurst, Kent					Fr. house and land, New-house-farm.

NAMES.	D.	F.	Ch.	Cs.	QUALIFICATION AND WHERE SITUATE.
Shoosmith, John					Fr. house and ld., Knowl-hill-house.
Smith, Stephen, Salehurst, Sussex ..					300 acres of land as ocp., Park-farm.
Thomas, Rev. John Godfrey ..					Vicarial tithes and glebe of Bodiam.

BRIGHTLING.

NAMES.	D.	F.	Ch.	Cs.	QUALIFICATION AND WHERE SITUATE.
Carley, Jesse					Freehold h. and garden, Hollingrove.
Cheall, William					Freehold house and land.
Fuller, A. Elliott, Esq., ..					Freehold house and land, Rose-hill.
Fuller, Rose, ...					Land as occupier, Homestead.
Harmer, Henry					Land as occupier, Browns, Noaks, and Twyfords-farms.
Hayley, J. Burrell, Rev. ..					Tithes of Brightling.
Hayley, Rev. Burrell, 32, Charlotte-street, Portland-place, London ..					Freehold cottage and gn. and stables.
Hermitage, Henry					Freehold house and land, Davell-hole.
Holloway, John					Fr. house, lands and manor, Socknersh
Holloway, Thomas					Freehold house and lands, Old-hole & Piddlehurst-farms.
Lovell, George					Land as occupier, Brightling-place.
Meyrick, Fuller O. J. A., Bodorgan, Anglesea, North Wales ..					Rent charge on mansion & lds. Rose-hill
Reynolds, Joseph					Land as occupier, Hollingrove-farm.
Smallfield, John					Land as occupier, Great Worge-farm.
Smith, Edward William, London ..					Copyhold lands, Bowdens-wood.
Smith, Charles, Edgar, Canterbury..					Copyhold lands, Bowdens-wood.
Smith, Walter Austen, London ..					Copyhold lands, Bowdens-wood.
Veness, Thomas..					Freehold house and garden.

CATSFIELD.

NAMES.	D.	F.	Ch.	Cs.	QUALIFICATION AND WHERE SITUATE.
Ashburnham, Denny, Rev. ..					Freehold Rectory of Catsfield.
Adams, James					Ld. as ocp., New Barn and Down-lds.
Redingfield, Francis Philip, Esq. ..					Freehold house and land, Park-gate.
Bontor, Robert					Leasehold houses.
Blackman, John					Freehold houses.
Davis, Thomas					Freehold house, White Hart Inn.
Farmer, James					Fr. h. and land, Hope House farm.
Lade, John Trill					Land as occupier, Tilton-farm.
Mugridge, Richard					Freehold house and land.
Pilkington, Andrew, Esq... ..					Freehold land, Church and other fms.
Plumbley, Uriah					Leasehold houses.
Smallfield, Thomas					Land as occupier, Bromham-farm.
Smith, Francis, St. Clements, Hastings					Freehold house.
Wrenn, Benjamin, Ninfield ..					Freehold mills and houses.
Wrenn, Frederick					Freehold house.
*Waters, Richard					Land as occupier, (part in Crowhurst), Franks and Broad-lands.
Wrenn, James					Land as occupier, (part in Bexhill), Henley-down-farm.

CROWHURST.

NAMES.	D.	F.	Ch.	Cs.	QUALIFICATION AND WHERE SITUATE.
Cooke, Joseph					Lands as occupier, High-house.
*Coppard, Charles, Findon ..					Freehold house and land, Crowhurst.
Hoper, George, High-street, Lewes..					Freehold land, Adams-farm.
Harding, Rev. Sir C., Tonbridge, Kent					Rectory of Crowhurst.
Harmer, Henry, Esq.					Land as occupier, Crowhurst-place.
Pelham, J. Cressett, Esq., Shrewsbury					Freehold h. and land, Crowhurst-place

NAMES.	D.	F.	Ch	Cs.	QUALIFICATION AND WHERE SITUATE.
Rush, Rev. Henry John	—	—			Freehold h. and land, Ransoms-farm.
Reeves, Thomas	—	—			Land as occupier, Sampsons-farm.
Sharp, Thomas	—	—			Crowhurst.
Wood, William . ..	—		—		Ld. as ocp , Adam's & Croucher's-fm.

DALLINGTON.

NAMES.	D.	F.	Ch	Cs.	QUALIFICATION AND WHERE SITUATE.
Barrow, Thomas, Hawkhurst, Kent..			—		Fr. house and land, Padgham-farm.
*Bates, Simon, Dallington ..		—		—	Freehold shop and ground.
Bourner, P., Brigden-hill, Ashburnham	—				F. houses and land, Red-pale-farm.
Bartlett, Wm. John, Woods corner, Dallington					House and land as occupier, Graylings-woods and Stackendens.
Gosling, William		—			Freehold h. and land, late Ledbetters.
Honeysett, John	—				Fr. houses and land, Dallington-street
Marchant, Thomas	—				Land as occupier, Gisfords-farm.
Peters, John	—				Fr. houses and gns., Dallington-street
Pilbeam, George	—				Land as occupier, Woodsell-farm.
Pound, Henry Bedder	—				Freehold houses and land.
Randoll, John, Esq. ..		—			Freehold houses and land, Castle-farm
Reeves, Francis, Delmonden green, Hawkhurst, Kent			—		Land as occupier, Padgham-farm.
Russell, Francis			—		Freehold house and land, Rabbitts-fm.
Sands, George	—				Freehold house and garden.
Sawyer, J., Lodge-farm, Ashburnham					Freehold and copyhold houses and land, near Woods-corner.
Taylor, Samuel	—				Land as occupier, Herrings-farm.
Veness, John	—				Land as occupier, Hayselden-farm.

ETCHINGHAM.

NAMES.	D.	F.	Ch	Cs.	QUALIFICATION AND WHERE SITUATE.
Austin, Daniel					Land as occupier, Bellhurst-farm.
Anderson, Ambrose		—			Freehold house and gn., Hurstgreen.
Baker, Thomas					Land as occupier, Burgham-farm.
Clulow, Rev. Geo., Epwell, Banbury		—			Fr. house and buildings, Church-farm.
Dumbrill, John		—			Freehold house.
Ditch, George					Land as occupier, Boarders.
Garner, George	.				Fr. house and land, part of Barnhurst.
Garner, George, jun., Salehurst ..		—			Freehold house and land, Hurstgreen.
Haddon, Wm. Charles ..		—			Freehold house and land, Hurstgreen.
Overy, Cater					Land as occupier, Ketchingham-farm.
Palliser, Richard ..		—			Freehold h. and land, Seacocks-heath.
Page, Thomas		—			Freehold house and land, Hurstgreen.
Russell, Samuel			—		Fr. house and land, part of Barnhurst.
Standen, Thomas ..		—			Freehold house and land, Miskins.
Sperrling, Charles Robert		—			Fr. house and land, Etchingham-lodge
Snepp, John		—			Freehold house and land, Haremare.
Snepp, William		—			Freehold house and land, Hurstgreen.
Tottie, the Rev. Hugh		—			Glebe lands of Etchingham.
Wood, Edmund			—		Freehold house and land, Hurstgreen.
Willsher, Robert, jun. ..		—			Land as occupier, Church-farm.

EWHURST.

NAMES.	D.	F.	Ch	Cs.	QUALIFICATION AND WHERE SITUATE.
*Austin, Thomas					Land as occupier, Sempsted-farm.
Apps, Edmund	—				Land as occupier, Beacon-farm.
Ayerst, Thomas, Newenden, Kent ..	—				Freehold land, Stockwood-farm.
Beck, William . ..			—		Cp. house and land, at Staple-cross.
*Beecham, William Pain, Esq., Hawk-hurst, Kent					Freehold land tax, on glebe and tithes.

NAMES.	D.	F.	Ch	Cs.	QUALIFICATION AND WHERE SITUATE·
Boots, Benjamin				—	Cp. house and land, at Staple-cross.
Burgess, John					Land as occupier, Brosses-farm.
Butler, Edward				—	Fr. house and land, at Cripps's-corner.
Copper, William					Freehold office, parish Church clerk.
Challen, Henry, Hawkhurst, Kent					Freehold land, Stockwood-farm.
Doxat, Alexis James, 13, Bishopsgate- street, London					Freehold land, Sparkes-farm.
*Daws, Thomas				—	Freehold land, Soggs-farm, &c.
Eldridge, James				—	Freehold land, Stock-wood-farm.
*Eldridge, Thomas				—	Land as occupier, Rawles-farm.
Henley, Joseph				—	Freehold h. and land, at Staple-cross.
*Henley, Thomas				—	Freehold land, Prawls-farm.
Hyland, John ..					Copyhold h. and land, Shedders-farm.
Hoffman, John, Hanover-crescent, Regents-park					Freehold land, Court-lodge-farm.
Hyland, William				—	Freehold land, Dykes-farm.
Harmer, Richard				—	Cp. house and land, at Ewhurst-green
Luck, Richard				—	Land as occupier, Sparkes-farm.
Luxford, Henry, High Holden, Kent					Freehold land, Spanyards-farm.
Mercer, Richard, Battle				—	Fr. house and land, at Crips's-corner
Reed, William				—	Freehold land, Bredehigh-farm.
Richardson, Thomas				—	Freehold land, Piddlehurst-farm.
Richardson, John, Ore				—	Freehold land, Miles's-farm.
*Smith, Tilden				—	Land as occupier, Newhouse-farm.
Smith, John					Freehold land, near Lordine-farm.

HURSTMONCEUX.

NAMES.	D.	F.	Ch	Cs.	QUALIFICATION AND WHERE SITUATE·
*Allfree, William, Southborough, Kent				—	Freehold land, Mill-fields.
Arkcoll, Thomas				—	Fr. house and land, Nunningham-farm
Barnard, Thomas				—	Cp. house and garden, Church-rod.
Barton, John, Bexhill				—	Herstmonceux.
Beadle, James				—	Copyhold house and land, at Foulmill.
Beney, Edward				—	Freehold mill & house, Windmill-hill.
Brook, James ..				—	Freehold house, Gardner-street.
*Cosham, Thomas Shadwell				—	Freehold land, Whitefields.
*Colbrand, John, All Saints, Lewes ..					Freehold house and garden, Cowbeach.
Colman, James ..				—	Cp. houses and ld., near Coopers-croft
Crouch, William				—	Copyhold house and garden.
Daw, Edward ..				—	Freehold cottages & gn., Chapel-row.
Edmonds, Moses				—	Three freehold cottages, Gardner-st.
Everest, James				—	Freehold house, Gardner-street.
*Everest, James, jun.					Brewhouse & ld. as ocp., Gardner-st.
Friend, Thomas					Land as occupier, Breach-fields and late Chandlers.
Gillon, William Down, Esq., Wallhouse				—	Fr. h. and lands, Herstmonceux-place.
Guy, David, Cowbeach					Land as occupier, Cowbeach-farm.
Hare, Julius Charles, Rev.				—	Rectory of Herstmonceux.
Harmer, John, Cowbeach					Fr. house and land, Little Bakehurst.
Harmer, William, Bodle-street				—	Fr. house and land, Gardner-street.
Hunniset, William				—	2 copyhold cottages.
Lock, William, Windmill Hill				—	Cp. h. and garden, Comphurst-lane.
Martin, Henry				—	Land as occupier, Herstmonceux.
Miller, Thomas ..				—	Fr. house and garden, late Eastlands.
Miller, Thomas, Windmill Hill				—	2 cp. houses and garden, at Failmill.
Mills, Thomas, Esq., Hunton, Kent ..					Freehold house and land, Wargroves.
Morris, Samuel				—	Br. h. and ld. as ocp., New Brewhouse.
Noakes, Samuel				—	House and gn. as ocp., Gardner-street

NAMES.	D.	F.	Ch	Cs.	QUALIFICATION AND WHERE SITUATE.
*Oxley, David, Findon Park	..			—	Freehold house and garden.
Parris, Edward, Wartling	..			—	Freehold h. and land, Maypoles-green
Pursglove, Robert	..			—	Cp. house and garden, Flowers-green
*Pursglove, Richard	..			—	Copyhold h. and land, Church-road.
Sampson, Thomas Shadwell	..			—	Freehold land.
Simmonds, Thomas	..			—	Land as occupier, Chilthurst-farm.
Smith, Jesse ..	..			—	Land as occupier, Church-farm.
Smith, Isaac ..	..			—	Cp. house and garden, Gardner-street
*Stone, Peter ·..	..		—		Fr. house and land, Gardner-street.
Stubberfield, John	..			—	Fr. h. and premises, Windmill-hill.
Tayler, Edward	..			—	H. & ld. as ocp., Pope's & Rockfields.
Vinall, Thomas	..			—	Freehold house, Gardner-street.
Vine, Richard			—		Land as occupier, Blackford.
Wagner, Geo. Henry Malcom, Esq..		—			Freehold land
*Winchester, Richard, Cowbeach ..		—			Freehold house.
Winchester, Joseph, Cowbeach	..				Two cp. cots., Foulmill & Trallilows.
Woodhams, William	..			—	Ld. as ocp., Chilsam fm. & Jeffreys.
Wratten, Isaac	..			—	Cp.h.& ld.Kingsbrook & Milking-fields
Whitbread, Francis, Foulmill	..			—	Ld. as occupier, Clippenham-farm.
Young, James, Harper-street, Blooms-bury, London	..				Land as occupier, Lime-farm.

HOOE.

	D.	F.	Ch	Cs.	
Blackman, Benjamin	..			—	Freehold land, Hunts & Bunce-farms.
Coleman, John	..			—	Land as occupier, Holmes'-farm.
Carey, Peter	..			—	Ls. house and gn., on the common.
Colbran, Thomas, Ninfield	..			—	Land as occupier, Sadlers-farm.
Fox, Stephen	..			—	Land as occupier, Quiddleswell.
Haygarth, George, Rev., Henfield	..				Vicarage of Hove.
Henbury, Robert	..			—	Freehold land, School-farm.
Lewis, William	..			—	Land as occupier, Sandhill-farm.
*Martin, Edwin, Battle	..			—	Freehold house.
Mitten, Joseph	..			—	Land as occupier, Longdown-farm.
Noakes, James	..			—	Freehold house and land, Spencers-fm.
Pennefather, E., Fitzwilliam-street, Dublin ..	..			—	Freehold house and land.
Pilbeam, Robert	..			—	Freehold houses.
Pilbeam, William	..			—	Leasehold houses.
Relfe, Thomas ..	..			—	Leasehold houses.
*Waghorn, Edward, No. 10, South Colonnade, St. Leonards	..			—	Freehold marsh land.
*Waghorn, Mercer, No. 12, Castle-street, Hastings	..			—	Freehold marsh land.
Walter, William	..			—	Land as occupier, Broad street-green, and Gilberts-farm.
*Whitmarsh, Henry, Thos., Blackheath	—			—	Freehold house and garden.
Walter, Stephen, West Farleigh, Kent					Freehold house and land, Olives-farm.

MOUNTFIELD.

	D.	F.	Ch	Cs.	
Butchers, Daniel, Tonbridge, Kent ..					Fr. h. and garden, near John's-cross.
Christmas, Robert, Park Pale	..			—	Land as occupier, Park-pale-farm.
Daws, George, Cross farm	..			—	Land as occupier, Cross-farm.
Hickes, Francis, Castle farm	..			—	Land as ocp., Castle and Hoth-farms.
Hook, John, Darwell Beech farm	..			—	Land as ocp., Darweel-beech-farm.
Howe, Samuel, Salehurst	..			—	Freehold land and hs., Birch-ford.
Kenward, George, Salehurst	..		—		Land as occupier, Baldwins-farm.
Martin, William, Salehurst	..				Fr. house and garden, near the Cross.

NAMES.	D.	F.	Ch	Cs	QUALIFICATION AND WHERE SITUATE.
Margesson, Rev. Wm., Courtlodge..					Vicarage of Mountfield.
Nicoll, S. J. Esq., Lyndhurst, Hants.					Freehold manor, Courtlodge.
Smith, Tilden, Vinehall					Freehold land and houses, Vinehall.
Shorter, John, Banks farm ..					Land as occupier, Banks-farm.

NINFIELD.

Bateman, Wm., Bunhill-row, London					Freehold land, Morehall-farm.
*Carrick, William					Freehold house, Ninfield-green.
Colman, Hugh					Freehold house, Ninfield-green.
Collins, Christopher					H. and ld. as ocp., King's Arms-Inn.
Crisford, Henry					Ld. as ocp., Upper Standard-hill-farm
Cuthbert, Joseph					Freehold house, Ninfield-green.
Coleman, John, Ashburnham ..					Land as ocp., Moons and Church-fms.
Coleman, Alexander, Ashburnham ..					Land as ocp., Moons and Church-fms.
Davey, George					Freehold houses, Lower-street.
Esdaile, J.,Upper Bedford-row,London					Freehold land, Morehall-farm.
Farmer, John					Land as occupier, Pashley-farm.
Hilton, James, Finsbury-sq., London					Freehold land, Morehall-farm.
Holland, James					Freehold house.
Holland, Reuben ..					Freehold house and land.
Lee, Henry, Lewisham, Kent ..					Freehold land, Morehall-farm.
Lemmon, Levi, Ashburnham ..					Land as occupier, Waits-farm.
Mills, Samuel, Russell-sq., London ..					Freehold land, Morehall-farm.
Morris, Thomas					Freehold house, Russell-green.
Phillips, John, Rev. ..					Fr. house and land, Little Park-farm.
Pierce, Joseph, Tonbridge Wells ..					Freehold house, Ninfield-green.
Sampson, William					Freehold land.
Sheather, John					Freehold house
Tutt, James					Ninfield.
Waters, John					Land as occupier, Ingrams-farm.
Wilson, Glocester, Hastings ..					Freehold land, Moons and Church-fms.
Wrenn, Walter					H. and l. as occupier, Russell-green.

PENHURST.

Smith, Tilden . ..					Land as occupier, Church-farm.
Sinden, Joseph, Catsfield ..					Land as occupier, Peans-farm.

PEVENSEY.

Ashburnham, Rev. John, Hawkhurst					Vicarial tythes and glebe of Pevensey.
Avery, James					Freehold land, Marshfoot
Copper, Edward, Westham ..					Freehold house and land, Rickney.
*Deudney, Charles, St. Leonards ..					Land as occupier, Redhouse.
*Filder, Moses, Eastbourne ..					Freehold land, Maynards Marshes.
Gorringe, Nathaniel Wm., .					H. and ld., Pevensey-st. & Marshfoot.
Gorringe, John Pennington .					Freehold land, Church acre drove.
Gurr, Richard, Rickney ..					Ld. as ocp., Rickney and Handcomb.
*Holland, John					Fr. house and gn., Pevensey-street.
*Horton, Robert, Peasmarsh ..					Land as occupier, Bucksbridge.
Payne, William, Wadden, Croydon..					Freehold land.
*Phillips, John					Freehold house and land, Pevensey.
Plumley, Alfred					Ld. as ocp., Chilly, and near the street.
*Plumley, Thomas					Fr. h. and ld., Chilly, & nr. the street.
Russell, John					Freehold house and ld., Pevensey-st.
Simes, Rev. William, Westgrinstead .					Freehold land, near the street.
Thomas, Samuel, 104,Cornhill, London					Freehold land.
Waters, Benjamin, Eastbourne ..					Freehold land, Bucksbridge.
Woodward, Rev. Wm., Plumpton ..					Freehold land.

NAMES.	D.	F.	Ch	Cs.	QUALIFICATION AND WHERE SITUATE
SALEHURST.					
Ayerst, Francis, Hawkhurst					Land as occupier, Moat-farm.
Adams, Henry, Salehurst					Fr. h. and garden, Northbridge-street.
Adams, Thomas, Salehurst					Cp. hs. and gardens, Robertsbridge.
Buss, Thomas					Land as occupier, Merriments-farm.
Buss, John					Freehold house & garden, Hurstgreen.
Campany, John					Land as occupier, Cold Harbour-farm.
Croft, Edward					Freehold house and garden, Silverhill.
Cruttenden, John					Freehold land, Bourne-farm.
Cruttenden, William, Ashford, Kent.					Moiety of freehold land.
Cheesman, Thomas, Stone					Freehold land, Willardshill-farm.
Cocker, A. R., Nassau-st., Soho, Midx.					Freehold house.
Crouch, James					Ld. as ocp., Jollys & Baldocks-farms.
Davenport, Richard					Fr. h. and land, Darvel Bank-farm.
*Detrazaylle, Peter					Fr. house and land, Barnhurst-farm.
Daws, Thomas					Freehold h. and garden, Robertsbridge
Dunk, Robert, Rolvenden, Kent					Freehold house and garden.
Daws, James					Freehold house and land, Coldslide.
French, George, Hawkhurst					Freehold house and shop.
*Gregson, John, Angel Court, Throgmorton-street, London					Fr. houses and farms, Wigsell-farms.
Hilder, James					Freehould house, mill and land, near Northbridge-street.
Hilder, John					Fr. h. and garden, Northbridge-street
Hartnup, Thomas					Land as occupier, near Silverhill.
Harman, Anthony, Tonbridge					Copyhold house, Robertsbridge.
Jones, Robert					Cp. h. and ld. and fr. ld.,Robertsbridge
Luxford, John					Freehold house and land, Higham-fm.
Lusted, Thomas					House and land as occupier, North-bridge-street, and Silverhill.
Luxford, John Odian					Freehold house and garden.
Lusted, Joseph					Land as occupier, part of Higham and Campanyse-farms.
Micklethwait, Sotherton, B. Peckham					Freehold land, Iridge-farm.
Martin, Henry					Cp. hs. and garden, Robertsbridge.
Martin, Thomas					Land as ocp., part of Church-farm.
*Marchant, Robert					Fr. house and garden, Robertsbridge.
Munn, George					Land as occupier, Robertsbridge.
Mantle, Thomas					Fr. hs. gns. and bgs., Robertsbridge.
Miller, Giles, Goudhurst, Kent					Freehold house and buildings, George Inn, Robertsbridge.
Nash, John, Etchingham					Freehold house and garden, Swiftsden
Nicolls, James					Fr. h. and garden, Northbridge-street.
Noakes, W. Lawrence, Etchingham.					H. mill and land as ocp., Bugsell-mill.
Noakes, Thomas Lawrence					H. mill and land as ocp., Bugsell-mill.
Putland, Henry					Freehold land, part of Stockwell-farm
Piper, Jesse, Hawkhurst					Freehold land, part of Wigsell-farm.
Piper, John					Cp. house and garden, Robertsbridge·
Pemble, Stephen					Copyhold land, Robertsbridge.
Pemble, Henry					Fr. houses and land, Robertsbridge.
Pemble, Thomas					Moiety of copyhold-house,Blacksmith's shop and land, Robertsbridge.
Pemble, Paul, Battle					Freehold land, near Forebridge.
Pemble, William, Ashburnham					Moiety of copyhold house, Blacksmith's shop and land, Robertsbridge.
*Richardson, Edmund					Moiety of freehold land.
~ ·'h, Richard, Lewisham, Kent					Fr. house and land, Cold Harbour-farm

NAMES.	D.	F.	Ch	Cs.	QUALIFICATION AND WHERE SITUATE.
Standen, Henry					Fr. house and garden, Northbridge-st.
Smith, Benjamin, Hastings					Freehold land, Browns farm.
Springett, John, Hawkhurst					Land as occupier, Salehurst.
Springett, T. Brook, Hawkhurst					Fr.hs.& lds., Northlands & Gaters-fms.
Stone, Robert					H. & ld. as ocp., part of Bantonys-fm.
Smith, Charles Henry					Freehold houses, Hurstgreen.
Southwell, Thomas					Cp. hs. and gardens, Robertsbridge.
Tooth, Robert, Cranbrook					Freehold land, part of Walters-farm.
Tindell, Stephen					Fr. h. and land, near Salehurst Church
Wrench, The Rev. Jacob George					Vicarial tithes of Salehurst.
Winchester, Henry, Hawkhurst					The Advowson of Salehurst.
Weekes, Thomas					Freehold h. and land, Robertsbridge.
Weston, Henry					Freehold h. and lands, Robertsbridge.
Waters, Joseph					Freehold h. and gn., Robertsbridge.
Watson, Daniel					Land as occupier, Ockham-farm.
Weekes, Samuel					Land as occupier, Sealand-farm.
Weekes, Henry, Hawkhurst					Moiety of cp. h. & gn., Robertsbridge
Weekes, John					One share of freehold brewhouse and house, Robertsbridge.
Weekes, Thomas					One share of fr. hs., Northbridge-street
Young, William					Fr. h. and garden; Northbridge-street.

SEDLESCOMB.

NAMES.	D.	F.	Ch	Cs.	QUALIFICATION AND WHERE SITUATE.
Bishop, John, Esq.					Freehold land, Great Sanders.
Byner, Thomas					Freehold house and land, in the village
Baker, John					Cp. and fr. h. and gn., in the village.
Barton, Edwin					Land as ocp., Swails Green-farm.
Butler, Philip					Freehold house, in the village.
Cook, Henry, Brede					Freehold house, in the village.
Crisford, Spencer					Freehold houses, in the village.
Dennett, Thomas					Freehold houses and ld., in the village
Eldridge, John					F. ld. and house, Swails Green-farm.
Eldridge, William					Fr. and cp. hs. and land, in the village.
Eldridge, William					Freehold houses, in the village.
Grace, Henry					Fr. houses and land, in the village.
Pratt, John, Rev.					Rectory and glebe land of Sedlescomb.
Simes, John					Land as occupier, Hancox-farm.
Smith, Richard, Whatlington					Freehold house and ld., Footland-farm
Weston, Robert					Fr. houses and land, in the village.
Weston, James, Westfield					Freehold hs. and land, in the village.

WARTLING.

NAMES.	D.	F.	Ch	Cs.	QUALIFICATION AND WHERE SITUATE.
*Akehurst, John, Wartling Hill					Land as occupier, Hoopers Hoad's-hill and Sand-hill-field.
Avery, Robert, Pevensey					Freehold house and land, Marsh-foot.
Attwood, Thomas, Boreham street					Freehold house and garden.
Baines, William, Wartling hill					Copyhold houses and gardens.
Blackman, William, Boreham street					Freehold house and garden
Bray, George, Boreham street					House and land as occupier, William's, Railfield, and Bull Head Inn.
Blackman, Edward, Boreham street					Freehold house and lands.
Barden, James, Boreham street					Freehold house and garden.
Collins, John, Rocklands					Ld. as ocp., Rocklands and Richards.
Dann, David, Cowbeach					Copyhold lands.
Duke, Thomas, Bexhill					Freehold house and lands.
Dawes, Alfred, Boreham					Freehold and copyhold hs. and lands.
Elwood, Chas. William, Clayton Priory					Freehold rent charge on Windmill-hill

NAMES.	D.	F.	Ch	Cs.	QUALIFICATION AND WHERE SITUATE.
Elphick, William, Wartling ..					House and land as occupier, Marshfoot and Tindul's-marsh. .
Fuller, John Thomas, Boreham street					Freehold house and lands.
Filder, Joseph, Eastbourn ..					Freehold lands, Patchurst.
Gillon, William D., Esq., Saint Albans-place, London					Freehold lands, Rocklands, Hopers, and Hoad's-hill.
Harmer, James ..					Land as occupier, Twyshurst-farm.
Holland, Francis, Wartling hill ..					Fr. lands, Hollands, Jess, & Jarratts.
Hall, Henry, Cowbeach ..					Freehold and copyhold lands, Worms.
Harmer, Thomas ..					Land as ocp., Beards and Bemsell's.
Jenner, Thomas, Boreham street ..					Land as occupier, Boreham-farm.
Jenner, John, Millses ..					Freehold h. and lands, Hunter's-croft.
Kenward, James, Cowbeach					Land as occupier, Whimsup-farm.
Lade, Daniel, Hellingly ..					Land as occupier, Cowbeach-farm.
Lade, James					Copyhold house and lands, Studdens.
Miller, John					Ld. as ocp., Tilley & Browning's-fms.
Noakes, Henry, Boreham street					Freehold house and land.
Pierce, Samuel Eyles, Tonbridge, Kent					Rent charge on hs. & gn.,Windmill-hill
Pinyon, Thomas.. ..					Land as occupier, Prinkle farm.
Simmons, John, Windmill hill ..					Leasehold house and shop.
Smith, Richard, Hurstmonceux ..					Freehold house and lands.
Thorpe, Thomas					Freehold house and gardens.
Woodhams, John					Land as occupier, Stunts-green-farm.

WESTFIELD.

NAMES.	D.	F.	Ch	Cs.	QUALIFICATION AND WHERE SITUATE.
Baker, William					Freehold house and land, The Moor.
Baker, William, jun, ...					Land as occupier, Widows-farm
Baker, Robert					Land as occupier, Rocks-farm.
Baker, Samuel					Freehold house and land.
Baker, Thomas					Copyhold house.
Bray, George					Land as occupier, Place-farm.
Brook, John					Freehold house and land.
Camac, William, Esq. . ..					Freehold land, Buckhurst-farm.
Catt, John					Freehold house and shop.
Catt ,Stephen					Land as occupier, Loms-farm.
Catt, William					Land as occupier, Pattletons-farm.
Crisford, Edmund					Land as occupier, Moor-farm.
Crisford, Stephen, jun.					Freehold house and land.
Gill, Gideon					Freehold house and land.
Gardiner, Jeffrey James, Yalding, Kent					Freehold land.
Hyland, John					Freehold house and land.
Lewry, Thomas					Land as occupier, Crowham-farm.
Mawle, John					Land as occupier, Platnix-farm.
Noakes, Robert					Land as occupier. Oakes-farm.
Osburn, David					Land as occupier, Lankhurst-farm.
Selmes, James					Freehold house and land.
Selmes, Stephen					Freehold house and garden.
Stunt, Thomas					Freehold house and land.
Stunt, Thomas, jun.					Freehold house and garden.
Turner, Richard					Freehold house.
Tyhurst, John					Vicarage and tithes of Westfield.
Vernon, Mark Henry					Freehold house and land.
*Weller, John					Land as occupier, Westbrook-farm, and part of glebe land.
Watson, Stephen					
Wilson, Glouster, Esq., Hastings..					Freehold land, Knights-farm.

NAMES.	D.	F.	Ch	Cs.	QUALIFICATION AND WHERE SITUATE.
WESTHAM.					
Allfrey, William, 36, Lincoln's Inn-fields, London					Copyhold land.
Arkcoll, William					Land as occupier, Langney-farm.
Breton, Robert					Land as ocp., Hankham-Hall-farm.
Cavendish, G. H., Hon., Belgrave-square, London					Fr. house and land, Montague-farm.
Crisford, Samuel					Freehold windmill.
Delves, Thomas ..					Freehold house and gn., Handcomb.
Filder, James, Eastbourne					Copyhold land.
Geering, Aaron					Freehold house and land, Blacknest.
Geering, James					Fr. house and land, Westham-street.
*Geering, Moses					Freehold house and land, Handcomb.
*Geering, William					Freehold land, near the mill.
Grace, Henry Thomas, Rev.					Vicarial tithes of Westham.
Gurr, Richard, Pevensey					Land as occupier, with part in Pevensey, Handcomb.
Hawes, Robert					Land as occupier, Glynlee-farm.
Hunt, Thomas					Freehold house and ld., Hope-cottage.
Kenward, William					Fr. house and land, Westham-street.
Langford, Charles					Land as occupier, Montague-farm
Leigh, Henry					Land as ocp., near Westham-street.
Lewis, Thomas					Copyhold house and land, Langley.
Miller, William					Freehold house and land, Handcomb.
Roods, Samuel					Freehold land, Handcomb.
Spice, Henry					Fr. h. and gn., near Westham-street.
*Streeter, Nathaniel					Freehold house and land, near the mill
Webb, William,					Fr. house and garden, at the Horns.
White, Thomas, Yalding ..					Freehold land.
Whiteman, John					Freehold land, The Rattle.
Woodhams, Francis					Cop. h. and land, Friday-street-farm.
WHATLINGTON.					
*Bates, William, Whatlington mill ..					Fr. h. mill and land, Whatlington-mill
Daws, James, Robertsbridge					Freehold h. & land, Poppinghole-lane
Daws, William					Land as occupier, John's-cross, Dorrell's green and Eastland-farm.
Durrant, John, Hawkhurst, Kent ..					Freehold land, Poppinghole-lane.
Honeysett, Edward, No. 11, Argyle-street, London					Freehold cottage and land.
Margeson, Wm., Rev., Court Lodge, Mountfield					Parsonage house, and rectorial tythes of Whatlington
*Martin, Horace, Battle ..					One undivided fourth part of a farm in Whatling, Mountfield & Sedlescomb
Overy, Robert					Freehold land, Lee-ford-farm.
Overy, Stephen					Copyhold hs. and land, Home-place.'
Overy, Thomas					H. and land as ocp., Wood-place-farm.
Polhill, Nathaniel, Poole, Dorset					Copyhold land, Records-farm.
Simes, John					Ld. as ocp., Vinehall and Farn-farms
Stanford, Charles					Freehold cottage, near the Church.

NAMES.	D.	F.	Ch	Cs.	QUALIFICATION and WHERE SITUATE.

HASTINGS.—ALL SAINTS.

NAMES	QUALIFICATION
Beck, William, No. 6, East Ascent, Saint Mary Magdalen..	Part of a fr. bg., Great Bourne-street.
Bell, Isaac, 37, All Saints- street	Freehold house, 38, All Saints-street.
Beck, Henry, No. 3, Russell-street	Part of a fr. bg., Great Bourne-street.
Burchatt Edward, All Saints-street	Freehold house, Mercers-bank.
*Campbell, John, East-hill..	Freehold house, 27, All Saints-street.
Carpenter, George, All Saints-street..	Freehold house, near the Bourne.
Coussens, John, Ship Inn, Bourne-st.	Freehold house, 21, All Saints-street.
Cramp, Richard, 99, All Saints-street	Freehold house, No. 6, Union-row.
*Day, Peter, 31, Russell-street	Fr. h., Waterloo-row, All Saints-street
Ditch, George, Courthouse-street	Part of 2 fr. hs., Great Bourne-street.
Duly, John, Swan yard, St. Clements	Freehold house, No. 1, Waterloo-place
Fenner, David, No. 109, High-street	Freehold Chapel, Ebenezer Chapel.
Gallop, Joseph, All Saints-street	Freehold house, No.1, All Saints-street
Gausden, Charles, Battle	Freehold house, All Saints-street.
George, George, West Beach-street..	Freehold house, East-well.
Haiselden, Edward, 15, Wellington-sq.	Fr. h., Buxton-house, Bourne-street.
Harper, Joseph J., Blidlow, Risboro, Bucks	Six freehold houses, High Wickham.
Harvey, Anthony, sen., 4, Bentinck cottages, East hill	Freehold houses, East-hill.
Hall, William, at Mr. Lucas Shadwell's, All Saints-street	Three fr. hs. and gns., All Saints-street
Hannay, Joseph, 105, High-street	Freehold house, 35, All Saints-street.
Hide, Thomas, All Saints-street	Freehold cottage, in his garden.
Hinkley, John, Bourne-street	Freehold house, Bourne-street.
Jackson, George, George-street	Freehold house, East-hill-house.
Jeudwine, Chas. J., 121, All Saints-st	Freehold ground, All Saints-street.
Mills, John, East hill	Freehold house, East-hill.
Morfee, Thomas, 4, George-terrace, Park-road, Old Kent-road, London.	Freehold house, Pleasant-row.
Moore, Charles, 71, High-street	Part of a fr bg., Great Bourne-street.
Pearse, William, Minchinhampton, Gloucestershire	Eight fr. hs. and gns., Chapel-house, Chapel-cot., & 6 other hs. nr. adjoining
Perry, George, All Saints-street	Freehold house, East-hill-passage.
Pickerden, Thomas, 3, Cavendish-terrace, Saint Clements	Freehold house, East-well.
*Phillips, George, 33, All Saints-street	Freehold h., No. 88, All Saints-street.
Phillips, William, jun., East hill	Freehold house, 73, All Saints-street.
Prior, Joseph, Beach cottages	Freehold house, All Saints-street.
*Ridley, William, All Saints-street	Freehold house, East Bourne-street.
Riley, Wm. Felix, Forest hill, Clewer, Berks	Freehold house, Hastings-house.
Russell, Thomas, Hallaway-place	Freehold house, Hallaway-place.
Shorter, J. Goldsworthy, 85, High-st.	Fr. h. & gn., No. 24, All Saints-street
Sinden, George, 88, All Saints-street	Freehold house, Union-row.
Snaith, John, Henry's terrace	Freehold h., No. 25, All Saints-street.
⁻⁻ⁿford, George, 129, All Saints-st.	Freehold house, All Saints-street.

NAMES.	D.	F.	Cb	Cs.	QUALIFICATION AND WHERE SITUATE.
*Taylor, Richard, Red Lion Court, Fleet-street, London					Freehold house, All Saints-street.
Thwaites, Henry, Providence house, East hill					Freehold house, Melbourne-cottage.
Tichbon, Thomas, All Saints					Freehold house, All Saints-street.
Tree John, Queen's Head Inn					Part of two fr. hs., Great Bourne-street
*Tree, William Went, All Saints-street					Part of a fr. bg., Great Bourne-street.
Tutt, George, sen., East hill					Freehold houses, East-hill.
Tutt, Richard, Albion-st., St. Clements					Freehold house, No. 8, Pleasant-row.
*Tutt, Thomas, All Saints-street					Freehold h., No. 96, All Saints-street.
Vine, John, All Saints-street					Freehold house, near the Bourne.
Wallis, Wm., Blyvers, High Wickham					Freehold house, High Wickham.
Weston, Edward, 43, High-st., Lewes					Freehold houses, Westons-cottages.
*Whiting, Thomas, 35, All Saints-st.					Freehold house, Union-row.
*Whiting, Job., No. 4, Stone-street.					Freehold house, Union-row.
White, Thomas, 75, All Saints-street.					Freehold house, All Saints-street.
White Austin, All Saints-street					Freehold house, All Saints-street.
Wood, Daniel, No. 19, All Saints-st.					Freehold house, All Saints-street.
Wrenn, John, Prospect-h. East-hill.					Part of a fr. bg., Great Bourne-street.

BEXHILL.

NAMES.	D.	F.	Cb	Cs.	QUALIFICATION AND WHERE SITUATE.
Amoore, Edward					Freehold house and land.
Barrow, Stephen					Land as occupier, Braggs-farm.
Brook, Arthur					Freehold land, Chantries.
Breton, Thomas					Freehold land, Barrack-fields
Beeching, S., Boulogne sur mer France					Freehold land, Picknell-green.
Beeching, Thomas					Freehold land, Sprotts-farm.
Barton, John					Freehold land, Herstmonceux.
Beeching, William					Freehold house.
Bennett, James					Freehold house, White-hill.
Barnard, Thomas					Leasehold house
Borradaile, Robert					Land as occupier, Sandhurst-farm.
Birch, Rev. Thomas					Glebe, house, land and tithes of Bexhill
Chrismas, Thomas					Land as ocp., Barnhorn-hill-farm.
Chrismas, Stephen					Land as ocp., Lower Barnham-farm.
Coleman, Samuel					Copyhold farm, Wakehams.
Chester, Charles					Fr. house and land, Little-common.
Crowhurst, John					Cp. houses, Sidley and Holliers-hill.
Cramp, Samuel					Freehold house and land.
Coe, Jas., St. Andrews-ter., Hastings					Share in building, Wesleyan Chapel.
Duke, Walter					Copyhold land, Preston.
Dyke, Sir P. H., Lullingstone, Kent					Freehold woodland, Staple-wood.
Day, Richard					Cp. house and land, Bexhill-street.
Deudney, James					Freehold land, Pages.
Deudney, Thomas					Annuity of £35. a year, on Pages-fm.
Dallaway, Thomas					Freehold house, Bexhill-street.
Duke, Thomas					Freehold land, Birchington-farm.
Devall, Thomas					Freehold house and land, Burchington
Earry, William					Land as occupier, Mount Pleasant and Shortwood-farms.
*Fuggle, John, Brenchley, Kent					Freehold house and land.
Gorringe, James					Land as occupier, Collington-farm.
Gordon, William, Bromwick, Stafford					Freehold land, Barnhorn.
*Gasson, Wm., 12, West-st., Hastings					Freehold house.
Holland, Samuel					Freehold land, Great Burchingtons.
Hammond, Thomas					Ld. as ocp., Freeseland & Bank-farms.
Holland, Thomas					Copyhold land, Whydown.
Holland, Henry					Copyhold land, Glovers.

NAMES.	D.	F.	Ch	Cs.	QUALIFICATION AND WHERE SITUATE.
Hayward, Samuel					House, land and mill as occupier, on Bexhill Downs
Larkin, Thomas					Copyhold land, Downgate & Hoynes.
Lingham, Benjamin					Freehold land, Barnhorn.
Lansdell, Edward					Land as occupier, Actons-farm.
*Mooreman, Thomas, Lambeth, Surrey					Freehold land, Worsham.
*Mooreman, J., Clapham-road, Surrey					Freehold & copyhold farm, Sandhurst.
Mitchell, John					Freehold house, Freesland.
*Mathis, Richard					Freehold house, Hooe-common.
Mitten, William					Freehold house and land.
Miller, Thomas					Copyhold house, Wheat Sheaf Inn.
Manley, John					Copyhold house and garden.
Neeve, George					H. land and mill as ocp., Sidley-green
Osborn, Lavett					Freehold land, Cheesemans.
Ockenden, Samuel					Freehold land.
Ogle, Sir Chas., Bart.,Belgrave-square, Middlesex					Freehold land, Marsh.
Oliver, James					Freehold house and land.
Prior, Edward					Freehold house
Pomphrey, Joshua,George-st.,Hastings					Copyhold houses, Bexhill-street.
Parker, John					Copyhold house, Belly-hill.
Prior, John					Copyhold house and garden.
Pelling, Dearing					Freehold land, Barrack-land.
Peppercorn, William, Vauxhall, Surrey					Freehold land, Clinch-green.
Russell, James					Land as occupier, Worsham-farm.
Russell, Wm., 14, Bishopsgate-street, London					Freehold house and land, Bexhill-street
Reeve, Henry					Freehold house and land, Gunters.
Rich, Henry					Copyhold house and garden, Ashes.
Rawlins, Geo., Saint Martins, London					Freehold land, Broad Oak.
Ransom, Stephen					Freehold house, Sidley-green.
Ransom, William					Freehold house.
*Shaw, Wm., George-street, Hastings					Copyhold house.
*Stride, Robert					Freehold house.
Sinden, Thomas					Cp. house and land, Cramps-farm.
*Sinden, John					Copyhold house and land.
Sinden, William					Copyhold shop, Blacksmith's-shop.
Sinden, Samuel					Copyhold shop.
Spray, James					Ld. as ocp., Lunsfords-cross-farm.
*Thomas, James					Copyhold house and garden.
Thomas, William					House ld. & mill as ocp., Sidley-mill.
*Thomas, George					Land as occupier, Ingrams-farm.
Thomas, Stephen					Ld.as ocp., Mayos & M.-Pleasant-fams.
Thwaites, Thomas					Ld. as ocp., Grinses & Gunters-farms.
Wedd, James, Yalding, Kent					Fr. house and garden, Bexhill-street.
Wedd, George, Yalding, Kent					Fr. house and garden, Bexhill-street.
Winborn, Arthur					Freehold house and land, self-occupier
Young, Isaac					Freehold house and land, Kites-nest.
FAIRLIGHT.					
Batty, Robert					Fr. house and land, Fairlight-lodge.
Crisford, William					Mill, h. and ld. as ocp., Fairlight-mill.
De Vandes, Alex., 38, George-street, Hastings					Freehold house and land.
Flood, Luke Thomas					Ls. h. and land, Downe, Belle-vue-cot.
Field, James					H. & ld. as ocp., Lower Stonelynk-fm.
Field, Samuel					Parish Clerk of Fairlight.
⁓ ⁓a, Joseph, Right Honourable					H. and land as ocp., Fairlight-place.

NAMES.	D.	F.	Ch	Cs	QUALIFICATION AND WHERE SITUATE·
Pearse, Rev. Wm., Wellington-square Hastings					Freehold land, near the Church.
*Shadwell, Wm. Lucas, Esq., Hastings					Freehold house and land,Stonelink-fm.
Thorpe, Christopher					Fr. house and land, Wakehams-farm.
Thorpe, Benjamin					H. and land as ocp., Winterstow-farm
Thorpe, James Manser					Fr. house and land, Warren Church and Knowles-farms.
Thorpe, Charles, jun. .... * ..					House and land as occupier, New-barn and Lowinters-farms.

GUESTLING.

NAMES.					QUALIFICATION AND WHERE SITUATE·
Ashburnham, Sir Wm., Bart. ..					Freehold house and land, Broomham.
Ashburnham, John, Rev. ..					Fr.ld., Shelhurst-green & Ganders-fms
Beale, David					Mill as occupier, Batchelor's-bump.
Benfield, Nathaniel					Land as occupier, Pickham-farm.
Bourne, John..					Ld. as ocp., Lower Lidham-hill-farm.
Cloke, William					Freehold houses.
Cloke, Moses					Land as occupier, Stock-farm.
Cloke, Aaron					Part of freehold houses, Stock-green.
Flood, Luke Trapp, Esq., Fairlight..					Freehold and copyhold houses and ld., Lower Lidham-hill-farm.
Gilfin, John					Ld. as ocp., Upper Lidham-hill-farm.
*Gilfin, William..					Ld. as occupier, Great Maxfield-farm.
Harman, George .. .					Freehold house, White Hart Inn.
Hoad, Christopher					Land as occupier, Scrag Oak-farm.
*Honeysett, David, Rye					Freehold houses.
Hay, Robert Benjamin, Esq. ..					Fr. ld., Part of Shelhurst-green-farm.
Overy, Robert					Land as occupier, Snailham-farm.
*Scrivens, William, Esq., 92, High-street, Hastings					Leasehold house.
Standen, John					Freehold house, Mount Pleasant.

HASTINGS.—HOLY TRINITY.

NAMES.					QUALIFICATION AND WHERE SITUATE·
Bennetts, Frank, 3, Castle-st., Hastings					Gas shares in fr. property, St. Andrews
Dunk, Henry, 45, High-st., Hastings					Three gas shares in freehold property, Saint Andrews.
*Hazell, Robert, Maidstone, Kent ..					Ten shares in freehold buildings, cots. and land, Saint Andrews.
*Randall, Alexander, Maidstone, Kent					Ten shares in freehold buildings, cots. and land, Saint Andrews.
*Rock, Jas., 6, Stratford-pl., Hastings					Freehold house, Saint Michaels.

HOLLINGTON.

NAMES.					QUALIFICATION AND WHERE SITUATE·
Cossum, Richard					Freehold house and land.
*Farncomb, William					Freehold house and land, Castle-ham.
Lamb, Sir Chas. Montolieu, Bart. ..					Freehold mansion and land, Beauport.
Maplesden, Richard, Bulverhythe ..					Land as occupier, Beach-farm.
Pocock, William..					Land as occupier, Wilton-farm.
Reed, Jonathan, Precurser-place, St. Michael, Hastings					Freehold Chapel, Wesleyan Chapel.
*Starr, Thomas					Freehold house and land.

ORE.

NAMES.					QUALIFICATION AND WHERE SITUATE·
Benson, Joseph, Rev., Hounslow, Midx.					Fr. house and land, Bungerhill-farm.
Brisco, Musgrave, Esq.					Freehold h. and land, Coghurst-farm.
Chester, Samuel, East Ascent, Saint Mary Magdalens, Hastings ..					Four ls. houses, near the Londo

NAMES.	D.	F.	Ch.	Cs.	QUALIFICATION AND WHERE SITUATE.
Elphinstone, Sir Howard, Bart., C.B.					Fr. house and land, Ore Place-farm.
Elphinstone, Howard, Esq., 19, Eaton-place, London					Freehold land, Part of the Hole-farm.
Eliot, Wm. Granville, Esq.					Freehold house and land, Vale-brook.
Easton, Joseph					Leasehold houses, Fountain Head.
Eldridge, Wm., High-street, Hastings					Freehold house and gn., Cackle-street
Fearon, Devey, Rev. Dr.					Rectorial tithes and glebe of Ore.
Henbrey, Thomas					Freehold house and land, Down-farm.
Levett, Charles Valentine, Mercoatoria, Saint Mary Magdalens, Hastings					Six leasehold houses, North-row.
Phillips, Henry					Freehold houses, Littleworth-cottages.
Putland, James					H. and land as ocp., Bungerhill-farm.
Stace, John, jun.					Leasehold houses, Coast-cottages.
*Smith, John					H. & ld. as ocp., High Lankhurst-farm
Taught, John					Leasehold houses, Woodbine-cottages.
Wyatt, Henry Earley					Fr. house and land, Mount Pleasant.
Woodroofe, William					Freehold h. and land, Partridge-farm.
*Ward, Thomas Newman					Leasehold houses, Orotava cottages.

PETT.

NAMES.	D.	F.	Ch.	Cs.	QUALIFICATION AND WHERE SITUATE.
Cruttenden, Thomas					Freehold house and land, Pett street.
Harman, John Reed					Freehold house and land, Pett farm.
Hills, Robert					Freehold house.
Hoad, Frederick					Freehold house and land, Elms farm.
Hoad, Henry, Ickesham					Freehold house and land, Elms farm.
Luck, Richard					Land as occupier, Elms farm.
*Overy, Thomas					Freehold house, Pett street.
Thorpe, John					Land as occupier, Gatehurst farm.
Filden, John, Winchelsea					Freehold land.
Wynch, Henry, Rev., Brighton					Freehold tithes and glebe of Pett.

HASTINGS.—SAINT CLEMENT.

NAMES.	D.	F.	Ch.	Cs.	QUALIFICATION AND WHERE SITUATE.
Amoore, William, High-street					Freehold house, High-street.
Butler, John, Cinque Port Arms Inn					Freehold house, 5, Waterloo-passage.
Banks, Benjamin, Winding-lane					Freehold houses, late Barrack ground.
Breeds, Thomas James, High-street					Freehold house and brewhouse, Hill-street and Court house-street.
Breeds, Thomas, High-street					Fr. brew-h. & whs., near High-st.
Bragg, Joshua Delve, Christow, Devon					Freehold house, High-street.
Bayley, William, High-street					Freehold house, George street.
Chandler, Benjamin, 5, Alfred-street, Reading, Berks					Moiety of freehold house, High-street.
Clement, George, 24, George-street					Fr. house, near the Cutter, Hastings.
Chapman, William, High-street					Freehold house, High-street.
Cork, John, St. Mary Magdalen					Freehold house, Winding-lane.
*Coussens, Henry, Ship Inn, Hastings					Freehold house, Winding-lane.
Crouch, Nathaniel, Saint Clement					Freehold house, 30, Church-street.
*Daniel, Thomas, George-street					Freehold house, West-street.
Duke, George, High-street					Coach-house & stable, adjoining No. 8, High-street.
Edwards, William, The Croft					Freehold house, the Croft.
Eaton, Henry, 28, Eaton-street, Pimlico, London					Freehold house, High-street.
Fagg, Matthew, Lydd, Lent					Freehold houses, Exmouth-house, Exmouth cottage, and in George-st.
*Foyster, John Goodge, High-street					Rectory of Saint Clement & All Saints

NAMES.	D.	F.	Ch	Cs.	QUALIFICATION AND WHERE SITUATE.
Harvey, Anthony, jun., 4, Bentinck cottages, All Saints					Freehold house, late Barrack ground.
Hinkley, Robert, Bourne-street					Freehold house, Winding-street
*Hayes, James Barrack ground					Freehold house, Barrack ground.
Hutchinson, Thomas, George-street..					Freehold house, George-street.
Harman, Benjamin, High-street					Freehold house, High-street.
*Jones, Geo. Clarke, 53, All Saints-st.					Freehold houses, late Barrack field.
Jordan, Thomas, No. 31, Hill-street					Fr. h., Wandsworth house, nr. Hill-st.
*Jordan, William, Beach cottages					Freehold house, Walbrook cotttage.
Longley, William, West-street					Freehold house, Gloucester-place.
Lewis, Fuller W., Westerham, Kent					Fr. h., whs., and bgs., High-street.
Lewis, John W., Westerham, Kent..					Fr. h., whs., and bgs., High-street.
Lewis, Robert, Westerham, Kent					Fr. h., whs., and bgs., High street.
Lewis, E. S., St. James's-pl., London					Fr. h., whs., and bgs., High-street.
Milward, Henry Collier, 2, York-street, Portman-square, London					Freehold house, West hill.
Morris, William, Eastbourne					Freehold house, Hill-street.
*Martin, Thomas, East Peckham, Kent					Freehold house, 91, High-street
*Mose, Jonathan, George-street					Freehold house, 31, High-street.
Masters, Moses, York gardens, St. Mary in the Castle					3 freehold houses, Halton field.
Mannington, John, High-street					Freehold building, George-street.
North, Frederick, Esq., Hastings lodge, Hastings					Freehold house, Devonshire cottage.
Pung, William, Bartholomew-street, Newbury, Berks					Moiety of freehold house, High-street.
Pearse, William, Minchinghampton, Gloucestershire					Fr. house, Zuriel cot., nr. Zuriel-place.
Penfold, Richard, Mount House					Freehold house, Mount house.
Russell, John, George-street					Freehold house, George-street.
Robinson, George, sen., Beach in St. Mary in the Castle					Freehold houses, High-street.
Ryall, James, 67, High-street					Freehold house, 3, Court-house-street.
*Radford, John, 10, Marine-parade..					Freehold house, West-street.
Stace, John, Ore					Fr. hs. & shop, West-st. & John-st.
Stubbs, Eli West, George-street					Freehold house, West-street.
Stickles, Henry, West-street					Freehold house, West-street.
Strickland, George, Harpsicord-house, Hill-street					Freehold house, Saint Clement.
Sinnock, Thomas, Saint Clement					Freehold houses, late Barrack ground.
Standen, William, Croft-lane					Freehold house, No. 7, Croft.
Thorpe, William, Miness, All Saints					Freehold house, No. 107, High-street.
Thwaites, John Dungate, 7, Meadow Cottage, Castle					Fr. land & houses, Lennox-st., Halton
Williams, John, High-street					Freehold house, High-street.
Wingfield, Henry, George-street					Freehold house, Hill-street.
*Wellerd, William, George-street					Freehold house, George-street.
*Wood, William, Winding-lane					Freehold house, Winding-lane.
Wood, Joseph, All Saints					Freehold building, Winding-lane.
*Wheeler, John, High-street					Freehold house, High-street.

HASTINGS.—SAINT LEONARD.

Burton, S., 10, New-sq., Lincoln's Inn					Freehold houses, West Ascent.
Cooper, Rev. Geo. Miles, Wilmington					Freehold houses, Marina.
Deudney, Robert, Gensing, Saint Mary Magdalen					Land as occupier, Great & Little Gensing farms and Smiths farms.
Fraser, G., 10, New-sq, Lincoln's Inn					Freehold house, Quarry cottage.

NAMES.	D.	F.	Ch	Cu.	QUALIFICATION AND WHERE SITUATE.
Farncomb, Edward, Filsham.		—			Land as occupier, Filsham farm.
*Overy, Charles, the Grove		—			Land as occupier, Grove farm.

HASTINGS.--SAINT MARY IN THE CASTLE.

NAMES.	D.	F.	Ch	Cu.	QUALIFICATION AND WHERE SITUATE.
Akehurst, John Wm., Prospect-row, Stonefield					Freehold house, Stonefield.
Breeds, James, Saint Clement					Freehold house, Wellington-square.
Baldock, John, Castle-road					Freehold house, Castle-street
Brown, John, Stonefield		—			Freehold house, No. 30, Stonefield.
*Bayley, John, jun., George-street		—			Freehold house, West-street.
Brice, John, 3, Wellington-square					Freehold house, Stone street.
Bayley, R. R., Basinghall-st., London					Freehold houses, Bedford-place.
Bolingbroke, Chas. Wm., Stone-street					Freehold house, Lion Inn, Stone-street
Browne, Joseph, High-street					Freehold houses, Stonefield buildings
*Campbell, Wm., York cottages					Two freehold houses, York cottages
*Comber, Joseph, 12, Stonefield street					Freehold house, Stonefield.
*Chandler, Richard, Pelham Arms		—			Freehold house, West-street.
Crake, Wm., Notting hill, Kensington					Freehold house, Pelham-place.
Dunn, Richard, near the Battery					Freehold house, George-street.
Duke, George, High-street					Freehold house, No. 4, Breeds-place.
Edwards, Wm., Summer Hill, Willsborough, near Ashford, Kent					Freehold house, George-street.
Eaton, John, High-street					Freehold house, Wellington-square.
Elphinstone, Howard, 19, Eaton-place, Westminster					Freehold house, Little Bridge-farm.
Emary, James, Castle Hotel					Freehold house, Meadow-cottages.
*Farncomb, Henry, Icklesham					Freehold house, Wellington-square.
Farncomb, Thomas, Harleyford-place, Kennington					Freehold house, Castle Hotel.
Foster, Thomas, George-street					Freehold house, St. Mary's-terrace.
Gallop, George, Castle-street					Freehold house, Castle-street.
Holmes, Thos., 5, St. Mary's terrace					Freehold house, 6, St. Mary's-terrace.
Hutchings, Henry Peter, South-Saxon Hotel, St. Mary Magdalen					Fr. h. Saint Andrew-terrace, Stonefield.
Hayward, John, Baldsloe					Freehold house, Baldsloe.
Hutchinson, T. C., St. Mary's-terrace					Freehold house, Hanover-house.
Kelland, M., High-street, St. Clement					3 Freehold houses, Stonefield-bgs.
Kent, Philip, All Saints-street					Freehold house, Kentish-buildings.
Kaye, Joseph, Gower-street, Bedford-square, London					Freehold house, Pelham-crescent.
*Kirby, Robert, 29, Chester-terrace, Regent's-park, London					Freehold houses, No. 3, 4, 5, 10, and 11, Pelham-crescent.
*Kirby, William, Denmark cottage					Freehold house, Denmark-cottage.
Murray, John, Castle-street					Freehold land, Breeds-place.
Mawdett, John, Castle-place					Fr. houses, No. 2 and 3, Castle-place.
Norris, James, Stone-street					Fr. house, in the terrace, Stonefield.
Noon, William, Winchelsea					Freehold rent charge, Castle-street.
*Nash, Richard, 1, Kentish buildings					Freehold house, 10, Albion-terrace.
Prior, John, sen., Cross-st., Stonefield					Fr. h., 23, Saint Andrews'-terrace.
Plummer, John, Castle-hill					Freehold house, Castle-street.
Phillips, John, High-street					Freehold house, Wellington-square.
Phillips, Henry Barry, High-street					Freehold house, Wellington-square.
Risby, James, Primus-place, St. Mary Magdalen, and Coach-office, Castle-street, Hastings					Fr. houses, York-bgs., & York-gardens.

NAMES.	D.	F.	Ch.	Cs.	QUALIFICATION AND WHERE SITUATE.
Roe, Thomas, York-buildings					Freehold houses, Stonefield.
*Ridley, William, York-buildings					Freehold houses, York-buildings.
*Reeves, George, Swan Tap					Freehold house, Stonefield.
*Ransom, Wm., sen., York-buildings					Freehold house, Wellington-library.
Ranger, William, St. Mary's-terrace					Fr. houses, Saint Mary's-terrace.
Robinson, Geo., jun., St. Mary's-terrace					Freehold hs., Saint Mary's-terrace.
*Ranson, Wm., jun., Blackland-cottage					Leasehold farm, Hole-farm.
*Smith, Timothy, Prospect-row					Freehold house, No. 4, Stonefield.
Stonestreet, Rev. George Stonestreet					Freehold land, near the Fighting-cocks, called Hamton.
Griffin, Halton					
Stace, Samuel, West-st., St. Clement					Freehold houses, St. Mary's-terrace.
Standen, Benjamin, The Croft					Freehold house, Wellington-square.
Simmons, John, York Cottages					Freehold house, York-cottages.
*Smith, J. B., High-st., St. Clement.					Freehold house, Castle-street.
Standen, Thomas, Silverhill, Hastings					Land as occupier, Silverhill-farm.
Tutt, James, Ninfield					Freehold mill, Castle-hill.
Thwaites, G., Ivy Cottage, West-hill.					Freehold house, Meadow-cottages.
*Tree, John, Meadow Cottages					Freehold house, York-gardens.
Williamson, J. Wilkins, Beaulieu-H.,					Freehold house, Beaulieu.
Waghorn, John, 49, High-street					Land as occupier, Little Ridge-farm.
Wingfield, George, All Saints					Freehold house, Beach-cottages.
Wallinger, The Rev. Wm., Iford					Fr. house and school, Castle-down.
Winter, William, Meadow Cottage					Freehold house, Meadow-cottages.
Wimble, N. Harrison, The Croft					Freehold tenement, Castle-street.

HASTINGS.—ST. MARY MAG-DALEN.

NAMES.	D.	F.	Ch.	Cs.	QUALIFICATION AND WHERE SITUATE.
Baldock, Robert, Warriors-gate					Freehold house, New London-road.
Burton, Septimus, 10, New-square, Lincoln's Inn					Fr. h., East Ascent and Maize-hill.
Beecham, Wm. Pain, Hawkhurst, Kent					Freehold house, 4, Primus-place.
Brisco, Wastel, Esq., Bohemia					Freehold lands
Chester, Samuel, St. Mary Magdalen					near the London-road.
Eldridge, William, Swan Hotel					Freehold stables, coach-housess, and cottages, Norman-road.
Duke, George, High-street					Freehold house, East Cliffe-place.
Honiss, Edward, York-place					Fr. h., No. 2, Verulam-buildings.
Jenner, James, Rolvenden, Kent					Fr. houses, Nos. 1 and 2 Primus-place.
Jeffries, Joseph, Saint Leonards					Freehold houses & land, Adelaide-place
*Manser, David, Winchelsea					Freehold house, No. 3, Primus-place.
Payne, William, No. 1, Adelaide-place					Freehold houses, Gensing-road.
Putland, Stephen, Saint Mary's-place					Fr. warehouses, stables, and Smith's shop, Saint Mary's-yard.
Spink, John, Highbury h., Froyle, Hants					Freehold stables and coach-houses, East Ascent and Mews-road.
*Tree, Benjamin, 10, York-buildings					Freehold house, No. 6, Prinus-place.
Troup, Jas., New-sq., Warrior's-gate					Fr. lds., New-square, Warrior's-gate.
Voysey, George, New London-road, Warrior's-gate					Freehold house, New London-road.
Vincent, Thomas, 6, Old Church-street, Paddington					Fr. hs., No. 2 and 3, Seymour-place.
*Waghorn, W., UnderCliff, St. Leonards					Freehold ground, Seymour-place.

NAMES.	D.	F.	Ch	Cs.	QUALIFICATION and WHERE SITUATE.

BREDE.

NAMES.		QUALIFICATION and WHERE SITUATE.
*Ades, John		Freehold land, Rose and Gate-land.
*Austen, Thomas		Freehold land, Broad Oak-land.
Apps, William		Freehold land, Maplestone-farm.
Baker, James..		Freehold house.
Blake, Stephen		Freehold house.
Bourne, John		Ld. as ocp., Soudens & Pickdick-fms
Bourne, F., tendered for Cavendish		Freehold farm, Brede.
Bourne, Thomas		Land as occupier, Reasons farm.
*Coleman, W., jun.		Freehold land, Conster Furnace-land.
Campbell, Harry		Leasehold house and Blacksmith-shop
Coleman, John		Freehold house.
Coleman, John		Land as occupier, Purster & Bonster Furnace-farms.
Ditch, John		Copyhold house and shop.
Gorringe, Stephen, Udimore		Ld. as ocp., Road-end, & pt. of New-h.
Hele, Rev. R. H. S.		Fr. land and wood, Powder-mills-wood
Inman, John		Freehold house.
Langford, J. C., Udimore		Freehold houses and land.
Mercer, Robert		Freehold house and land.
*Milham, William		Fr. ld. Highfield, & pt. of Spell-lands.
Pain, Thomas..		Freehold house, King's Head Inn.
Piper, William, Westfield		Freehold house.
Richardson, J. W.		Fr. h. shop and land, near the Church
Richardson, James		Freehold land, Little Udimore.
Sloman, John, Udimore		Freehold land, Goldfins-farm.
Skinner, James,		Land as occupier, Stone Link-farm.
Smith, David, jun.		Land as occupier, Coggers-farm.
Powes, P. A., Medmenham, Bucks		Freehold land, Maidland-farm.
Smith, David		Freehold mills and land.
Smith, Henry		Land as occupier, Brook-lodge, and Loneham-farm.
Tucker, T., 5, Henrietta-st., London		Freehold land and houses, Church-lodge, and Loneham-farms.
Vincett, Stephen, Bexhill		Freehold land, Lazy-field.
Woodhams, John, Udimore		Freehold land, part of Pound-farm.
Young, Edward, Hawkhurst		Freehold land, Maitland-farm.
Young, Richard..		Freehold house, on the hill.

BECKLEY.

NAMES.		QUALIFICATION and WHERE SITUATE.
Baker, William, sen.		Freehold houses.
Blackman, Alfred		Land as occupier, Gate-farm.
Curteis, Reginald, Windmill hill		Freehold land, Odean-farm.
Curteis, Edw. B., Esq., Windmill hill		Freehold land, Eastland-farm.
Cooper, Stephen..		Ld. as occupier, Great Oxenbridge-fm.
Cooper, Charles..		Land as occupier, Kitchenor-farm.
Cooper, Benjamin		Fr. house and land, nr. the Four Oaks
Cole, John		Freehold house, near the Four Oaks.
Dennis, Richard, Rye		Freehold house, Four Oaks.

NAMES.	D.	P.	Ch	Cs	QUALIFICATION AND WHERE SITUATE
Elfick, Thomas, sen.					Freehold house and land, Four Oaks.
Elliott, Thomas					Freehold chapel and land, Beckley-st.
Fairhall, Edwin					Freehold house and land, Birds-farm.
Fairhall, William					Freehold h.and land, Whatcomb-farm.
Gilbert, John					Ld. as ocp., Oden and Goosleys-farm.
Gilbert, James					Cp. h. and land, Little Harmers-farm.
Gilbert, Thomas..					Ld. as ocp., Tile Barn-fm. & Swifts.
Hollands, William					Land as occupier, Hope-farm.
Hodges, Rev. Henry					Rectory of Beckley.
Kenerick, W., Esq., Bourne-place,					
near Canterbury					Wood land, near Gate Lower-land.
*King, Richard					Fr. h. and land, Great Harmers-farm.
Munn, Rev. J. Reid, Burwash					Freehold house and land.
Norris, John					Ld. as ocp., Eastland-fm. & other ld.
Norris, Edwin					Freehold house and land, Beckley-st.
Oxley, William ..					H. & ld. as ocp., Rose and Crown-Inn.
Parsons, James, sen.					Cp. house and land, Beckley-street.
Parsons, Humphrey					Cp. house and land, Beckley-street.
*Parton, Peter, Tenterden					Freehold house.
Reeves, Thomas Walter					Freehold h. and land, near the Church.
Russell, John, sen.					Freehold house, near the Four Oaks.
Ranger, Sampson					Freehold houses.
*Selmes, Samuel					Land as occupier, Great Knell-farm.
Stonham, John					Land as occupier, Conster-farm.
Stonham, Thomas					Land as occupier, Hays-farm.
Stonham, Samuel					Freehold house, Beckley-street.
Thomsett, John					Fr. house and ld., near the Brickfields
Vincett, James					Cp. house and land, Beckley-street.
Wybourne, Stephen					Freehold house and ld., Beckley-street
Wybourne, John, tendered for Caven-					
dish and Curteis					Beckley-street.
Waterman, William, Tenterden					Fr.wood-l., adjoining Kitchenour-fm.

BROOMHILL.

*Burling, Isaac, Brooklands, Kent					Feeehold land, Little Innings, and part of Gilbert-field.
*Butler, Thomas, Ivychurch, Kent					Freehold land, Great Innings, and part of Gilbert-field.
*Grist, William, Brookland					Freehold land, Pell-field.
Pankhurst, George, East Guildeford..					Freehold land, near Jewry's-gut.

EAST GUILDEFORD.

Austen, Thomas, Kippington, Kent..					Freehold land, East-end.
Elliott, James, Playdon					Land as occupier, South-end.
Monypenny, I. Isaac, Hadlow, Kent					Freehold house and land, South-end.
Offin, John					Freehold house and land.
Pain, Thomas, Appledore					Freehold land, High-road.
Pankhurst, George					Land as occupier, near the Church.
Selmes, James, Rye					Freehold land.
Wells, Samuel..					Freehold land.

ICKLESHAM.

Amos, Daniel, Boughton, Kent					Freehold land, Crutches-farm.
Beale, John..					Freehold house, Icklesham-street.
Carey, Lewis					Freehold house, Icklesham-street.
Carey, Thomas					Freehold house, Icklesham-street

NAMES.	D.	P.	Ch.	Cs.	QUALIFICATION AND WHERE SITUATE.
Carey, Jacob					Freehold house, Cut Thorn.
Crassingham, Richard					Freehold house, Icklesham-street.
Fuller, Stephen, tendered for Darby					
and Fuller					
Griffin, Richard, Winchelsea ..					Ld. as ocp., part of Sheep-house-farm
Hoad, John					Freehold house, Hog-hill.
Monk, John					Freehold house, Icklesham-street.
Martin, Edward..					Freehold house, Icklesham-street.
Richards, Thomas					Glebe land and tithes of Icklesham.
Simmons, John, Wittersham, Kent..					Freehold house, Parsonage-farm.
Simmons, John					Freehold land, Little Scrag-oak.
Veniss, Isaac					Freehold house, Hog-hill.
Venis, James, Hastings, tendered for					
Darby and Fuller					Icklesham.

IDEN.

NAMES.	D.	P.	Ch.	Cs.	QUALIFICATION AND WHERE SITUATE.
Blackman, William, Rolvenden ..					Freehold land, near New-bridge.
Bowels, Jeffery					Fr. house and land, near Iden-street.
Bousfield, Geo., 60, Gracechurch-st.,					
London					Fr. h. and garden, near Iden-street.
Catt, James					House and land as ocp., Iden-street.
*Care, John, Peasmarsh					H. and land as ocp., Oxenbridge-farm.
Ditch, William					Copyhold house, & shop, Iden-street.
Elliott, James, Playden					Land as occupier, Glebe.
Haizell, Robert, Maidstone, Kent ..					Freehold land, near the Military-lock.
Lamb, Rev. G. A.					Freehold land, adjoining Tyes-wood.
Morris, William, jun., Peasmarsh ..					Freehold land, Ashfields.
Mortimer, John, Lewisham hill, Kent					Freehold land, Willow-house.
Norman, Rev. J. H., Deal, Kent ..					Freehold land, Oxenbridge-farm.
Olliver, John					Freehold field, Iden-street.
Pelham, Thomas, Kennardington ..					Freehold field, Iden-street.
Pix, Thomas Smith, Peasmarsh ..					Fr. house and land, Barn Grange-farm
Pomfret, R. C., High-street, Rye ..					Freehold land, near the Military-lock.
*Pomfret, Virgil, Tenterden ..					Freehold land, near New-bridge.
Phillips, Charles, Hoddeston, Herts..					Freehold land, near New-bridge.
Smallfield, Thomas, Wittersham ..					Freehold land, near New-bridge.
Tuck, John					Freehold land, near Iden-street.
Terry, Thos., 5, Church-st., Deptford					Freehold land, Tysons.
Terry, John, Minerva-place, New-					
cross, Surrey					Freehold land, Groves-farm.
Unwin, Edward, Sutton in Ashfield,					
Nottinghamshire					Freehold land, Park-farm.
Winser, John					Parish clerk of Iden.

NORTHIAM.

NAMES.	D.	P.	Ch.	Cs.	QUALIFICATION AND WHERE SITUATE.
Austen, Edmund					Land as occupier, Blackets.
Ashenden, John					Freehold house.
*Beale, James					Freehold house, near the Six Bells.
Beale, Thomas					One fourth part of fr. houses and land
Body, Moses					Land as occupier, Copland-farm.
*Bishop, George					Freehold h. and land, Hays & Goatley
Blundell, Stephen, Cranbrook, Kent					Freehold houses, Clinch-green.
Booth, Stephen					Copyhold house and land.
Booth, Daniel..					Freehold house.
Brown, E. Wright					Copyhold house, Hermon-hill.
Chester, Richard					Freehold house and land, Horns-cross.
Chester, Jasper					Copyhold house and land.

NAMES.	D.	F.	Ch.	Cs.	QUALIFICATION AND WHERE SITUATE.
Chester, Richard					
Comport, John ..					Fr. and copyhold houses and lands.
Coleman, Joseph					Fr. house and land, near the Turnpike.
Coppinger, Thomas					House & land as occupier, Six Bells Inn
*Curteis, William, Tenterden					Trustee to leasehold land, gate-farm
Davis, John, Rye					Freehold house and land.
Edwards, John, Newenden, Kent					Copyhold house.
Elfick, William					Freehold house.
Farrance, Thomas					Land as occupier, Goatley-farm.
*Field, Thomas					Freehold h. and mill, High Park-mill.
Frewen, M., Chevely green, Suffolk..					Freehold house and land.
Gibbs, Joseph					Fr. h. and land, near High Park-mill.
Gilbert, John ..					Freehold house and land.
Hanson, William, Newenden					Freehold houses.
Harman, John, Croydon, Surrey					Freehold house.
Harris, John					Fr. house and land, near the Turnpike
Hilder, John, Sandhurst, Kent					Freehold house.
Hilder, Thomas, Catsfield					Freehold house.
Hilder, Thos. Paine, Kingsnorth, Kent					Land as occupier, Cooks-farm.
Kelly, Anthony P., 12, Charles-square, Oxford, Middlesex					Fr. house and ld., Church-house-farm.
Lord, Rev. William Ed. ..					Rectory of Northiam.
Larkin, Thomas					Two mills as ocp., Mill Corner-mills.
Lord, Edward					Land as occupier, Crockers-farm.
Longley, John, Tenterden					Copyhold house and land.
Luxford, Joseph					Ld. as ocp., Lueford, near Tufton-place
*Musgrave, John, Hackney					Fr. farm and bgs., Yew-tree-farm.
Munk, Isaac					Freehold house.
Marlow, Valentine					Freehold house and buildings.
Newington, John					Land as occupier, Common-woods.
Parsons, William					Land as occupier, Yew-tree-farm.
Peen, William ..					Freehold house.
Perigoe, William					Freehold h. & land, nr. the Turnpike.
Pix, John					Fr. h. and ld., Higham & Little Dixter
Piper, John					Freehold house and land.
Powell, H., 71, High-st., Whitechapel					One undivided sixth part of freehold-land, Hunts-farm.
Powell, Wm. Mark, ditto					One undivided sixth part of freehold-land, Hunts-farm.
Powell, James, Pallant, Chichester ..					One undivided sixth part of freehold-land, Hunts-farm.
Russell, E., High-st., Croydon, Surrey					Freehold house.
Ranger, George..					Freehold house and ld., in the village.
*Ransom, Henry..					Cp. h. and ld. warehouse and stables.
Rocks, Thomas ..					Land as occupier, Stent-farm.
Santer, David ..					Freehold house and shop.
*Selmes, James					Land as occupier, Tufton-place.
*Selmes, Henry, Beckley ..					Freehold house.
Sevenoaks, William					Freehold house, near mill corner.
*Sharpe, Hercules, Esq. ..					Fr. house and ld., Dornans and Hurst.
Springett, George					Freehold land, Great Dixter.
Tomsett, John ..					Freehold house.
Turner, Thomas Frewen					Fr. house and garden, Brickwall-house
Walpole, Edward, Esq., 12, Dowing-street, Westminster					Freehold land.
West, Daniel					Freehold house.
Wood, Richard ..					Copyhold houses, Cotlands.
Waddell, John					Freehold house and stable, High-street

o

NAMES.	B.	F.	C.	C.	QUALIFICATION and WHERE SITUATE.

PEASMARSH.

NAMES.					QUALIFICATION and WHERE SITUATE.
Ashdown, Thomas					Freehold land, Main-street.
Baker, William, Beckley					Freehold house.
Banister, William					Freehold house.
Bates, William, Ivy church, Kent					Freehold house and land.
Banister, Edward					Freehold house.
Cooper, William					Freehold house.
Curteis, H. B.					Freehold house.
Cruttenden, William					Freehold house.
Edmonds, William					Freehold house.
Hodges, Thos. Law, Benenden, Kent					Freehold land, near Blackwall.
Jury, William ..					Freehold house.
Kenerick, William, Esq., Bourne-place, near Canterbury					Freehold land, Gate Low-land.
Morris, Wm., sen.					Freehold house and land, Main-street.
Monypenny, Thomas, Rolvenden					Freehold land.
Philcox, John ..					Freehold house, Main-street.
*Packham, William					Freehold house.
Pix, Thomas					Freehold land, Blackwall.
Reeve, Laurence, Udimore					Freehold house and land, Bailing-farm
Stonham, James					Freehold house.
Stileman, Richard, Winchelsea					Freehold house, and land.
Standen, Samuel.					Freehold house, Main-street.
Smith, John ..					Freehold house, Main-street.
Standen, Isaac					Freehold house.
Smith, William					Freehold house.
Thomas, Edward Smith					Freehold house.
Ticehurst, M. Cleve					Freehold land, near Dinglesden.
Wimark, John ..					Freehold house, and Tan-yard.
Wait, Richard ..					Freehold land, Brick-yard-field.
Woollett, Thomas					Freehold house.

PLAYDEN.

NAMES.					QUALIFICATION and WHERE SITUATE.
Austen, Richard, Guildford					Freehold house, Horton-green.
Bellingham, James, Wartling					Freehold land, near the Church.
Collyer, Ralph					Freehold land, near Horton-green.
Curteis, Reginald, Wartling					Freehold land, near the Church.
Dawes, Weeden, Rye					Freehold field.
Dawes, Edward Nathaniel, Rye					Freehold field.
Lovett, John, 3, Old Kent road					Freehold h. and land, near Head-mill.
*Pilcher, Charles					Land as occupier, Mockbeggar-farm.
Smith, John ..					Land as occupier, Wollett-farm.
*Smith, Henry ..					Land as occupier, near the Church.
Vennall, Thomas, Rye					Freehold field, near the Church.
Wilson, Richard					Freehold h. and land, near Hoad-mill.

RYE.

NAMES.					QUALIFICATION and WHERE SITUATE.
Aylward, Thomas W., High-street					Freehold house, Mint-street.
*Allen, Justinian, Watchbell-street					Freehold house, Green.
Alce, Robert, Landgate					Freehold house, Landgate.
Amon, John, Watchbell-street					Freehold house, High-street.
*Aylward, William, Rope Walk					Freehold house, High-street.
Aylward, Charles, Rope Walk					Freehold house, Mint-street.
Austen, Edmund, Winchelsea					Freehold house, Landgate.
Apps, William, jun., Landgate					Parish Clerk, St. Mary's.
*Austen, S. Chalk, Mint-street					Freehold house, Mint-street

NAMES.	D.	F.	Ch.	Cs.	QUALIFICATION AND WHERE SITUATE.
*Austen, John, Playden					Freehold house, Landgate.
Barber, Wm., Leadenhall-st., London					Part of fr. hs., Mint-st. and Liberty.
•Burkitt, John, High-street					Fr. house and land, Mermaid-street.
Barnes, Edward, Rope Walk					Leasehold house, Rope-walk.
Brazier, Henry, Winchelsea road					Freehold warehouse, Winchelsea-road.
Batchelor, John, Custom House-street					Freehold houses, Landgate.
Blake, James, High-street					Freehold warehouse, Mint-street.
Butler, Richard Weeden, Market-st.					Freehold house, Watchbell-street.
Brockett, S. B., High-street					Freehold stable and land, Rope-walk.
Barry, Frederick, Wishward					Land as occupier, Rye-hill.
Bellingham, Thomas, Fairlight					Freehold house, Middle-street.
Bourn, Henry, High-street					Freehold house, High-street.
Chatterton, E., jun., Mint-street					Freehold house, East-street.
Collett, S. R., the Jingle, near Lincoln					Freehold land, Leasam.
Curteis, E. B., Windmill hill					Freehold land, Cadbro'-farm.
Clark, Thomas, Mint-street					Freehold house, Mint-street.
Cuff, Christopher, jun., Landgate					Leasehold house, Tower-street.
Cooper, Henry, Vicarage					Vicarial tithes of Rye.
Chatterton, Edward, Watchbell-street					Freehold house, Watchbell-street.
*Clark, Thomas, Watchbell-street					Freehold house, Market-street.
Clark, John, Watchbell-street					Freehold house, Gun-garden.
•Curd, William, Watchbell-street					Freehold house, Watchbell-street.
Clark, Thos. Staffell, Winchelsea-road					Freehold house, Pump-street.
Clark, Fisher, High-street					Freehold house, Ferry-road.
Crowhurst, Thomas, Canterbury					Freehold house, Landgate.
Crowhurst, James, Playden					One-third of freehold-h., Mint-street.
Dive, William, Watchbell-street					Freehold house, Watchbell-street.
*Daniel, John, sen., Tower-street					Freehold house, Tower-street.
Dyson, T., Myddleton-sq., London					Ls. house and garden, East-street.
Edmonds, James, Playden					Freehold mill and land, Rye-hill.
*Fryman, St. Gilbert, Market-street					Freehold premises, Ockhams-lane.
French, Charles, High-street					Freehold house, High-street.
Frise, George					Freehold house, High-street.
*Forster, John, Market-street					Freehold house, Mint-street.
Furby, Samuel, High-street					Freehold house, Strand.
Finis, John, Dover					Freehold ground, Winchelsea-road.
Goble, Ilias Thos., Walworth, Surrey					Freehold house, Watchbell-street.
*Gibbon, Thomas, Landgate					Freehold house, Landgate.
Gibbs, Walker, J. Waterstock Wheat- ley, Oxfordshire					Part of freehold house.
Giles, John, Landgate					Freehold house, Landgate.
Godfrey, Thomas, Hawkhurst					Freehold house, High-street.
*Hearsfield, Thos., Watchbell-street					Freehold house, Watchbell-street.
Heath, James, Strand					Part of freehold houses, Mint-street.
Heath, Henry, Biddenden, Kent					Part of freehold houses, Mint-street.
*Harman, T. Clark, Wisbeach, Cam- bridgeshire					Part of fr. hs., High-st. & Mint-street.
Hoad, James, Winchelsea-road					Freehold ground, Winchelsea-road.
Hatter, Thomas, Rope Walk					Part of freehold house, Gun-garden.
*Harman, James, Parade, Hastings.					One fourth part of 10 fr. hs., Landgate
Hilder, Edward, High-street					Freehold house, High-street.
Hicks, Charles, High-street					Freehold house, Landgate.
Holloway, William, High-street					Freehold house, High-street.
Hollis, William, Landgate					Freehold house, Landgate.
Hunter, William, Wishward					Freehold house, Wishward.
Hessell, James, Strandgate					Freehold house, Watchbell-street.
Harvey, Nicholas, Rock-channel					Leasehold premises, Rock-channel.
*Huggins, W. O., Pump-street					Freehold house, High-street.

NAMES.	D.	P.	Ch	Co	QUALIFICATION AND WHERE SITUATE.
Hatter, William, Fish market					Part of freehold house, Gun-garden.
Hyland, William, Mint-street					Freehold houses, Hylands-yard.
Jubb, William, Watchbell-street					Freehold house, Hucksteps-row.
Judge, John, Lion-street					Freehold house, High-street.
*Jarrett, Thomas, Market-street					Part of freehold house, Market-street.
Jarrett, William, Market-street					Part of freehold houses, Market-street.
Jarrett, Richard, Market-street					Part of freehold house, Market-street.
Jarrett, James, Week-st., Maidstone					Part of freehold house, Market-street.
Kennett, John, Tower-street					Freehold house, Market-street.
King, Edward, Spring-place					Freehold house, Landgate.
Kennett, Henry, Clapham Rise, Surrey					Freehold house, Market-street.
Laurence, Charles, Mint-street					Freehold house, Watchbell-street.
Lardner, J. H., Middle-street					Freehold house, High-street.
Leaver, Thomas, Strand-gate					Freehold house, Strand.
Lightfoot, John, Lion-street					Freehold house, Wishward.
Laurence, John, High-street					Freehold house, High-street.
Manser, David., sen., High-street					Freehold house, Tower-street.
*Mills, Joseph, High-street					Freehold house, Brocks-row.
Meryon, John, High-street					Freehold house, Lion-street.
Miller, S., 21, Bedford-row, London					Leasehold house, East-street.
*Norley, William, Bethersden					Freehold houses, Landgate.
Payne, H. T., East Guideford					Freehold house, Strand.
Procter, Thomas, Rye					Freehold house, Mermaid-street.
Prosser, James, Loudwater, Bucks					Freehold house, Watchbell-street.
Pain, George, Lion-street					One-third of freehold house, Landgate
Pain, Edward, Lion-street					One-third of freehold house, Landgate
Pain, Charles, St. Leonards					One-third of freehold house, Landgate
Piper, Jesse, Hawkhurst					Freehold warehouse, Strand.
Pain, H. C., Pump-street					Pump-street, Pump-street.
*Rubie, George, Mint-street					Part of freehold house, Lion-street.
Ramsden, Wm., Market-street					Freehold house, Market-street.
*Reynolds, John, Rope Walk					One-fourth freehold-hs., Rope-walk.
*Reynolds, Charles, Green clift					One-fourth freehold hs., Rope-walk.
*Reynolds, Henry, Rope Walk					One-fourth freehold hs., Rope-walk.
Reynolds, James, Rope Walk					One-fourth freehold hs., Rope-walk.
*Rubie, Geo., jun., Hucksteps row					Part of freehold house, Lion-street.
Rubie, Edward H., Watchbell-street					Part of freehold house, Lion-street.
Seymour, James, Landgate					Freehold house, Middle-street.
*Smith, Wm., Strandgate					Freehold ground, Winchelsea-road.
Smith, Jeremiah, Cadbro					Freehold ground, High-street.
Skinner, Edward, High-street					Part of freehold houses, High-street.
Smith, Andrew, Mermaid-street					Baptist Chapel, Strand-hill.
Stonham, David, High-street					Freehold house, High-street.
Skinner, George, Little Cadbro'					Land as occupier, Wadland-farm.
Turner, Charles, Mint-street					Freehold house, Watchbell-street.
Turner, John, Uckfield					Freehold house, Market-street.
Turner, James, Bexhill					Freehold house, East-street.
Tutt, Thomas, Rye, tendered for Darby and Fuller					
Taylor, David, High-street					Freehold house, High-street.
Thomas, Charles, Middle-street					Freehold house, Middle-street.
Thorpe, Thomas, High-street					Freehold house, High-street.
*Thomas, Charles, High-street					One-third of freehold-h., Mermaid-st.
Turner, Francis, High-street					Freehold house, East-street.
Thomas, George, Church-street					Freehold house, Brocks-row.
Vidler, John, Watchbell-street					Freehold house, Watchbell-street.
Willmore, Thos. John, Mermaid-street					Independant Chapel, Watchbell-street.
Wright, James, Wishward					Freehold houses, Wish-ward.

NAMES.	D.	F.	Ch	Cs	QUALIFICATION AND WHERE SITUATE.
Waters, Edward, Landgate				—	Freehold house, Landgate.
Woollett, William, Landgate				—	Freehold house, Watchbell-street.
Wood, Thomas, Pump-street				—	One-third freehold house, Pump-street
Wood, John, Pump-street				—	One-third freehold house, Pump-street
*Wood, George, Pump-street				—	One-third freehold house, Pump-street.
*Whiteman, George, Taylor's corner				—	Freehold house, Little Lea.
Whitehead, John, Yalding, Kent					Freehold warehouse, Strand.
Wood, William, Mint-street					Freehold house, Pump-street.
Worsell, Richard, Rye, tendered for Darby and Fuller					
Worsell, Richard Webb, Rye, tendered for Darby and Fuller					
WINCHELSEA.					
Alce, Robert				—	Freehold house.
Alce, Thomas				—	Freehold house.
*Amen, Thomas				—	Freehold house.
Barham, Henry, tendered for Darby and Cavendish					
Benfield, Joel, Icklesham				—	Freehold Clift, the Clift.
Bennett, William				—	Freehold house.
Chatterton, Wm., Market-place, Rye				—	Freehold house.
Colebrook, James, Benenden				—	Freehold house.
Curteis, Thomas, Sevenoaks				—	Freehold ld., part of Camber-point-fm.
Dawes, Thomas, Camberwell, Surrey					Freehold land.
Denne, Wm. John, Doctors Commons					Fr. ld., part of New-h. & Roadend-fms.
Elliott, William, 19, Seymour-place, Bryanstone-square					Freehold house.
Fuller, Walter				—	Freehold shop, Castle-street.
Fuller, William					Share of freehold house.
*Farncomb, Henry				—	Share of land.
Farncomb, Henry, tendered for Darby and Fuller					
Holt, Jacob					Share of freehold houses.
Heamden, Isaac				—	Freehold house.
Harrod, George				—	Freehold house.
Hollingbury, John, Northiam				—	Freehold house.
Jones, Joash				—	Freehold house.
Laurence, David					Share in freehold shop.
Longley, William					Freehold house.
Laurence, Stephen				—	Freehold house, German-street.
Martin, Thomas, Beverly, Yorkshire				—	Freehold house.
Osborn, Richard					Share in freehold shop.
Smith, James, Icklesham				—	Freehold stables, New-stables.
Smith, John, Hastings				—	Freehold house.
Sargent, William				—	Freehold house.
Stileman, Richard				—	Freehold land, The Friars.
Terry, Charles, Litlington					Freehold house, Adelaide-place.
West, Rev. J. J., Southborough, Kent					Freehold house.
Wilson, James, Icklesham				—	Freehold land, Knelstone-farm.
UDIMORE.					
Colbran, George				—	Freehold house and land, Jordans-farm
Colbran, Thomas				—	Freehold house and land, Jordans-farm
Francis, John, Cranbrook, Kent				—	Freehold house, Little Udimore.
Filmer, William				—	Freehold house, Cockmailings.
Freeman, Henry				—	Land as ocp., Wickham & Carltor

NAMES.	D.	F.	Ch	Cs.	QUALIFICATION AND WHERE SITUATE.
Freeman, Edwin	—			—	Land as ocp., Wickham and Carltons.
*Gorringe, Stephen	—			—	Land as occupier, Road-end-farm.
*Ker, Henry John, Eymsford, Kent ..	—				Freehold house and land, Cross-house.
*Langford, T. C., Rye				—	Freehold land, Shedwicks-farm.
Smith, Jeremiah . ..					Freehold house and land.
Smith, Stephen Woodhams, Iden ..					Land as occupier, Spudland and Fagg.
Smith, James Allen, ...					Freehold glebe land.
Ward, Thomas Newman, Ore ..					Freehold land, Knelstone-farm.

TABLE OF THE VOTES

GIVEN IN THE SEVERAL POLLING DISTRICTS.

POLLING DISTRICTS.	FIRST DAY.				SECOND DAY.				TOTAL.			
	D.	F.	Ch.	Cs.	D.	F.	Ch.	Cs.	D.	F.	Ch.	Cs.
Lewes, ...	472	368	429	342	53	44	69	43	525	412	498	385
Cuckfield, ...	98	90	93	95	15	20	14	15	113	110	107	110
Brighton, ...	203	164	215	201	92	85	135	92	295	249	350	293
East Grinstead,...........	211	146	155	119	32	34	36	39	243	180	191	158
Mayfield, ...	450	378	123	136	43	36	22	31	493	414	145	167
Battle, ...	219	157	159	186	18	17	33	35	237	174	192	221
Hastings, ...	142	93	114	101	40	23	41	14	182	116	155	115
Rye, ...	135	73	126	137	33	21	29	33	168	94	155	170
Total,..........	1930	1469	1414	1317	326	280	379	302	2256	1749	1793	1619

INDEX.

R

ERRATA.

West, Rev. Harvey, page 4,—*read* West, Rev. Harry.

Marsham, Dr., page 41,—polled for Curteis by mistake, he corrected himself immediately, and stated he intended to Poll for Darby and Fuller, before he left the polling booth. A memorandum to that effect was made by the *Poll Clerk*.

Spratt Water, Esq., page 68,—*read* Sprott Walter, Esq.

Dadswell, Edward Ohill,—*read* Dadswell Edward Okil.

BAXTER, AND SON, PRINTERS, LEWES.

CPSIA information can be obtained
at www.ICGtesting.com
Printed in the USA
BVOW06s0846240417

482096BV00016B/272/P